The Everyday Autism Handbook for Schools

60+ ESSENTIAL GUIDES FOR STAFF

Claire Droney and Annelies Verbiest

Illustrated by Melanie Corr

Jessica Kingsley Publishers
London and Philadelphia

First published in Great Britain in 2022 by Jessica Kingsley Publishers
An Hachette Company

1

Copyright © Claire Droney and Annelies Verbiest 2022
Illustrations copyright © Melanie Corr 2022

'Alone we can do so little, together we can do so much' quote by Helen Keller,
reproduced with kind permission of the Helen Keller Foundation.
'Plan your work and work your plan' quote by Napoleon Hill reproduced with kind permission
of the Napoleon Hill Foundation, One College Avenue, Wise, Virginia USA 24293, naphill.org.
'Case study: Five-week autism peer awareness project' re-published
with kind permission of the Chartered College of Teaching.
Figure 1.4 reproduced with kind permission of Rebecca Burgess.
Appendices 15 and 16 reproduced with kind permission of Scoil Triest Special School.

Front cover image source: Shutterstock®.

All appendices marked with ⬇ are available to download as PDFs, and can be
photocopied and downloaded for personal use with this programme, but may not be
reproduced for any other purposes without the permission of the publisher.

A CIP catalogue record for this title is available from the
British Library and the Library of Congress

ISBN 978 1 78775 428 7
eISBN 978 1 78775 429 4

Printed and bound in Great Britain by CPI Group

Jessica Kingsley Publishers' policy is to use papers that are natural, renewable and recyclable
products and made from wood grown in sustainable forests. The logging and manufacturing
processes are expected to conform to the environmental regulations of the country of origin.

Jessica Kingsley Publishers
Carmelite House
50 Victoria Embankment
London EC4Y 0DZ

www.jkp.com

'A welcome "toolkit" of enlightening guidance and practical strategies valuable to teachers, parents and practitioners across education, health and social care. This book is divided into easy to find (and read) "guides" across themes with associated activities and techniques, all anchored in evidence-based practice. Content such as the "tips", monologues and frequently asked questions also illuminate the child's perspective and their needs, as well as their abilities.'

— *Dr Áine de Róiste, psychologist and senior lecturer in social care in the Department of Applied Social Studies, Munster Technological University, Cork, Ireland*

'This is a must-read handbook for school staff working with autistic young people. It is written by educators who share their rich and varied experience in a clear and friendly style that is both accessible and informative. Autistic voice and experience inform each section of the book. This is sure to be a much read and recommended resource in schools.'

— *Claire O'Neill, autism class teacher, teacher–educator and neurodivergent coach*

'A comprehensive and accessible volume that combines theory, practical strategies, checklists, templates and downloadable resources for busy professionals. Just as the authors identify visuals as the "WD40 of the autism world", this book can be described as the "WD40 autism manual" for schools, full of practical and energy-saving tips to support ease of learning for staff and pupils alike. I wish it had been around when I was teaching!'

— *Mary McKenna, teacher, lecturer and early years autism consultant with The Children's Clinic*

'A tour-de-force of practical teaching strategies contextualized in relevant literature and the in-depth pedagogical experience and expertise of both authors. Clear, accessible guidance is accompanied by short vignettes which bring the book to life. The section on teaching strategies comprises subtitles written from the perspective of the child, e.g. "Make Everything Visual for Me", "Motivate Me", "Give Me a Schedule", which forefronts the experience of the learner. Core aspects of learning such as oral language and communication are examined in depth with insightful suggestions for teaching approaches to enable learning and progress. The authors explicitly enable the learning of teachers and schools by providing useful suggestions for creating inclusive environments and developing collaborative practices. An entire section is devoted to the effective establishment and use of the special class model of support, an issue which is very pertinent in the Irish context at the moment... This is the first book I have read in a long time that combines theory and practice in a manner accessible to a wide range of readers. I will be adding this book to the reading list for my own student teachers.'

— *Ann Marie Farrell, assistant professor, School of Inclusive and Special Education, Institute of Education, Dublin City University*

of related interest

Inclusive Education for Autistic Children
Helping Children and Young People to Learn
and Flourish in the Classroom
Dr Rebecca Wood
Illustrated by Sonny Hallett
Foreword by Dr Wenn B. Lawson
ISBN 978 1 78592 321 0
eISBN 978 1 78450 634 6

Simple Autism Strategies for Home and School
Practical Tips, Resources and Poetry
Sarah Cobbe
Foreword by Glenys Jones
ISBN 978 1 78592 444 6
eISBN 978 1 78450 817 3

Education and Girls on the Autism Spectrum
Developing an Integrated Approach
Edited by Judith Hebron and Caroline Bond
ISBN 978 1 78592 460 6
eISBN 978 1 78450 837 1

What brings you joy?

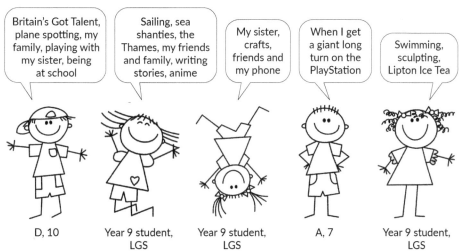

Source: Gustavo Rezende

Contents

Acknowledgements

I would like say thank you to everyone who inspired this book.

- To my colleagues and friends in Scoil Eanna and Scoil Triest special schools where I took my first tentative steps towards learning about autism, guided by some amazing special needs assistants.
- To the Bridge London Trust Outreach Team – Dani, Sarah, Clare, Jamie, Menita and Rosie – with whom I spent five glorious years celebrating, discussing and arguing about autism at our desks, on buses and while walking through Islington streets to visit schools. Thanks also to Dani for sharing his expertise about autism and disability awareness programmes, and to Jamie for his much appreciated input on some of the earlier drafts of this book.
- To the staff in St Maries of the Isle primary school, which is one of the most inclusive mainstream schools I have ever worked in.
- To the autistic children, young people and adults and their families who gave of their time and expertise to add so much colour and depth to this book.

Claire

Thank you to Aoife, Bláthnaid, Jacinta, Jessica, Karen, Liz, Mags, Marcella, Maria, Michael and Sinéad for their words of wisdom, insights, and thoughtful contributions.

I would like to thank all the staff in Scoil Triest special school and Berrings National School, in particular Liam Walsh, former principal of Berrings National School, for continuously supporting me throughout our shared time in Berrings.

I would also like to thank Judie Chalmers for her wisdom and support.

A special thanks to Melanie Corr for drawing the illustrations.

Annelies

We would like to thank Geraldine Bond and all the staff in Scoil Triest special school, where we both learned so much about best practice in autism and where staff enthusiastically supports each student to 'be as good as you can be' on a daily basis.

Thanks to our editors Sarah Hamlin, Isabel Martin and Karina Maduro.

This book is dedicated to everyone who works with children and young people with special educational needs, and to their families. They are the real experts.

Claire and Annelies

About This Book

This book is a practical handbook for anyone working with primary-aged autistic children. It contains a mixture of theory and practical strategies, written in an entertaining, easy-to-read format.

Who this book is for

This book is for principals, teachers, teaching assistants and after-school staff, in both mainstream and special primary schools. It is also very suited to parents or guardians looking to deepen their understanding of autism.

How this book works

The book is divided into six sections, each based around a specific topic. Each section is further divided into a number of guides that correspond to different parts of this topic.

Every guide contains:

- easy-to-read explanations of each topic
- case studies to illustrate the topics
- personal insights from a range of autistic children, young people and adults, as well as parents and teachers
- practical strategies.

Each guide is designed so that it can be read on its own. Instead of starting at the beginning of the book and working through it in chronological order, you may prefer to choose a section that interests you, or that is particularly relevant to the young person that you are currently working with, and read the guides in that section.

All guides contain symbols to clarify different aspects. These are:

 Simple theory and explanation

 Practical strategies

 Checklists

Practical housekeeping tips

 Top tips or important considerations

 Bespoke, downloadable resources available online

 Useful guides on related topics

Some guides also contain a list of frequently asked questions (FAQs). The FAQ section at the end of many of the guides is based on questions that have arisen time and time again during training and consultation sessions with school staff over the years. We try to answer them in these sections.

> This book has an accompanying PDF containing Appendices as well as some bonus online content. The accompanying PDF can be downloaded from https://library.jkp.com/redeem using the code QFTPGWK
> The PDF contains all the Appendices mentioned in the text. It also includes a curated list of easily digestible autism resources for school staff to dip in and out of, with suggestions for books, films, podcasts, articles, websites, video clips, poetry, graphic novels, cartoons and social media channels.

Aims of this book

The Everyday Autism Handbook for Schools aims to be a one-stop shop for school staff to dip in and out of as and when the need arises. It is designed to serve as both a roadmap and a comfort blanket, to guide staff in the right direction, as well as reassuring them that they are on the right track.

Having worked with autistic children and young people in mainstream, special class and special school settings for many years, we want to share the experience and knowledge we have developed through teaching and training, and through plenty of our own trial and error.

This book contains everything we know about autism – and want you to know, too.

Please note

Throughout the book, we have included insights from a variety of autistic people and their families. Listening to autistic voices helps to illuminate staff understanding of autism, and the reasoning behind why we use certain approaches. We acknowledge that these thoughts and opinions are those of individuals, and in no way represent the entire autistic community.

The book is jam-packed with *practical examples* and *case studies*. These are based on situations that commonly occur in a classroom, rather than on any particular students.

Consistent with a Universal Design for Learning (UDL) approach, we hope that many of the strategies and resources we suggest in this book can be applied flexibly and can be used to meet the needs of *all* students in the classroom.

Rather than being treated as a separate entity, the concept of *well-being for both staff and students* is woven throughout the book. This is reflected in the choice of suggested strategies, a consistent student-centred approach, and a positive behaviour management approach, as well as an acknowledgement that school staff also need positivity, praise and a range of self-care strategies.

Part 1

Introduction to Autism

Introduction to Autism: Six Key Points

1. Definition

Autism is 'a lifelong developmental disability which affects how people communicate and interact with the world' (NAS 2020a).

Lifelong means that a child is born with autism, and an autistic child will become an autistic adult.

2. Prevalence

The number of people who have an autism diagnosis (outlined in Figure 1.1) varies in different countries and has gradually increased. This may be due to an increased awareness and understanding of autism, which has in turn led to earlier diagnosis and increased rates of diagnosis.

UK 1 in 100
Ireland 1 in 65
USA 1 in 54

FIGURE 1.1 AUTISM INCIDENCE
(NAS 2020a; Department of Health 2018; CDC 2020)

3. Causes

There is lots of interest in identifying factors that may be associated with autism. It is thought that there may be a number of *genetic* and *environmental factors* involved that may play a role. However, there is currently no known cause of autism.

Note: Environmental factors can also impact on whether or not autism is identified or diagnosed. For example, if your environment is particularly autism-friendly and structured, and if others are particularly understanding and supportive, then you may not ever want or need to seek a diagnosis.

4. The dyad of impairments

If a person receives a diagnosis of autism, they will have differences or difficulties in two main areas (see Figure 1.2). Known as the dyad of impairments (APA 2013), these two areas are:

1. social interaction and social communication
2. restricted, repetitive patterns of behaviour, interests or activities (RRBs). This includes:

- sensory processing needs
- special interests
- stereotyped movements or speech
- a need for structure and predictability.

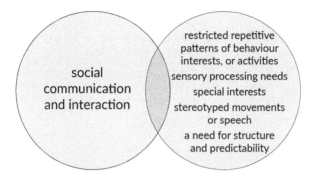

FIGURE 1.2 DYAD OF IMPAIRMENTS

In order to receive an autism diagnosis, a person must have difficulties or demonstrate differences from both sides of the dyad, and across a number of different areas (APA 2013).

Please note: Deficit-based language is often used by clinicians (rather than strengths-based language), hence the use of the word 'impairment' here.

5. The autism spectrum

Autism researcher Lorna Wing first introduced the concept of the autism spectrum (Wing 1996). This suggests that while every autistic person has core differences or difficulties in a number of key areas (the dyad of impairments), not everyone will be affected in the same way, nor will they act in the same way. In other words, autism manifests in different ways in different people, and it is not simply a cut-and-dried case of 'you either have it or you don't' (Happé and Baron-Cohen 2014).

The autism spectrum is often depicted as a line or a rainbow, as depicted in Figure 1.3 on the following page.

However, visualizing the spectrum as a line that appears to go from 'not autistic' to 'very autistic' can be problematic, because it can lead to lowered expectations for someone like Peter, and potentially unrealistic expectations and lack of understanding for someone like Harry.

Peter, 14	Laura, 8	Harry, 40
Loves music and going for walks	Loves drawing and Japanese Manga	Loves photography
Speaks in single-word sentences	Has a great sense of humor	Is an expert in his field of work
Doesn't read or write yet	Has a best friend in school	Finds it difficult to figure out what to say when he goes to the supermarket
Can use the toilet independently	Finds it hard to remember what homework she is supposed to do	
Wears a jumper all summer long as he dislikes the feeling of air on his skin	Often daydreams during class and needs to be reminded to focus	Often forgets to put his shoes on before he leaves the house
Caregivers plan to support Peter to live in assisted accommodations when he is 18, if that is something he opts for in the future	Wants to be an animal scientist when she grows up	Needs a calendar on his phone to keeo himself on track
	Can be quite sensitive to perceived insults	Dislikes the noise of an ambulance siren going past
	After school, she needs an hour to relax in her bedroom with a book	Married with two children

FIGURE 1.3 A LINEAR SPECTRUM

Artist Rebecca Burgess prefers to consider the spectrum as a wheel (see Figure 1.4), with different strengths and needs highlighted for different people at different times in their lives.

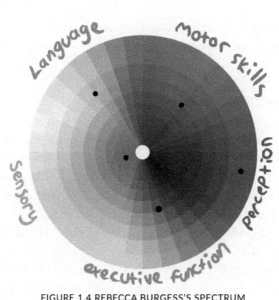

FIGURE 1.4 REBECCA BURGESS'S SPECTRUM

❝ Autism has a history of being defined by how 'high functioning' or 'low functioning' the person is on a spectrum. The problem with this is that each autistic individual will appear to be 'high functioning' in some situations, and not in others, depending on the environment, how tired they are and the specific kind of difficulties they might have. Someone might be very good at socialising, but only if they are doing it somewhere free of sensory overload.

Another person might never be good at socialising, but still have a successful career.

I created the image of 'the autism spectrum' as a colour wheel to help express this complexity. Every autistic individual has different 'points' along each area of the spectrum, indicating how much they struggle, or don't struggle at all, with things such as executive functioning, socialising, and sensory intake. ”

Rebecca Burgess

6. Getting a diagnosis

There are two main manuals used to classify autism. These are:

- *The Diagnostic and Statistical Manual of Mental Disorders, 5th Edition* (DSM-5) (APA 2013)
- *The International Classification of Disease 10* (ICD-10) (World Health Organization 2004) (the ICD-11 is due to be formally published in January 2022).

These manuals provide an official description of what autism is. Clinicians then use these manuals to help them diagnose autism in tandem with:

- observation of the child in the home, school and clinical setting
- an interview with the child, if appropriate
- a parental questionnaire and/or an interview with the parents.

Observations gathered from the above are then used to fill out an official diagnostic test/tool, such as the Autism Diagnostic Observation Schedule (ADOS), or the Diagnostic Interview for Social and Communication Disorders (DISCO).

Ten Things Every Teacher Should Know About Autism

1. Girls and autism

Until recently, the ratio of autistic boys to girls was thought to be four to one. However, more recent studies suggest that that the figure is closer to three to one (Cridland et al. 2014; NAS 2020b).

Girls are often misdiagnosed or remain undiagnosed until later in life. This is due to a number of reasons, including:

- The assessment tool used to diagnose autism was initially developed with boys in mind and so may not accurately reflect the differences in the way both genders present with autism.
- Girls can be much better at pretending, imitating, masking and modifying their behaviour than boys. For example, in order to blend in, girls can copy their friends' behaviours.
- Girls may have more socially acceptable special interests. Examples include drawing, horses or fashion.
- Some girls have other conditions that can overshadow their autistic traits. For example, a clinician might focus more on an eating disorder or anxiety, which hides the fact that these issues may stem from undiagnosed autism.

(Cridland et al. 2014; NASEN 2016; Ratto et al. 2018)

2. Asperger syndrome (AS)

The term Asperger syndrome is gradually disappearing. The international manuals for diagnosing autism (the DSM-5 and the upcoming ICD-11) have both removed Asperger syndrome as a separate diagnosis and have put this under the umbrella of 'autism spectrum disorder' (ASD).

One of the main differences between AS and autism is that children with AS do not display a significant language delay in their early years. Some people with AS prefer to hold on to their AS label as it forms an important part of their identity.

3. Spiky profile

The term 'spiky profile' highlights the fact that many autistic children will display strengths in some areas and needs in others. This can be confusing for teachers, as it is often assumed that high performance in one area correlates to high performance across all other areas.

Consider a 9-year-old boy who excels at maths, but who is not able to make his own bed or walk to school independently. Or a 14-year-old girl who is top of her class in every subject, but who is afraid to go to the shop on her own in case she forgets what to say at the counter.

" I did really well academically and ended up going to Oxford university... That ended up becoming my downfall. I came up against this, 'She gets good grades, what's the problem? When actually, everything else was the problem.' "

Georgia Harper, autism advocate and Embracing Complexity lead at Autistica

4. High functioning and low functioning labels

The labels 'high functioning' and 'low functioning' are often deemed to be pejorative for both parties.

Using the label 'high functioning' can lead to a lack of support and empathy for any student who struggles to do a seemingly easy task. The converse is also true. Referring to someone as 'low functioning' can diminish the perceived capability of the child, leading to lowered expectations for that child.

Alternative terms include:

- someone with low support needs currently
- someone with high support needs currently.

5. Hidden disability

Autism is known as a 'hidden' or 'invisible' disability because it is hard to tell if someone has autism just by looking at them. As a result, people can sometimes ascribe intentionality to an autistic child's behaviours instead of taking their autistic differences into account.

They ask 'Is she acting like this because she's wilful?' when her behaviour is probably due to a number of differences that arise as a result of her autism. For example, she might be acting in this way because she finds it hard to cope with a new supply teacher, the lights are too bright or she simply does not understand the lesson because it has all been delivered verbally.

Just as a wheelchair user uses a ramp to board a bus, so should an autistic child have access to any of the additional supports that may make their school day easier.

These include: visual schedules, sensory breaks, reward systems, playground structures or homework emailed at the end of the day rather than asking the child to write it out.

Autism awareness sessions for staff and students are also very important to increase understanding and compassion for everyone.

6. Models of disability

Society is becoming more autism aware. From silent hours in supermarkets to sensory rooms at airports and stadiums, from relaxed cinema screenings to downloadable photo stories on restaurant and theatre websites, there has been a slow but definite sea change towards a more inclusive understanding of autism.

This demonstrates a palpable shift away from a medical understanding of a disability towards a more social one.

The medical model: This model seeks to fix or change the person's disability. It focuses on the disability, believing that the autistic person needs to change or adapt to fit in with the non-autistic world.

The social model: This model believes that society should change, rather than the individual. Practically speaking, at school this means adapting the learning environment (classroom, hall, toilets) to suit the needs of autistic pupils (lower lighting, silent projectors, silent hand-dryers, visual schedules in each classroom).

CASE STUDY: CLONAKILTY, COUNTY CORK, IRELAND

The small town of Clonakilty is an excellent example of the social model of disability in action. In 2017, it became Ireland's first autism-friendly town. Local organizations, including businesses, schools, doctors, the fire service, sports organizations and those in the hospitality industry all volunteered to become 'autism-friendly champions' by pledging to complete a number of agreed aims. These included:

- ensuring all staff receive autism training
- making photo stories available online to prepare autistic people for a visit
- displaying assistance dog-friendly stickers in many businesses
- catering to the sensory needs of autistic clientele, for example, by having a quiet space available.

Accredited by Aslam, Ireland's national autism charity, Clonakilty also has a public sensory garden in the town centre, has made signage more visually clear in key public areas, hosts an annual Autism Awareness day and gives a monthly tip on its website about how to gain a better understanding of autism.

www.clonakilty.ie

7. Autism supports

66 Over the last fifteen years, I have spoken to many parents about the different supports they have used with their children. The bottom line is that they are all eager to try different supports that will help their child to be as good as they can be. 99

Claire

The choice of autism interventions and supports available is immense. A quick Google search of 'autism supports' yields almost 30 million results. These include dolphin therapy, equine therapy, CBD oil, sensory therapies and fish oil to name but a few. Some are supported by evidence-based research and others anecdotally by parents and professionals. In a bid to help parents and educators to navigate the sea of conflicting and confusing information available out there and to make informed decisions both for and with their children, some organizations have produced reports featuring lists of evidence-based practices (EBPs).

EBPs are those practices that are considered by researchers to be safe and effective and to produce positive outcomes when used with autistic children and young people.

- **National Clearinghouse on Autism Evidence and Practice (NCAEP):** Following extensive literature reviews, this report identifies 28 evidence-based practices for autistic people (Steinbrenner et al. 2020). These include: reinforcement of desired behaviours, exercise and movement, modelling, peer-based instruction and interactions, reinforcement, Sensory Integration® (SI), social narratives, social skills training, technology-aided instruction and interaction, video modelling and visual supports.

   One recent addition to this list is Sensory Integration® (SI), specifically that as outlined by Dr A. Jean Ayres and not currently including weighted vests or sensory diets.

   https://ncaep.fpg.unc.edu
- **Autism Focused Intervention Resources and Modules (AFIRM)** is a useful website produced by NCAEP. It contains online modules with videos and activities to teach practitioners how to actually plan for, use and monitor an evidence-based practice with autistic children and young people aged 0–22 years.

   https://autismpdc.fpg.unc.edu/evidence-based-practices
- **'Autism Spectrum Disorder in Under 19s: Support and Management'** (NICE 2013) gives informed advice about autism supports, as well as advising against using certain practices, including exclusion diets (gluten- and casein-free diets), hyperbaric oxygen therapy and chelation.

   www.nice.org.uk

- The **National Autistic Society (NAS)** website contains advice about choosing the right approach, as well as a regularly updated information page in their news section about new autism supports (NAS 2020c).
  www.autism.org.uk

It is worth noting that some supports have not yet been identified as an EBP. This does not mean they are ineffective, but rather that there is currently a lack of available evidence to determine their effectiveness.

There are so many tried-and-tested strategies and resources that autistic people and their families can use to help reduce any stress that may arise from living in an environment that is not always autism-friendly. We will outline many of these ideas throughout the book.

8. Neurodiversity and focusing on strengths

66 It seems sometimes you need a dash of autism so you can look at things from a totally different perspective and create new, untrodden ways. 99

Lenore Good, autistic advocate, blogger and mother of six

In recent years there has been a move away from viewing autism as a deficit towards a focus on strengths and a celebration of neurodiversity. Embracing neurodiversity means recognizing and celebrating the many different ways that humans have of thinking and looking at the world (Kapp et al. 2013).

Workplaces are now recognizing the unique potential of autistic people, and companies such as Microsoft Ireland and the software company SAP are actively recruiting autistic employees. There are realistic autistic characters portrayed in the media, in books and on children's television programmes, as well as autistic artists and programmers, authors, mathematicians, psychiatrists, surfers and singers.

We are very much moving away from a deficits-based view of autism to a strengths-based model.

- **A deficits-based view** focuses on what you cannot do. It highlights all the negative aspects of a disability.
- **A strengths-based view** focuses on strengths and what you can do. It uses positive language to describe autism and highlights the strengths of autistic people. It celebrates difference. Such strengths include attention to detail and a visual orientation.

9. Words matter!

'He suffers from autism', 'She's affected by autism', 'He's an ASD child' and even 'ASD unit' are all terms heard from school-based professionals or seen in newspapers lately. If language shapes the way we think, then it is important to consider the language we use every day to discuss autism.

Identity-first or person-first language?

The debate about whether to use 'identity-first' or 'person-first' language to describe autism is ongoing.

For example, which is more correct?

'Jenny is autistic' or 'Jenny is a woman with autism.'

Does it matter, and if so, who does it matter to?

Person-first language: *'Jenny is a woman with autism.'* This implies that Jenny is far more than her disability. She should not be defined by it, nor should it be used as an adjective to categorize her. Autism is just one part of her. The person comes first, and the disability comes last.

Identity-first language: *'Jenny is autistic.'* This posits Jenny's autism as such an intrinsic part of Jenny's identity. Autism is not something that can be cast off or hidden. It is inseparable from Jenny, like the writing that runs through a stick of rock from a beachside shop. Indeed, every person is made up of different traits, but autism is such an important part of them that it must be included as an adjective that describes that person.

The thinking around this has changed, with identity-first language coming to prominence in recent years. This change has been led by some of the autism community themselves. The #ActuallyAutistic community are particularly vocal about these terms, their very name implying a preference towards identity-first language.

" Autism is part of who I am. "

Year 9 student, Limpsfield Grange School for girls aged 11–16
with communication and interaction difficulties

ASD, ASC or autism?

Which of the following terms do you prefer to use?

- autism spectrum disorder (ASD)
- autism spectrum condition (ASC)
- autism.

Autism spectrum disorder, or ASD, is still very much used in schools, in journal articles and by professionals. However, the term 'disorder' can imply deficit, or 'something wrong with'. Some schools and professionals have moved away from the term ASD towards the seemingly gentler term 'autism spectrum condition', or ASC. But does the word 'condition' still suggest 'disorder/illness/ailment', and something that needs to be cured?

In a 2015 study (Kenny et al.), researchers surveyed and interviewed 3470 people (autistic individuals, parents and professionals) in the UK about their preferred terms to describe autism.

Results indicated that:

- Autistic adults and their families preferred the term 'autistic'.
- Almost half of the professionals preferred the term 'person with autism'.
- The most highly endorsed terms were 'autism', 'autism spectrum' and to a lesser extent 'autism spectrum disorder'.

66 One father made the point that we only hear the opinion of verbal autistic people who are able to tell us what they prefer. His pre-verbal son wasn't yet able to offer his opinion about it. 99

Claire

At the end of the day, it always comes down to personal choice. If you are not sure, just ask the person themselves.

66 The correct choice is the wording that people want used about themselves. 99

Stuart Neilson, autistic author and scientist (Neilson 2019a)

Upon reflection, we have decided to use identity-first language throughout this book, while also respecting the views of anyone who might instead prefer person-first language.

10. Autistic children grow up to be autistic adults

If you work with an autistic child, always ask yourself one question: 'What skills will be most useful for her as she moves through her life?'

For example, if you are teaching your student how to wait by using a 'Wait' card, think about why you are doing it. Is it so that you can proudly show her parents and other staff that she can now 'wait' for ten seconds to take her turn, using a timer and a 'Wait' card?

Or is it so that ultimately she can participate in a group game, manage a cinema queue or go out for dinner to celebrate her big brother's birthday and be fully part of the celebration, without anyone having to take her outside and miss everything – all because she understands and has practised the idea of waiting?

Thinking like this will help you to focus on your students' specific strengths and needs, to always consider the reasons behind why you have chosen to focus on certain skills and to have a longer-term view of what they need. What you teach in primary school will form the first important links in a lifelong chain of learning.

Part 2

Top Autism-Friendly Strategies

Make Everything Visual for Me

 If you stand outside Old Street Station in London and look down, you will see a thick green line painted on the pavement that weaves across roads and around corners, all the way to Moorfields Eye Hospital. Instead of having to ask someone for directions outside the underground station and instantly forgetting them, or depending on others to lead them, a patient can simply follow the green line all the way to their destination.

There is no doubt that visuals can make life easier in so many ways. There's Google Maps or Citymapper to find your way on city walks or cross-country drives, step-by-step photo recipes or Instagram Live cook-alongs online to help you whip up something nice for dinner. Or how about simply using the notes app on a phone to jot down a shopping list before a quick dash to Tesco Extra.

Autism and visual supports

Many autistic children may learn better by seeing and doing, rather than simply by hearing. As you read through this book, you will notice that every single chapter hinges on choosing, creating and using different visual supports to suit different situations.

Visual supports (VS) are the linchpin upon which all good autism practice is based. In fact, VS are considered one of the 28 evidence-based practices for autistic children and young people aged 3–22 years (Steinbrenner et al. 2020). Studies on the use of visual supports with autistic children and young people detail improvements or changes in social interaction, communication, behaviour, play, cognitive ability, academic work, motor activities and adaptive outcomes (Sam et al. 2020).

> **Why use visuals?**
>
> - Many autistic children have *language and auditory processing difficulties* (APA 2013), As outlined in ☞ 'Help Me to Communicate' later in Part 2, an autistic child's expressive language skills may be better than their receptive language skills, which means that understanding spoken language can be more difficult.

- Many autistic children have *a strong visual processing sense* and may be more inclined to focus on visual details than other forms of communication.

Autistic author and animal scientist Temple Grandin has described how she 'thinks in pictures'. Grandin has also described how she can visualize exactly how her machinery will work before she ever builds it. 'Many people with autism are visual thinkers. I think in pictures. I do not think in language. All my thoughts are like videotapes running in my imagination. Pictures are my first language, and words are my second language' (Grandin 2002).

As a result, using visual supports in your classroom can really play to the strengths of some of your autistic students, as well as compensating for any language processing difficulties.

What visuals?

Visual supports are 'concrete cues that provide information about an activity, routine or expectation, and/or support skill demonstration' (Steinbrenner et al. 2020, p.139).

This includes sign language, gesture, concrete materials, pictures, written text and video.

Visual supports:

- make everything more predictable
- are more concrete and longer lasting than words
- can be checked repeatedly, as and when needed by your students.

Visuals are the WD-40 of the autism world. Used correctly, they can be used to support your students with absolutely everything.

Guide 3

Six Ways That Visuals Can Help at School

1. Understanding of classroom routines

Tuesday 17th November 2020
Register
Handwriting
maths
Small break
Irish
Art
meditation

FIGURE 2.1 WHOLE-CLASS SCHEDULE

In one morning, Lizzie, 7, had asked her teacher five times about her favourite subjects: 'When's Irish? Do we have Drama today?' The teacher directed her to the whole-class schedule (Figure 2.1) that was written in marker down the side of the class whiteboard and asked her to check it whenever she felt worried or unsure about Irish or Drama.

2. Understanding and enjoyment of lesson content

Philippa, 8, looked bored as her class listened to an audio story of a Greek myth. However, once the special needs assistant pulled up a few pictures of 'Theseus and the Minotaur' on the class iPad, Philippa perked up and said, 'Oh, that's just like our Greek project' and pointed to the Greek myth display.

3. Differentiation of lesson content

Visuals can help to differentiate the curriculum in a way that will suit most students. For example:

- **Literacy and Numeracy:** Have 'Maths' and 'Literacy' boxes/folders (Figure 2.2) at hand to pass out to students, as needed. These boxes could contain:

FIGURE 2.2 MATHS BOX

- – **Numeracy:** mini whiteboards and pens, blank flashcards, dice, hundred squares, number lines, Dienes cubes, mini clocks, real coins, money number lines.
- – **Literacy:** blank bingo boards, magnetic letters, phonics letter sound cards, mini whiteboard and pen, blank flashcards.
- **Science:** If the class has to draw a picture of a Venus flytrap, look at a variety of photos and pictures on the interactive whiteboard and watch a video of one opening and closing online.
- **P.E.:** Use pictures to show your students what to do during a P.E. lesson. For example, hold up a picture of 'hop' as well as saying the word. Use pictures to explain games such as 'Chasing' or 'Traffic Light Game' (red light = stop, green light = run, orange light = walk).
- **Art:** Draw pencil dots to show a student where to dot glue on a page.
- **Music:** Make PowerPoints or find YouTube videos of favourite songs to make them more tangible.

" When I first started teaching in a special school, I couldn't figure out how to teach music. We worked our way through a music programme but the students were never very keen on just listening to and learning the songs. I decided to make a PowerPoint presentation for every song, with some relevant images. All of a sudden, they were intrigued. By the end of the year, my students could play our 'Name That Song' competition just by listening to the opening bars of each tune. The visuals helped them to focus, understand what the songs were about and the activity enhanced their listening skills to no end. For me, it felt miraculous! "

Claire

4. Information processing

Charles, 8, loved swimming but often forgot what sequence to put his clothes on after swimming. He always tended to start with his socks, then his T-shirt, and then finally put on his pants. Staff felt that as he became older, this way of dressing might become inappropriate or unsafe for Charles, particularly in an open-plan changing room with no cubicles. Class staff printed and laminated a visual sequence for dressing and stuck it in the changing room every week when they visited the pool. It helped Charles to remember the most efficient order in which to put his clothes on.

5. Motivation

BEAT THE TIMER

_____ Versus the Timer

Tick below if you manage to beat the timer! Get 3 in 1 session and win a reward!

Child	Timer
✓	
✓	

FIGURE 2.3 PETRA V THE TIMER

Petra, 9, had no interest in writing a new report about the Vikings, and told her teacher so.

Staff set the timer for 10 minutes, and asked Petra to complete 4 sentences about the Vikings using her initial draft as a guide. If she managed to 'beat the timer', she would be able to read her favourite book about planes. In this way, class staff were able to encourage Petra to start her work.

They continued to use the 'Petra V The Timer' chart for different tasks throughout the day, especially those that Petra found difficult to start (Figure 2.3).

6. Anxiety reduction

If Zach, 8, was worried about something at school, it often became 'stuck' in his mind, and he simply couldn't relax until the issue had been resolved. One day, he lost a letter that he was supposed to bring home and get signed in order to go on a school tour, and he wanted to get a replacement letter. For the first hour, he repeatedly asked his teacher 'Where's the note?', 'Can I have the note?' and 'Don't forget the note.' His class teacher knew she wouldn't be able to access a spare copy from the secretary's office until break time. So, she got a mini whiteboard and wrote 'Don't worry, I will get the note at lunch time and put it in your bag at home time' and gave it to him. When Zach asked again, she simply directed him to 'Check your mini whiteboard, Zach', or pointed to it. This proved to be calming for Zach, as every time he remembered his worry, he simply reassured himself by looking at the mini whiteboard and remembering that the teacher would get it for him later.

66 It was often the small, informal things that I found really helpful – like a teacher writing 'Don't worry' on top of a Post-it note. 99

Georgia Harper, autism advocate and Embracing Complexity lead at Autistica

General Classroom Visuals That Work for Everyone

By backing up spoken words with visual supports, you will enhance the understanding of everyone in the class, not just that of your autistic students. Visual supports help to make the classroom environment as accessible as possible for everyone, which is an excellent example of Universal Design for Learning (UDL).

> Universal design (UD) is the design of environments that can be accessed and understood by everyone. Some practical examples of universal design include:
>
> - OXO Good Grips vegetable peelers are designed for anyone to be able to easily hold and use.
> - The installation of ramps or lifts in all train stations ensures that everyone (wheelchair users, people with buggies, people with reduced mobility) can participate in train travel.
>
> Similarly, at school, UDL is a framework that aims to make learning environments and resources accessible to all.
> Some examples of UDL in school include:
>
> - writing down verbal information for students
> - setting up quiet spaces, fixing flickering lights and completing a sensory audit on a building
> - using a variety of multimedia resources during lessons
> - activating prior knowledge for comprehension
> - offering students a choice of assessment method
> - giving students slides or notes in advance of class so that they can adapt them to their preferred format.

Some basic visual supports to start with

1. Make general classroom rules and routines easier to understand and remember.
   - **Make posters** detailing any of following:
     - **'Good Listening' means:** 1) mouth closed 2) hands empty and 3) looking at teacher

- **When teacher claps:** 1) mouth closed 2) pens down 3) look at teacher
- **'Brain, Board, Buddy, Boss':** 'First I try by myself, then I check the board, then I ask a friend and if I still can't do it, I say to the teacher "I need help."'
- **Independent work:** 'When I work in my workbook, I read the words quietly to myself.'

In this way, your students can simply check the poster if they are stuck on something in class. Practice these rules with the whole class regularly for the month of September. Send them home too for your students to do as part of their homework.

2. **Use a whole-class daily schedule** written down the side of the whiteboard. Cross out activities as they are completed.

3. **Make spoken whole-class instructions really clear and visual** by writing down the essay title or questions you want the students to respond to on the whiteboard, so that everyone remembers what they need to do.

> 66 I once observed an older autistic student during an English lesson. The teacher called out an essay title for the class to write about and everyone got to work, including this particular student. He appeared to be very focused on his work. However, when I wandered over to see what he was writing, it had nothing to do with the essay question at all. He was just trying to look busy and hadn't thought of asking anyone for help. Simply writing the question on the whiteboard would have quickly solved this. 99
>
> *Claire*

4. Use WAGOLL ('what a good one looks like').
   - **Display an example** of what a neatly laid-out copybook page looks like on a poster so that your students can copy the layout, as needed.
   - **Use a visualizer** to help your students to see exactly how something is done, rather than seeing it demonstrated in a different format on the interactive whiteboard or on a Word document. This allows them to get on with their work, without having to first generalize the whole-class input to a new layout during individual work time.

5. **Annotate the classroom with pictures and labels** to make it really clear what happens in each area and where classroom items go.
   - Label the different areas of the classroom with photographs, pictures or words. For example, 'reading corner', 'maths table', 'literacy copybooks'.
   - Put photographs (or videos on an iPad) of what to do in different areas. For example, you could put a photo of someone sitting on the beanbag reading

in the reading corner, or a photo of your student with a speech bubble saying 'Can I take your order please?' in the home café area.

- Label drawers, boxes and shelves. For example, 'literacy copies', or 'LEGO®'.
- Have a seating plan to show students where they are going to sit throughout the day.

Visuals for independence

Ultimately, your goal in using visual supports is to enable your students to become more independent in everything they do and to help decrease any anxiety along the way.

Never, ever underestimate the power of a simple visual.

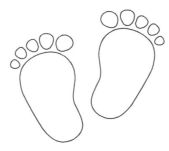

Dan, 8, found it hard to line up in the playground with his class after break and play time, and at home time. Instead, he tended to whizz around while the rest of the school lined up. Dan's mum was keen that he lined up with everyone else, particularly at home time, when all the other parents were present in the playground, waiting to collect their children.

Dan's teacher spent lots of time encouraging him to get into the line and walk back to the classroom with his classmates. He wrote a social narrative called 'Why I Must Line Up with My Class' and devised a reward system for Dan. But none of this seemed to help Dan to line up.

One day, when the playground was quiet, Margaret, an amazing special needs assistant, brought Dan to the playground, and together they painted an outline of his feet exactly where his class lined up, to show him exactly where to stand. The next day when the bell rang, she found Dan standing on two little red feet waiting for the rest of his class to come and line up too.

Guide 5

Top Tips for Using Visuals

Just make it visual

" I used to carry a pad of Post-it notes and a pen around in my handbag so that I'd always have a quick way of making things visual for my son whenever he needed it. "

Mother of a 16-year-old autistic boy

Autism and visuals go together like fish and chips, Woody and Buzz, peaches and cream or tapas and wine. To simply say that they are important is a major understatement. However, sometimes school staff forget about using visual supports and try to help a student using far more complicated strategies.

Remember, if in doubt, just *make it visual*. Once you get into this mindset and figure out what to use and how to use it, everything becomes easier.

Always try to back up any spoken language with an object, picture or written word.

- Remember, your students need to learn how to use and trust their visual supports, so only introduce one at a time.
- Be selective in the visual supports that you are using at any one time and remember to take down or put away the ones that no longer serve you. It is pointless to have a thousand beautifully laminated visuals stuck up around the classroom if they are not in use by either the students or staff.

" In my first year of teaching, a speech and language therapist came into my classroom and removed at least half of the visuals at one student's desk. There were Reward Boards, class rules, schedules, Choice Boards, scripts and Days of the Week Matching Boards. Her rationale was that the child no longer even saw some of these visuals anymore – they were just visual clutter at this stage. "

Claire

- Don't panic if you see lots of perfect visuals adorning the walls of colleagues' classrooms, or on Instagram classroom video walk-throughs. Visual supports really need to be personalized to suit the specific needs of each child, and there really is no one-size-fits-all approach.

And lastly:

- Rome wasn't built in a day. Initially, why not choose one focus topic or subject per month and make a few extra visual supports for this. Very soon you will have built up a bank of visuals, all stored neatly in plastic sandwich bags or boxes, ready for students to access as and when needed. For example:
  - September – schedules
  - October – classroom rules and routines
  - November – reward systems
  - December – Maths
  - January – Literacy

 ## Tools of the trade

Velcro: Make a rule and ensure everyone in the class knows that *hard Velcro goes on solid surfaces*, and *soft Velcro goes on moveable items*. This will prevent many unusable, unstickable disasters from happening when Velcro is stuck 'soft to soft' or 'hard to hard'.

Laminating: It's a boring job, but somebody has to do it. When laminating pictures for a schedule, cut out each picture first, glue them individually inside the laminating pockets and then laminate them all. This may seem overly labour intensive. However, it will ensure that your schedule pictures last much longer by avoiding nasty peeling corners, which invariably provide an irresistible invitation to your students to fidget with, tearing the visuals apart.

Snipping tool: This handy screen-shotting tool is available in any Microsoft package, even the older versions. Simply type 'snipping tool' into the computer search bar, right click and pin it to your taskbar for all eternity. Use it to snip the pictures you need from the internet or from documents without the need to 'save as' or to 'copy and paste'. It is particularly handy to make schedule photos with YouTube thumbnails featuring students' specific songs or favourite programmes.

Some very basic individualized visuals for daily classroom use include a schedule, timer, Reward Board, mini whiteboard and pen and a pad of Post-it notes.

Give Me a Schedule

 Coping with uncertainty

Imagine arriving at a one-day conference without knowing what time your coffee break or lunch will be at, who the speakers will be and what time it will finish. Imagine your anxiety building as the day wears on. You might wonder:

- How much longer do I have to concentrate for?
- When can I have a cup of coffee and a chocolate biscuit?
- When will I be able to go to the toilet without disrupting the whole room?
- What if it doesn't finish on time for me to collect my children?

As an independent adult, you can use coping skills (such as asking someone else or checking the agenda online) to calm yourself down and to find out what is going to happen throughout the day.

This ability to think flexibly and on the spot is something that many autistic people can find difficult. In fact, *flexible thinking skills* are one of the key areas looked at when diagnosing autism (APA 2013).

Flexible thinking skills: Being able to think flexibly means being able to accept change easily. For example, I was due to deliver training in a school on Monday morning, but my alarm clock didn't go off and I woke up late, panicking when I saw the time. However, due to my relatively flexible thinking skills, I was able to adapt to this new situation, quickly decide that I didn't have time for a shower or breakfast, and instead jumped straight into the car with a banana in my hand to eat while stuck in traffic.

Many autistic people can find it difficult to be immediately flexible or to remember the coping skills they used when a similarly unpredictable situation happened to them in the past. When an unexpected change happens, the autistic brain can go straight to panic mode. In fact, change can prove to be so anxiety-inducing to someone with autism that the rest of the day can feel off kilter and impossible to manage.

Let's think about this in terms of pasta. Uncooked spaghetti breaks under pressure (inflexible thinking) while cooked spaghetti can bend and flex as needed. Visualizing this can often help your students with metacognition, which essentially means being aware of their own thinking habits.

In fact, following lots of work around this, one student said 'I wish I was more like cooked spaghetti' when he knew he was finding it hard to process change one day.

Or how about imagining your students' brains as a jar full of water and glitter? An unexpected change is akin to shaking the jar, making the glitter swirl all around. Often, it can take the rest of the day for the glitter to fully resettle at the bottom of the jar.

66 The smallest change can make everything tumble down like an avalanche. I sat in the same place every day. One day the teacher changed our seats – the smallest change can throw me off for a couple of hours. Change is bad! Change makes all the happy, warm feeling go away. 99

Year 9 student, Limpsfield Grange school for girls aged 11–16
with communication and interaction difficulties

Guide 6

Using a Schedule

❝ I find knowing what to expect really helps. I try to get as much information beforehand as possible. So schedules and getting to know the setting and activities will go a long way. ❞

Tim Chan, autistic author

Many autistic people dislike change and prefer everything to be as predictable as possible. It makes them feel calmer to know exactly what is going to happen.

One way of making the school day more predictable is by using a schedule. This can show your students exactly what is going to happen throughout the day, provides a sense of certainty and can alleviate any anxiety about the unknown.

Learning to use a schedule leads to:

- increased independence ('I don't have to ask what's next, as I can just check my schedule')
- increased motivation to do non-preferred tasks ('I don't like English, but I can get through it as I know my favourite subject, Maths, is next')
- increased executive function skills ('I know how to look ahead and make a plan based on what activities I will be doing')
- decreased anxiety ('I know what I am doing all day today').

Schedules (under the banner of visual supports) are considered one of the 28 evidence-based practices for autistic children, youth and young adults (Steinbrenner et al. 2020).

What kind of schedule to use

There are four types of schedule that you can use. These are:

1. objects of reference (OoR)
2. photo schedule
3. symbol schedule
4. written schedule.

Figure 2.4 shows a useful hierarchy for using visual supports with our students. Once they have mastered the first step (objects), you can move on to the next step (colour photo). You can also use more than one step at a time, for example, by using a colour symbol with the word printed underneath.

FIGURE 2.4 HIERARCHY FOR VISUAL SUPPORTS

1. Objects of reference

OoR are objects used to represent an item on the student's visual schedule (Figure 2.5). It is often used for younger students who may not yet understand photographs or symbols.

Some objects of reference could include:

- home time: Barbie mini backpack
- toilet: dollhouse toilet
- drink: cup
- lunch time: lunch bag.

FIGURE 2.5 OBJECT-BASED SCHEDULE

2. Photo schedule

Using photographs of actual activities/things/places will hugely help your students to understand their schedule.

Take photos of every single activity, book and place that your students will experience and then print them out and laminate them.

FIGURE 2.6 TRANSITIONING FROM A PHOTO TO A SYMBOL SCHEDULE

If a student understands *photographs*, then it is often useful to gradually move him onto using *coloured symbols*. This can be done very simply by sticking a much smaller symbol square in the corner of a larger photo of the object (Figure 2.6). Gradually cut away the photo over a period of time until all that remains is the symbol.

3. Symbol/picture schedule

Use a commercial schedule maker (for example, Boardmaker or Communicate: In Print), or use simple images snipped from the internet. Just make sure that everyone is using the same pictures to denote activities or objects, both at home and at school, as otherwise it could get confusing for your student.

4. Word schedule

If the student can read fluently and understands what the words mean, you can then move on to using a word and/or picture schedule. This can be written in simple list form in a copybook, on a mini whiteboard or on a pad of paper on a clipboard. You can also use cut-out laminated words Velcroed down the left-hand side of a student's desk – as each activity finishes, he removes the word to a collection box on his desk.

It is very important to give your students a schedule type that is appropriate to their age and ability.

Alanna, 11, was able to read fluently. Her new teacher gave her a word–symbol schedule, which she kept losing, burying under books or ignoring completely. Alanna seemed a bit teary and uncertain in the mornings when she arrived at school, and her teacher put it down to getting used to a new school year.

Possible reasons

Alanna was really embarrassed by the fact that she had such a babyish schedule, so she kept hiding it. She was also too embarrassed to ask her teacher or the class special needs assistant what was happening next during the day, so spent her days in a state of uncomfortable uncertainty.

What to do

After a long chat and a walk with Alanna, Vicky, the special needs assistant, figured out what she needed, and together they decided to use a schedule written down in a copybook that she kept at her desk. Vicky also sent a copy of the weekly class timetable home so that Alanna would always have some idea of what was happening the next day.

Understanding the schedule

Most children will not automatically know how to use a schedule. They will need to spend some time learning:

- what each part means
- how to use it.

It is really important to check that the student understands the schedule, rather than it being a meaningless – albeit pristine – display of laminated symbols. You can assess understanding using the below activities or consult your speech and language therapist and parents for guidance as to where your student should start.

Teaching the schedule

A good way of assessing or teaching students how to recognize their schedule objects, photos or pictures is the 'matching, selecting and naming' process (Bird, Beadman and Buckley 2001). Take your time on each step, and only move on to the next step when your student is fully competent in the previous one.

- **Matching:** Give your student a photo of a lunchbox and ask him to find the matching symbol out of a few pictures laid out on the desk in front of him.
- **Selecting:** Place two photos/symbols in front of the student. Say 'Give me "lunchbox" please.'
- **Naming:** Hold up photos/symbols and say 'What's this?'

Ms Ryan was told that Jake, a 4-year-old autistic boy, would be enrolling in Reception in September. To prepare for his arrival, she created a workspace for him and spent lots of time printing out schedule symbols and stuck them in a full-day schedule on the workstation. However, when Jake arrived, he chose instead to sit with the rest of the class and didn't engage with his schedule at all. By October, Ms Ryan had stopped using it with him, as she said it wasn't working and he simply wasn't interested in it.

Possible reasons

If a student seems disinterested in his schedule, it may be simply because he does not understand it, or that it is too long for him.

What to do

Ms Ryan photographed the main parts of the school day, as well as some of the front covers of the books they were using in class. She allocated some time daily for one member of the class team to work with Jake on matching photos to the actual objects. She set him up at a table with his classmates. Once staff were sure that Jake fully understood what each photo meant, they started showing him a photo before introducing each activity. Jake usually then started to walk towards that activity, which demonstrated his understanding.

For Jake, this was just the beginning of understanding what using a schedule meant. He was beginning to trust that staff would always let him know what he was doing by using a picture.

Which to use: Full-day, part-day or First/Then/Next schedule

The length of schedule you use depends on your student's cognitive ability, and how much information they can take in at one time. Different lengths include:

- one activity at a time
- First/Then schedule throughout the day
- First/Then/Next schedule
- part-day schedule (one section put up in the morning, one in the mid-morning and one in the afternoon)
- full-day schedule.

Using a Schedule to Make Changes Easier

Inevitably, changes will occur during the school day. While some of your students will be able to cope with this, others may find it very stressful. You can prepare your student for any changes by purposefully introducing tiny changes into the school day. This promotes the ability to think more flexibly, as well as opportunities for practising coping strategies for any unexpected changes.

- **Always introduce 'change' in a gentle way by starting with a 'just as good' change.** This means changing a non-preferred activity to a preferred activity. For example, 'Maths is not on. Let's go for a quick walk instead.'
- **Put a 'Change' card on the schedule to show the student what has changed and what he will be doing instead.** In this way, students will begin to realize that 'change' can actually be manageable and does not always have to precede panic mode.
- **Start to introduce more change for neutral subjects/activities (that he neither loves nor actively dislikes)** once your student is used to small changes. Eventually begin to change preferred activities for non-preferred activities.
- **Do try to sweeten the deal for him a bit by offering something nice instead** if you need to cancel an activity your student absolutely loves and has looked forward to for ages. For example, 'Swimming is cancelled. Let's go to the canteen for a fruit pack instead.'
- **Try to use 'Change' cards, especially at times when there are so many different, unexpected activities happening, e.g. during the lead-up to Christmas or summer holidays.** If your student is well-versed in using a 'Change' card throughout the autumn term, he may find the unpredictability of the Christmas season a bit easier to manage. For example, 'Phonics is cancelled. Let's go to the hall to practise the play instead.'
- **Simply write any changes on the board for older students.** For example, 'Mrs Bee out tomorrow. Mr Smith here instead. Mrs Bee will be back on Wednesday.'

Using schedules to ease transitions

66 Sometimes it's hard coming into a new environment because I guess I take a lot in and it might be overwhelming walking into a new room because there are so

many details to take in and it would probably take me longer to get used to than NT people. 🙶

Year 9 student, Limpsfield Grange school for girls aged 11–16 with communication and interaction difficulties

'Transitioning' simply means moving from one place to another, or from one activity to another.

Transitions happen constantly throughout the school day. These include:

- going from home to school
- moving from the corridor to the classroom
- changing activities within the classroom
- going to the assembly hall, the toilet, the P.E. hall, the computer room or the sensory room.

Transitions mean change and uncertainty for your autistic students, and as a result can cause anxiety. Facilitate easier transitions by preparing your students. Pre-warn them when a task is about to end, and show them visuals about the next activity they will be doing or where they will be going to.

Alfie, 5, is an autistic, pre-verbal student in a mainstream primary school. Whenever staff ask him if he would like to go to the sensory room, Alfie appears reluctant to go, and often ends up sitting on the floor of the classroom.

Possible reasons

When someone says 'Let's go', your first question is usually 'Where to?' If a child doesn't know where he is going, then of course he is going to refuse to go! Alfie did not want to leave the classroom because he genuinely did not understand where he was going to, and this made him feel really anxious.

What to do

Staff used the following strategies to help Alfie cope with his fear of the unknown:

- Show Alfie photos and videos of the sensory room during work time to help him to get used to seeing these pictures and videos.
- Show Alfie his transition key ring containing a photo of the sensory room when he is about to go there or give him a photo of the sensory room to hold in his hand while walking there.*
- Bring Alfie's favourite dinosaur toy on the journey to help him to better cope with this trip that is nerve-wracking for him.
- Take the same route to the sensory room every time.
- Go directly to the sensory room, without stopping to talk to anyone.

- Stick a Destination Board on the sensory room door. A Destination Board is a board with a photo of the room on it. The student sticks his photo to a blank square on the Destination Board. Let Alfie Velcro his sensory room photo onto the Destination Board.
- Use a timer in the sensory room to help Alfie to realize when his session is over.
- Show Alfie a photograph of the classroom when it is time to return there.

* A transition key ring contains photos of all the different places that a student might go during the school day. Staff usually wear it on a lanyard around their necks, or clipped to their trousers. As Alfie grew more used to going to the sensory room, staff added more photos to his transition key ring (e.g. playground, assembly hall, kitchen) and worked on helping him to recognize these.

Guide 8

Using Schedules at Other Times

Mini activity schedules

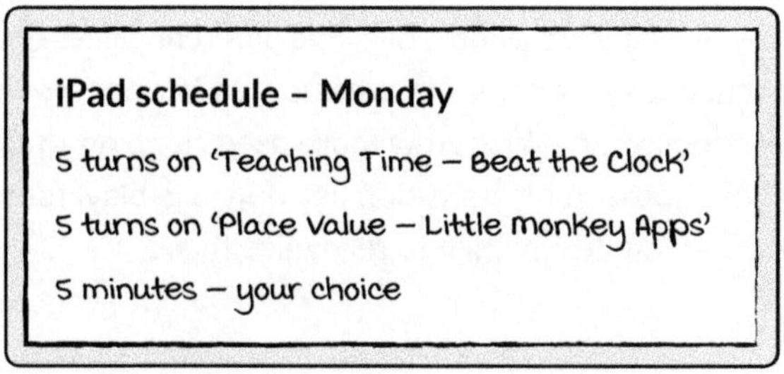

iPad schedule – Monday

5 turns on 'Teaching Time – Beat the Clock'

5 turns on 'Place Value – Little monkey Apps'

5 minutes – your choice

FIGURE 2.7 MINI ACTIVITY SCHEDULE

It may sound slightly meta to have a schedule within a schedule. However, it can be so useful to use a mini activity schedule for *activities that have more than one component* (Figure 2.7). These can be used during either group or individual activities sessions, including:

- **iPad activities:** write a list of the apps that he is going to use
- **morning meeting:** days of the week/weather/three songs/writing sentence/ finish
- **sensory activities:** smell box/massage/you choose/finish
- **P.E.:** warm up/two parachute games/cool down/finish
- **school tours:** bus/farm/playground/lunch/back to school.

Schedules at home

Peter, 8, used a written visual schedule throughout the day at school. It really helped to make the day predictable for him and alleviate any anxiety he might have. However, the weekend was a different story for Peter, with frequent tears and frustration when things didn't always go his way.

Possible reasons
Peter found it difficult to cope with all of the unstructured time at the weekend. Plans could change on a whim, and his parents' friends and their children often popped around to the house unexpectedly.

What to do

- His teacher recommended scribbling out a quick schedule for him, detailing what the family were going to do on Saturday.
- She also recommended that if anyone arranged a visit to simply put it on the schedule.

Three times that weekend, Peter told his mum that he loved his schedule and that it really worked for him and made him feel better.

66 The schedule really helps me, I like it! 99

Peter, 8-year-old autistic boy

Schedules on the move

Technology and the internet have made it much easier to instantly create high-quality visual supports for everyone. There are lots of schedule-maker apps available online, including Visual Schedule (Wizard Solutions Inc.), What's Next? (LifeAxis) and Choiceworks (Bee Visual, LLC).

However, sometimes it is just as easy to use the notes app on a phone to make a daily to-do list, or pull up some photos using the internet browser on your smartphone.

66 My teaching life got easier when smartphones were invented. One day, in a rush, I left the visual schedules for our school trip behind on my desk. When one student started to get anxious on the bus, I simply googled a picture of the farm and the playground that we were going to, and together we looked at them for a while. Instant schedule, and instant calm! 99

Claire

Offline, bullet journals and week-to-view fridge calendars are excellent options to help make life more predictable for everyone.

 It can be so easy to get lost in an online search for 'apps + autism'. For a wide range of app suggestions to suit users with different needs, see CALL Scotland: www.callscotland.org.uk.

It is heartening to see that in many schools, visual schedules are now par for the course, with both autistic and non-autistic children using them daily. This is a great example of Universal Design for Learning, which is concerned with strategies and resources that can benefit everybody and make learning accessible for all.

Learning to follow a schedule in primary school will develop vital organizational skills for secondary school, university and the world of work. For example, if a student at university feels anxious about his workload or having too many activities in the upcoming week, simply knowing how to create a list and tick off its items as each task is completed can be very calming.

" My son really loves secondary school, because it's so structured, and because he has a timetable to follow. He didn't like primary school as much, because it was the opposite. "

Parent of a 13-year-old autistic boy

Top Tips for Successful Schedules

1. **Don't get bogged down by perfection.** It is really important to remember that *a schedule does not have to be beautiful to work*. Write it on a Post-it note, a scrap of paper, or even a napkin. Whatever works to ensure that your student knows exactly what is going on that day and is forewarned of any changes coming up.
2. **Always print out extra schedule photos/pictures/words**, as they will inevitably get lost. You will probably find them in the back pockets of your trousers, in your car and on your kitchen table at home.
3. **Arrange your schedule pictures in alphabetical order** inside miniature plastic bank bags Velcroed to the back of a door. This really helps for ease of access, particularly in a special school setting. Store ten copies of the same picture in each little bag.
4. **Always have a few spare blank laminated squares** that you can quickly draw or write on, as needed.
5. **Remember, a schedule is for life.** School staff often wonder when they should stop using a visual schedule with their students. Fear of the unknown or intolerance of uncertainty can play a central role in anxiety for autistic children (Rodgers et al. 2016). (☞ See 'Teach Me Ways to Cope with Anxiety'.) At school, this could manifest as an inability to cope with unstructured parts of the school day.

   It is worth sticking with a daily schedule, even if you think a child no longer notices it. Often, they are glancing at it, and are comforted by the fact that it is there. It definitely helps to reduce any low-lying sense of uncertainty and keeps any anxiety down to a gentle simmer. To progress, simply replace a visual picture schedule with a word schedule, and then a written list, as appropriate.

Frequently asked questions

Q: He doesn't need a schedule. He never looks at it anyway, and he knows the class routine off by heart – he often reminds me what's next! Should we just stop using it altogether?

A: I would say keep using it, day in and day out. He may not appear to be looking at it, but it might be a nice comfort for him just to know it's there. He's also clearly very invested in reminding you about the order of the day, which shows how important it is to him. Also, think about the days when he is not feeling 'calm-alert'. Having access to and knowing how to use a schedule will provide great reassurance then.

Q: She has a meltdown at the start of every new lesson. What can I do?

A: She might need a visual schedule and/or a 'First/Then' reward system, so that she can clearly see what's going to happen next, and when she can have her reward. Why not try it for a few weeks and see if there is any change in her behaviour?

Remember, most children don't actively know that the schedule helps them to feel calm. Most children won't say 'I know why I feel anxious, and it's because I require a schedule, please, teacher.' It's up to us to provide our students with a schedule and notice and celebrate any changes in anxiety levels, however small.

Q: I'm afraid that using a schedule will just make him more rigid. He won't get a schedule in the real world.

A: We all use schedules – think about your work diary. We all use them to plan for the week ahead. It definitely won't make him more rigid, and in fact will help to lessen any anxiety. You could introduce tiny, manageable changes into the schedule so that he can increase his flexible thinking skills.

Q: Who's going to set it up? I just wouldn't have time in the mornings.

A: Why not teach your students or allocate one support staff member to write or set up the whole-class schedule at the start of every day? It could become part of the daily list of class jobs.

If the morning is too frenetic, why not arrange for them to have ten minutes to set it up every afternoon before home time?

Q: When should I start using a schedule?

A: Try to start from the very first day of the school year. Your students might need some time to fully understand how the schedule works, but it is so important to make it part of the routine from the very first day.

Motivate Me!

 ## Incentivizing schoolwork

Most people need a little incentive to do something they find difficult. Having something to look forward to can help you to:

- start a task
- focus on a task for set period of time
- persevere with a task as you know that the end is in sight, and that you will get something exciting afterwards.

Lots of children are highly motivated by social praise. A simple 'well done' from class staff, a table point or a marble in the jar towards earning a class prize can be enough to spur these students on to work harder. However, some children, including those on the autism spectrum, may not always be motivated by your approval alone.

In order to encourage a student to do something he is not particularly excited about, you may need to sweeten the deal for him by offering him something he is really interested in, perhaps related to a special interest, or by finding a way to get him fired up to do the task.

First: Work for two hours
Then: Watch Antiques Roadshow

FIGURE 2.8 CLAIRE'S PERSONAL FIRST/THEN BOARD (SEE 🔑 GUIDE 10: SETTING UP THREE TYPES OF REWARD SYSTEMS USING SPECIAL INTERESTS)

In this chapter, we will look at five different ways to motivate your students. They are:

1. using special interests:
   - Setting up Three Types of Reward Systems Using Special Interests (First/Then Boards, reward charts, learning contracts)
   - Five Ways to Use Special Interests During the School Day

2. other ways to motivate and increase engagement:
   - using competition to motivate
   - motivating using closed-ended tasks
   - motivating by making free-activity stations more finite.

Autism and special interests

66 Nothing can motivate me like my special interest… For me, my special interests are the greatest single source of pleasure in my life. 99

John Simpson (2019), autistic trainer, speaker and author

Many autistic children have a special interest in a particular topic. This can include movies, tall buildings, water bottles, lemmings, walking sticks, trains, dinosaurs, superheroes, hieroglyphics and World War 2, to name but a few. It is estimated that 75–90 per cent of autistic people develop one or more special interest early in life (Klin, Danovitch, Merz and Volkmar 2007) and that special interests remain important throughout a person's life.

Special interests:

- are highly rewarding
- may reduce stress.

They can be an all-consuming safety blanket to block out the world and retreat into a safe, comfortable and predictable place.

66 When I'm really stressed, I lean on my special interests more than other people…my reaction to stress…is to go to my local train station or bus station and either watch the buses and trains or get on and go on a journey… I will always talk eventually, it's just that the special interests help take the edge off my anxiety'. 99

John Simpson (2019), autistic trainer, speaker and author

As well as alleviating anxiety, engaging with special interests has also been shown to:

- increase self-confidence and peer interaction
- improve language and peer interaction
- allow your students to experience a sense of flow and achievement.

(based on Grove, Roth and Hoekstra 2016)

As a result, using special interests can be a teacher's top motivational tool. Harnessing the power of this special interest can really help with your students' focus, motivation and enjoyment of school. It also allows them to shine at something they are good at and very interested in.

Setting Up Three Types of Reward Systems Using Special Interests

A structured way of motivating your students is by using individualized positive reward systems. Often, these can be key to helping many of your students to stay on track at school.

It is worth noting that 'reinforcement of desired behaviours', which includes reward systems, is considered to be an evidence-based practice by the NCAEP (Steinbrenner et al. 2020).

Choosing a reward

Pip's reward list

5 minutes googling landmarks

5 minutes reading Landmarks of London book

5 minutes learning to draw The Shard from YouTube

5 minutes on bikes

FIGURE 2.9 AN EXAMPLE OF A STUDENT'S REWARD LIST

One of the most important parts of a reward system is the reward itself. After all, the success of a reward system depends on the student being really motivated to get this reward.

Draw up a list of rewards. Ask other teachers, parents and, of course, the student himself what he would like to work towards. Often your students have a whole secret life at home, where they are interested in things you have never heard them talk about.

Finding a suitable motivator for every child can be tricky, but not impossible. There is always something, although it might just mean doing a little detective work. Observe what your student gravitates towards in the classroom, in the playground or even in the class library.

Rewards must be specific to each student. The system simply will not work if the reward does not rock your student's world at that particular time.

Reward lists are working documents. If the reward system stops working, it is usually because the child is bored of the reward. The only solution is to go back to the drawing board to brainstorm some new rewards.

What type of reward system to use

Some different types of reward systems include:

- First/Then Board
- reward chart
- learning contract.

It is worth trying different versions with your students to find out what suits them best.

First/Then Board

A simple First/Then Board can be highly effective. However, it often causes the most confusion amongst school staff. Below is a simple step-by-step guide to using a First/Then Board.

FIGURE 2.10 REWARD BOARD

FIGURE 2.11 FIRST/THEN BOARD

1. Find five things that your student absolutely loves.
2. Photograph these items/activities and stick them on a Reward Board (Figure 2.10). You could also use symbols, or just words, depending on the cognitive ability of your student.

3. Before beginning a task, show the student the Reward Board, and ask him what he would like to work towards.

4. Then show your student the First/Then Board (Figure 2.11), already containing a specific task on the 'First' side of the board. Ask him to choose a reward and stick it on the 'Then' part of the First/Then Board.

5. Allow him to get to work. If he loses focus, remind him of the upcoming reward by pointing to the First/Then Board.

6. The minute he finishes his work, give him his reward and set the timer.

 Remember:

- The incentive always goes last. For example, 'Work' goes on the left, 'Reward' goes on the right.
- Ensure that the work is closed-ended or finite.
- Ensure that the reward is both or either timed or finite:
  - **Timed:** five minutes reading Harry Potter
  - **Finite:** do Harry Potter jigsaw.
- Make sure that all staff carry the First/Then Board with them at all times, including in the playground, the assembly hall, the lunch hall and when visiting other classrooms. In this way the student will be sure that it is always being used consistently.
- First/Then Boards can be particularly useful to aid transitions throughout the school. For example, if your student prefers to stay in the playground after the bell has rung, you could encourage him to return to class by showing him 'First: playground, Then: moon sand' (or whatever item he is currently highly motivated by).
- First/Then Boards can be easily adapted to be more age-appropriate for older students, as in the example below.

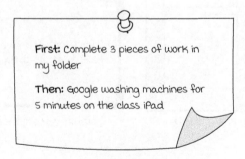

FIGURE 2.12 FIRST/THEN POST-IT NOTE

Daniel, 11, really loved washing machines and hand-dryers. In order to help him to focus on his work tasks, staff offered him a selection of rewards based on his special interests. Even though he needed the structure of regular rewards throughout the day, a pictorial First/Then Board was not age-appropriate for Daniel. Staff simply wrote his First/Then on a Post-it note (Figure 2.12).

First/Then Boards can also be used anywhere where your student needs help to manage situations that they may find tricky and to facilitate smoother transitions.

Alan, 9, found it hard to stay in the hall during assembly, preferring instead to wander around outside the hall door. His parents were very keen for him to participate in assembly, as they really wanted him to be able to attend church with them in the future. Alan absolutely loved playing his favourite maths app on the iPad. Staff introduced a simple First/Then Board and brought it to assembly with them. The deal was that once Alan had sat at assembly for the required time (one minute initially, and then staff gradually increased the time), he was allowed to go and sit at the back of the hall near the door with his headphones on, using the iPad for ten minutes. This incentive really helped him to begin to manage being in the crowded hall better.

In the above example, Alan's parents chose 'Staying in assembly' as one of his IEP (individual education plan) targets, so staff helped him to work on this. Some children will find participating in assembly or in other crowded, noisy situations really difficult, and it may not be a suitable target for them. As always, consider why you are focusing on a particular target, and whether it is really suitable for the child at this time. For some children, this could feel intolerable, and simply sitting near the hall or remaining in the classroom with a staff member would be preferable.

 There is often confusion between using a 'First/Then' as a schedule and using it as a reward system.

- **First/Then schedule:** 'First: Maths, Then: Irish'
- **First/Then Board as a reward system:** 'First: Maths, Then: Look at cranes for five minutes'.

A First/Then schedule is simply a much shorter version of a daily schedule, showing a child what is going to happen next. It is a schedule, rather than a reward system, and is used in a different way to that outlined above.

Reward charts

A reward chart is more long term than a First/Then Board. It can be used either at the end of a session, a day or a week. They are usually less immediate than a First/

Then Board, and often work better with older students, or those who have lower support needs.

> Grace, 8, was working on maths word problems as part of her learning targets. She found the language of maths really difficult, and often became discouraged while doing her work and would simply give up on it altogether.

What to do

- Class staff knew that Grace loved the 30-minute show 'Ace My Space', so they offered a reward of watching an episode of her favourite show on Friday afternoon in return for completing two word problems every morning.
- At the same time, staff tried to make the work easier and more palatable for Grace by teaching her a really concrete maths strategy: 'RUDE' (read, underline, draw, estimate), making 'Ace My Space' related word problems, and by giving her a specific number of sums to do per day (Figure 2.13).

Goal: To do 3 maths word problems every day with Sarah.

Reward: If I get 10 ticks, I can watch one episode of 'Ace My Space' on Friday afternoon at 1:30 p.m.

Monday			
Tuesday			
Wednesday			
Thursday			
Friday			

FIGURE 2.13 GRACE'S REWARD CHART

Once she was sure staff would allow her to watch her show during golden time on Friday afternoons, Grace was happy to stick at her difficult task of word problems. Over time, and as Grace became more confident in doing her work, staff were able to increase the number of word problems she had to do in order to achieve her reward and eventually were able to fade out the reward altogether.

Learning contract

A learning contract (Figure 2.14) is an age-appropriate way to help motivate older students. Sit down for a few minutes at the start of a lesson or support session and fill in the learning contract together with your student.

Learning contract between _____ & _____

Date: _____ Time: _____ Lesson: _____

I will: _____

I will earn: _____

FIGURE 2.14 LEARNING CONTRACT

Note: When your student is adept at using a reward system, you can begin to use a quicker, more casual version, if appropriate. For example, simply write the reward at the end of the student's daily schedule and tick off the tasks until it is reward time (Figure 2.15).

Tuesday

Emotions thermometer

Typing skills – stage 3

x9 tables in copybook

x9 song and iPad game

Reward: Draw Dogman for 5 minutes from YouTube

FIGURE 2.15 MINI WHITE BOARD WITH SCHEDULE AND REWARD

 Top tips for using reward systems

Remember:

- **Give your student his reward as soon as he has fulfilled his part of the deal.** This is particularly important when starting a new reward system, as it will help him to experience success early on.
- **Ensure you have left enough time after the work session for the student to get his reward.**
- **Initially, give your student easily achievable tasks** so that he can experience early success. Once he trusts the system, you can then gradually increase your expectations.
- **Always allow for some wiggle room (but don't let him know about it).** For example, if your student arrives into school exhausted because he did not sleep the night before, simply reduce his workload. Instead of ten sums, ask him to do 'First five sums, Then Shrek game for five minutes'. In other words, help him to achieve his reward by subtly reducing the amount of work that you expect him to do.

- **Never take away a reward that has already been earned.** This is unfair and will likely ruin any trust built between student and teacher, causing the student to never believe in the reward system again.
- **Some children do not need a formal reward system.** For example, a child might like to have the opportunity to earn stickers related to a special interest to stick on a personal sticker chart or on their book.

Recap on rewards

1. Identify a clear way of behaving that you would like your students to follow, or display a piece of work that you would like him to complete.
2. Create a list of suitable rewards together.
3. Design a visual reward chart to monitor progress.
4. Scaffold the task so that it is achievable.
5. Let your student complete the task.
6. Give your student his reward.

Five Ways to Use Special Interests During the School Day

Ultimately, if you can make a work task interesting enough for your students, they will be happier to do it. The possibilities are endless – it just takes a little imagination and confidence to just go for it. Below are some ideas about how to make an activity as intrinsically engaging as possible using a special interest.

1. Use what the student loves to help him to achieve a target

Class staff had one goal for Will, 4, which was to encourage him to focus on an adult-led task for up to one minute. He found this really difficult.

What to do
The staff knew that Will loved buses, so they made him an adapted book using *Buses for Kids* by Melissa Ackerman.

Making an adapted book

- Photocopy and laminate key characters or pictures from a book.
- Stick soft Velcro on the back of the laminated pictures and hard Velcro on the corresponding pages in the book.
- As you read through the book, ask your student to match specific characters or pictures to the correct pages.

Within a few days, Will was sitting at his desk waiting for the teaching assistant to arrive – he absolutely loved it! However, after three weeks, he flung the book out of the classroom door into the rain. He simply got bored of it. It was clearly time to move on to some different bus-related activities.

2. Slip in snippets of special interests throughout the day to encourage students to participate in different activities

Jake, 6, just wasn't interested in learning to sight read the days of the week during the daily morning meeting.

What to do

The teacher stuck Jake's favourite Julia Donaldson storybook characters on each of the days of the week flashcards. As a result, Jake was more than happy to look at them, and name both the day and the character.

3. Use a special interest to motivate a child to participate in group sessions

Melanie, 8, really loved Miss Trunchbull from the movie Matilda. She had been to the musical, had a toy riding crop and during playground time, she used to re-enact word-perfect scenes from the movie. During carpet time, Melanie tended to zone out and never put up her hand to ask or answer a question.

What to do

In order to encourage Melanie to put up her hand during class time, Ms Joanna, the special needs assistant, printed and laminated three particularly gruesome pictures of Miss Trunchbull and put them face down in front of Melanie. Whenever Melanie put up her hand to answer a question, she was allowed to turn over one of the pictures and look at it for two minutes. In this way, Ms Joanna encouraged her to answer three questions per day during class time.

4. Use a special interest but expand the focus of the topic

Temple Grandin advises that autistic children should be allowed to have their special interests, but that we should help them to 'broaden them out' to wider topics (Grandin 2009).

Staff often have concerns that harnessing a student's special interest in class will only serve to increase and deepen the interest into an obsession. Considering the above case study, it certainly would not be helpful to allow Melanie to watch the entire Matilda movie during school time, due to both lack of time and the fact that she may become over-stimulated by it. However, you can still use the essence of a special interest – just expand its range.

David, 9, was obsessed with tall buildings, particularly The Shard and Empress State Building in London. All he wanted to do was to google images of these buildings on the class computer. Class staff were focused on helping David to do more non-fiction writing, based on personal experiences. At this time, the whole class were working on recounts about personal experiences, but David had little interest in participating in this.

What to do

Staff worked with David's parents and decided that they would arrange for him to visit both buildings in one day over a weekend if he did some written work first. In preparation for the visit, this usually reluctant writer managed to create a Venn diagram, comparing and contrasting both buildings. He also wrote an acrostic poem about the Empress. Never, ever underestimate the power of a special interest!

The Empress
Every time we pass the Empress
My favourite landmark is the Empress
Perhaps we can go there someday
Really it is my favourite
Even better than The Shard
Someday I might work there
So I can see the view

5. Use a special interest to return to school

Jenna, 8, was beginning to refuse to attend school. She told her dad that she just didn't understand the point of school and that she hated it. School staff and parents were worried that Jenna would completely stop attending school. They worked closely with the multidisciplinary team to provide tailored support for Jenna both inside and outside of school.

What to do

Staff knew that Jenna really loved cats, particularly her cat, Jeffrey. In order to capture Jenna's interest and encourage her to come to school more often, class staff did the following:

- They asked Jenna if she would like to begin a project on 'All About Cats' to present to her class.
- They taught her how to use PowerPoint, how to snip pictures from the internet and how to create a presentation.
- They added some of her favourite cat characters to her worksheets.
- They supported Jenna to collect data on the different kinds of pets that other children had at home. In this way, she also practised and learned

some important social skills, such as knocking, interrupting politely, asking someone a question and ending the conversation. By collating the data and creating graphs, she also learned some maths skills.

- They helped Jenna to make a montage about cats, complete with typed sentences set to the theme of Jenna's favourite musical, *Cats*.

This project took a huge amount of staff time and resources, but for the duration of it, Jenna attended school far more regularly, simply because she was so interested in the topic.

Guide 12

Three More Great Ways to Motivate

> 66 While writing this book, I would do anything but write. I procrastinated by making banana bread, cleaning the house and scrolling through Twitter and Instagram. As the deadline loomed, I had to use the Pomodoro Technique to bribe myself to sit down on the chair, turn on my laptop and start writing. I told myself I'd be happy if I could just do 25 minutes. And, of course, I always managed to do much more than that. That first step is always the hardest. 99

Claire

Everyone has their own tips and tricks to force themselves to do painful tasks. Your students are no different. If you can make self-motivation easier for them by *structuring*, *limiting* or *timing* tasks, you can really take the sting out of a difficult piece of work and make life easier for everyone.

> **Pomodoro Technique**
> This is a cycle of short, 25-minute bursts of work, followed by a short break. Once you complete four cycles, you can take a longer break. The term was coined by Francesco Cirillo, who used a novelty tomato-shaped timer to time himself (Cirillo 2019).

1. Motivating using competition
Many children love it when an element of competition is thrown into the mix. It can help to spur them on to complete a task that they are not particularly enamoured with. You can do this in a number of ways.

Compete with the timer
A riff on the Pomodoro Technique, 'student versus the timer' is one of the simplest and most effective strategies you will ever use with your students. (See Guide 6, Figure 2.3 for a template.) Many children absolutely love beating the timer and ticking off the sheet or a mini whiteboard as they go along. Offer them a small reward after they beat the timer three times.

" I can never get over the respect some children have for that timer. "

Special needs assistant, special school for autistic children

Compete with the staff

Create competitions between a staff member and the student. For example, if a student is reluctant to read their sight word flashcards, staff and student can take turns to read a sight word each, and add it to a personal pile – who can get twenty flashcards first?

Compete with other students

Draw ten squares on the whiteboard and tell the students that they must work together to get all ten ticked off, by taking turns to answer questions about, for example, number bonds to 20. Working together removes the prospect of winning/losing, which can be difficult for many children, both autistic and non-autistic.

Compete with the computer

Many computer games and apps have timed elements in order to beat the computer. For example, 'Teaching Time' (Primary Games Ltd) has a really simple interface, with lots of graded and timed games such as 'Stop the Clock'. This can be really effective either working one-to-one with your students or as a whole class.

- Initially, offer your students more time than they need, so that they *always* beat the timer. This will give them confidence to continue to use the timer.
- Even though lots of children love using a timer, some will not. It is just a matter of personal preference.
- Adding a competitive element to a task is most suited for short, finite tasks, rather than long, written tasks such as writing an essay or reading a book.
- Be judicious about what you use competition for – as with everything, overuse can diminish its effectiveness.

2. Motivating using closed-ended tasks

" I like the tick boxes because they tell me how much I have left to do. "

10-year-old autistic boy

Making work tasks closed-ended or finite is an extremely important part of teaching autistic children. Many of your students can struggle with open-ended tasks. For example:

- creative writing
- reading for an unspecified amount of time
- being told to play with LEGO®.

They often prefer to do these closed-ended tasks, where there is a clear beginning and end. For example:

- matching
- making the same LEGO® object as in a picture
- doing a specified number of sums or sentences on a page.

Finite tasks are so comforting for anyone whose brain thrives on order and predictability. They can help to alleviate anxiety simply because it is clear when the task will end. Below is a selection of ideas on how to make everyday tasks in school more finite or closed-ended.

Worksheets

- Use a highlighter to show the student exactly what sums or questions he has to do on a worksheet.
- Cut the page in half so that he can focus only on what he has to do.
- Draw tick boxes beside the questions to be answered – he can tick them off as he goes along.

Reading

- Before you begin, tell your student how many pages of the book he is going to read.
- Decide that student and staff member read alternate pages until the end of a short book.

Writing

- Write numbers one to five on a blank sheet of paper to show your student exactly how much they have to write.
- Use a writing frame (Figure 2.16) for creative writing so the task does not appear endless.

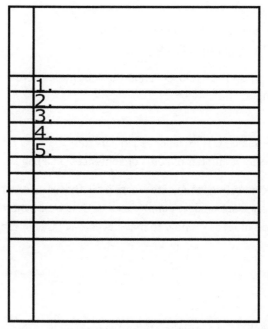

FIGURE 2.16 WRITING FRAME

“ One of my students really didn't want to start a seemingly endless writing task. However, when I wrote the numbers one to five on his page, he got to work immediately. Why? Because he could see exactly what he had to do, and crucially, he knew the end was in sight! ”

Claire

Oral work (e.g. reading flashcards, mental maths, answering questions)

- Only put the exact number of flashcards they have to read out on the table.
- Draw tick boxes on a mini whiteboard when asking your student a seemingly open-ended set of questions.

Mr Smith was working on telling time at o'clock with 7-year-old Amy. He drew five tick boxes on a mini whiteboard. Then he showed Amy the clock, asked her to say the time and ticked off the first box when she answered. He kept going until the five boxes were ticked. In this way, Amy was able to tolerate doing work she might otherwise find difficult or boring, as she could see the finish line.

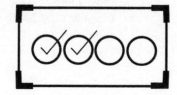

Technology

- Some computer games/apps have built-in tick boxes, which can really help autistic students to monitor their progress. For example, in 'Nessy Fingers' touch-typing programme, icons at the bottom of the screen are deleted every time the student completes an activity.
- Use a mini activity schedule for iPad or computer work time, so that your student knows exactly what games/apps he will be using and when the task will be over.

Naturally finite tasks

For younger students in particular, you can structure tasks so that they are very clearly and very naturally finite. These include:

- **Matching:** When everything is matched up, the task is over.
- **Adapted books:** When all of the laminated pieces are matched, the task is over.
- **Fine motor tasks:** Threading a number of beads, cutting tasks, opening and closing bolts, zips, completing jigsaws – when these are complete, the task is over.
- **Posting tasks:** Posting new vocabulary in a posting box – when the words have all been read, there are no more flashcards on the table.

3. Motivating by making free-activity stations more finite

> Ryan used to stand at the LEGO® tray sifting the LEGO® through his hands. He just wasn't sure what to do. When staff gave him a photograph of a simple structure to build, he smiled and began to build it.

While all children can benefit greatly from child-led and discovery learning, your autistic students may need some extra structure at freeflow activity stations or areas. These areas usually contain open-ended activities and require a child to make lots of choices.

Some of your students will need a specific task to do at every area, at least for some of their freeflow time. Otherwise, in the midst of all the noise and chatter of other children and adults, they often find it easier to retreat into their own private world or special interest, to stay at the same task or area every day or flit from area to area, not completing any tasks at all.

It is relatively easy to make these areas more autism-friendly, and many teachers are already very skilled at doing so. Some ideas include:

- **Art area:** Provide some sample drawings at the drawing station; put a dot in each area of the picture that a child must paint, colour or stick something on.
- **Maths area:** Put bowls labelled with numbers to show how many bricks to put inside each one.
- **Writing area:** Specify how many sentences you would like at the writing station, or give short, simple writing worksheets.
- **Fine motor skills area:**
  - Draw five dots on a piece of paper and ask your student to put glue on each of the dots, and then stick materials on the dots.
  - Provide a photo of the Play-Doh snake you want him to make, or provide a laminated Play-Doh mat with an outline printed onto it.
  - Provide a picture of the required peg board pattern or challenge him to get as many pegs onto the board as possible in one minute, using a timer.
- **Drawing area:** Instead of presenting your student with a blank sheet of paper, give them paper with a box drawn onto it. Provide some printed pictures to inspire them. Ask him to draw a specific picture in the box.

Once your student knows what to do at each area, he will be able to move independently and with purpose around the classroom, either with or without the use of a mini play schedule or by following numbered stations. Teachers often change the particular activity in each area every few weeks. This will work for your autistic students as long as the general structure of the activities stays the same.

 Why not choose one area that you would like to make more structured every week or fortnight?

> Always ask yourself: Does my student know exactly what he has to do in order to complete this task?

Frequently asked questions

Q: I really don't think he needs all that structure. He's well able and never asks us for it.

A: It is important to remember that mostly our students are not going to verbalize that they need everything to be made finite. Sometimes, they just don't know what they need to make things better in school.

Remember, even if you think there is no longer any need for structure, try to put it in anyway. Having it in place may help students to stay calm and prevent any behaviours that may challenge from arising in the first place.

Q: We've tried everything, and she just doesn't seem to be motivated by anything at all – what can we do?

A: It can take creativity to find something to motivate a child who seems oblivious to any reward offered. However, I guarantee you that there is definitely something she likes and will work for. It might just take a little longer to find it. Try sitting down with her and reading through a toy catalogue and see what she gravitates towards. Chat to her about her likes and dislikes, or watch what books and activities she engages in during golden time. Ask her parents or guardians what she loves at home and try to use this at school.

Help Me to Be More Organized and Independent

 " I'm always making lists: on my phone, on a Post-it note or on a calendar. It keeps me organized, allows me to plan my week and reminds me what I have left to do. This ability to organize myself is just one key part of my executive function (EF) skills. "

Claire

> The executive function system is like the air traffic control centre of the brain. It powers absolutely everything.

What is executive function?
Executive function: your personal life manager

Executive function helps you to manage your life. It is the rational, voice of reason that helps you to make decisions, plan for the future and respond coolly to situations rather than reacting hot-headedly. You may not have realized it, but you frequently employ EF skills throughout the working week. This includes:

- sitting quietly in an after-hours staff meeting and restraining yourself from taking out your phone, or running from the room
- chatting to a colleague in the playground while never once taking your eyes off the students and constantly scanning for any potential issues
- preparing for an important meeting on Tuesday morning by ironing your shirt on Monday evening, jotting down some key agenda points and getting an early night
- changing a lesson plan on the spot, because what you are doing is just not working and the students are getting restless
- staying outwardly calm during a difficult parent–teacher meeting and managing to keep your emotions in check until you arrive home that evening.

Autism and executive function

" I'm terrible at time management. My mum helps me. "

Student, Limpsfield Grange school for girls aged 11–16 with
communication and interaction difficulties

Many autistic people have difficulties with EF. At school, this means that your students may have difficulties with:

- managing time
- paying attention to a lesson
- structuring a task
- persevering with a task
- self-organization
- planning ahead for the week
- using working memory effectively
- problem-solving
- multi-tasking
- making decisions
- regulating emotions
- thinking flexibly.

Developing and improving executive functioning skills is crucial for improving readiness for learning (Pellicano 2012), as well as making life feel calmer and more predictable. Executive function skills allow your students to control and manage their own lives with varying degrees of independence, as well as helping to create a sense of calm and order.

Throughout this book, we have included many other strategies to develop EF skills particularly in:

- Make Everything Visual for Me
- Motivate Me
- Teach Me How to Recognize and Cope with My Emotions.

'Hot' and 'cool' EF skills

Executive function skills can be broken down further into two categories, each governed by different parts of the brain:

- **Hot EF:** emotional regulation, affective decision-making, delay-discounting (delayed gratification).
- **Cool EF:** planning, inhibition, working memory, set-shifting (shifting your mindset rapidly from one thing to another).

(Kouklari, Tsermentseli and Monks 2018)

Five important EF skills to develop at school

1. **Set-shifting (shifting your mindset rapidly from one thing to another).** Strategies include:
   - visualizing (mentally and using visual supports) and rehearsing what the day ahead might bring, including thinking about any potential changes or potholes
   - practising responses to change regularly using a 'Change' card
   - becoming used to using visual supports including schedules and weekly planners.
2. **Recognizing and regulating own emotions.** See ⚷ 'Teach Me How to Recognize and Cope with My Emotions' in Part 2.
3. **Persevering with a task.** Strategies include:
   - using reward systems
   - making work interesting and related to interests
   - helping to avoid distraction by specifying the exact work that needs to be done or putting up screens for concentration
   - using timers and an element of competition.
4. **Waiting skills.** Practice 'waiting' with your student, using a 'Wait' card and a timer. This needs to be well planned, with clear progression and an outline of what to do *while waiting*, gradually building up the amount of time needed to wait.
5. **Organization and Independence.** Please see strategies outlined in Guides 13 and 14.

Help Me to Be More Organized

Reduce the cognitive load

Autistic journalist and author Laura James has described how she breaks things into 'bite-size chunks' to avoid becoming overwhelmed by them (James 2018).

Similarly, autistic author Stuart Neilson (2018) has described some personal strategies that have helped him to reduce his own 'cognitive load' in order to make life easier for him at home, and to enable him to focus on more important matters. These include simple tricks such as using a three-in-one shampoo, conditioner and shower gel instead of having multiple bottles that all look the same in the shower tray, and supplementing his working memory with a notebook, mobile phone or Dictaphone to help increase productivity and efficiency.

Reducing this cognitive load is exactly what you are trying to do for your students at school. You can help your students to manage certain EF skills that they may find difficult by:

- adapting and setting up the classroom environment with systems and routines
- explicitly teaching self-organization skills.

Outlined below are some very simple ideas to help your students to develop organization and independence skills. Teaching self-organization skills requires lots of teacher modelling and explicit instruction in how to create and use these strategies and systems.

Adapt the classroom environment

- Have a designated, labelled place for coats, lunches and school bags. This will make it easier for your students to locate their personal items.
- Stick shadow outlines of items on the students' desks or in communal areas. For example, an outline of a pencil pot or pencil case, so they know exactly where to put items. In time, these outlines can be phased out.
- Have a consistent place or area for finished work that is clearly labelled.

🗝 For more classroom organization strategies, please see 'Make Everything Visual for Me' earlier in Part 2.

Explicitly teach self-organization skills

❝ I had some slides on the back of my phone that told me what I needed to remember for that day – it was quite useful and helped me. ❞

Year 9 student, Limpsfield Grange school for girls aged 11–16
with communication and interaction difficulties

- **Model how to use a week-to-view calendar with the whole class.** This could be done as a discrete lesson on the interactive whiteboard. Show students how useful it is to look ahead at the week, to think about what they will need each day and to plan for when to pack swimming or P.E. gear or what books to bring in for each day.
- **Colour code books with a simple sticker system to make it easier for students to locate them.** For example, use red stickers on maths books and green stickers on English books. Spend some time practising how to use this system, for example, by having a quiz about what colour goes with what subject, or a rapid-fire timed two-minute game of 'Take out your maths book! Take out your English book!'
- **Provide students with a visual reminder or Post-it note checklist of what they need to bring in each day of the week.** In time, teach them how to write and manage these notes themselves.
- **'Visualizing' is a really useful tool for self-organization, particularly for older students.** Getting into the habit of sitting down for a few moments every afternoon and mentally walking through what is going to happen the following day will really help your students to think about what they might need to bring, do or say. It might also help to make some of the day more predictable, as they have already imagined how parts of it might pan out. This cognitive rehearsal is used by athletes and surgeons – why not also teach our students to use it too?
  Essentially, this is a video walk-through in their minds of what might happen the following day ', and it may well help with set-shifting.'

Plan, do and tick off

Temple Grandin has described how she can find it difficult to remember 'long strings of verbal information' and prefers to write information down (Grandin 2014).

As always, writing down any directions you want your students to follow can really help them to remember what to do.

- Write an essay title or question on the whiteboard so that everyone remembers what they have to do and nobody has to feel awkward about asking.
- Provide your student with a written, tickable checklist to remind him what he has to do in order to complete a task, get ready for another lesson or get ready

to go home. State the order in which each part of the task can be done. This can be written on the interactive whiteboard, a mini whiteboard or a Post-it note.

- If the student prefers not to have specific visual supports just for him, simply ask the classroom support staff or a peer to write a communal checklist for the whole group.

" I gave a work checklist to a 10-year-old autistic boy who was struggling in class and watched from afar as he worked from it. When it fell on the ground, he bent up to pick it up, which showed me how important it was to him. "

Claire

Make planning fun

Why not teach your older students to use an on-trend bullet planner to stay organized? They often enjoy personalizing each page with drawings and fancy writing scripts, and it is an under-the-radar way of getting them into the habit of daily planning.

Highly visual apps such as To Round (write tasks in bubbles and watch them go down a funnel as you complete them), Trello (ticked off items are moved to another column), Tiimo (make a checklist, prioritize tasks, tick them off) or even the tickable lists on a smartphone notes function are other ways to stay on track as they move towards secondary school.

Ultimately, anything that encourages your students to *plan, do and tick off* is great.

Guide 14

Independence, Asking for Help and Developing Assertiveness

6 If you remove the scaffolding from a refurbished house before it can stand up on its own, it will inevitably fall. 9

Claire

Independence

Independence and the ability to generalize learned skills is paramount. However, in schools, there can often be a drive towards ensuring that children work independently of a teacher or teaching assistant without ever actually teaching them the necessary skills or giving them the required resources.

If you would like your student to begin to work independently, why not give him every chance to achieve this by:

- structuring the work
- giving him a work checklist
- making the task finite
- offering a reward, as appropriate.

6 I call TAs 'independence facilitators' for the students. 9

Emily Rubin, co-creator of SCERTS (2017)

Angela was a special needs assistant in a mainstream school, who mainly worked with two autistic 11-year-old boys in the same class. Class staff were keen to develop both boys' independence skills, as they rarely did any work task unless Angela sat right beside them, prompting continuously. Staff were also worried that the transition to secondary school may prove difficult for the boys, as they would probably not access the same level of in-class support there.

What to do

- Angela discussed the idea of independent work with both boys, and wrote a narrative outlining what independent work meant and would look like. She read this daily with them for five minutes for a few weeks.

- She set up a weekly reward system for each boy to complete an independent work session three times per week.
- Both boys were asked if they would like to sit at the same group table for Literacy and Maths so that Angela could monitor this independent work session.
- Angela gave each boy a checklist on a mini whiteboard, highlighted what they had to do on their maths worksheets and ensured they each knew what to do when the task was finished. She also put up a sign saying 'independent work happening here' on their table, for all students at the table to use.
- When Angela set the boys up to work, she physically stepped away to the other side of the classroom and pretended to do some work herself. The class teacher purposely never asked Angela to work with any other students during this time, as she knew she would need to keep an eye on both boys and walk back to redirect them to their visual supports and structure if she noticed they were going off task.

Asking for help

66 Most of the time, she'd rather get into trouble than ask for help at school. 99

Mother of an autistic 12-year-old girl

Knowing how to ask for help is a crucial part of developing independence skills. Some children may feel too shy or embarrassed to ask an adult or a peer, while others may not even realize that asking for help might actually solve the problem.

Learning how to ask for help involves knowing:

- Who could you ask?
- When is the best time to ask?
- What will you say?

Some students will need some targeted sessions around this. Sitting down together to discuss and write out an 'Asking for Help' prompt card will really help them to learn each step and use their own words to ask for help.

Asking for help

- Ask the person next to you: 'Do you know what we are supposed to be doing?'
- Put your hand up and wait for the teacher to come over. Say 'I need some help please.'

- If you need an object, say 'I need _____ please.' Say 'Thanks!' when they give it to you.
- If the teacher doesn't come over, walk up to her, wait for her to finish what she is doing, use her name and then say 'I'm a bit stuck on my work. Could I have some help please when you're ready?'

66 Anxiety is such a huge issue. To have a code word for the teacher, a safety letter in your bag that you could pull out without having to say anything when you were feeling stressed would be great. 99

Lenore Good, autistic advocate, blogger and mother of six

For students who prefer to use less overt or non-verbal means, you can use:

- **'Help' card system:** This is a laminated card with 'I need help' on the green side, and 'I'm okay' on the red side. During a lesson, the student places it on his desk to signal how he is doing to class staff. It would be even better if every student or every group table had a 'Help' card system in place.
- **Private 'Help' signal with teacher or special needs assistant:** Agree a signal for the student to be able to tell staff that he needs help, for example, placing a specific object on the desk, or simply putting up his hand during independent work sessions without being expected to say anything.

Assertiveness

Developing assertiveness skills will also help your students to become more independent.

Steve, 10, often just sat there in class, without a pen to begin his work, or in the dinner hall, without any cutlery to start eating his school dinner.

What to do

Staff focused on 'assertiveness' as part of Steve's Individual Education Plan (IEP) goals. This included:

- writing a social narrative outlining 'How to ask for something that you need' and reading it with Steve daily
- acting out different scenarios with puppets where one puppet needed to ask for a certain item and asking Steve to identify the correct and incorrect ways of going about this
- sabotaging lots of opportunities for Steve to practice this new skill. For example, they asked Steve to cut out something and 'forgot' to provide

scissors or requested that he rub out the whiteboard but had placed the eraser somewhere else. In this way, Steve had to ask for help

- asking Steve to do jobs around the school where he had to practice asking for different items from the secretary or from other classrooms. This ensured that the skills were practised in real-life situations too.

" Once I started working on assertiveness with one of my students, the change was almost immediate – it was as if it had just never crossed her mind to ask for help, but as soon as she was taught, she started to do it regularly. At the same time, she started having great fun with it in our one-to-one sessions, as whenever I sabotaged a situation to encourage her to ask for help, she laughed, knowing exactly what I was trying to do, and she would look all over the room to find the required item, in a bid to outsmart me and to not have to ask! "

Claire

Making school life easier

At the same time as teaching independence, it is also important to think about what systems your students actually need to learn to manage by themselves, and what you can do to simplify their day by helping them directly. While some people may call it 'spoon-feeding' or 'enabling', we consider it a system of allowing students to focus to the best of their ability on the task in hand.

" I once saw a 9-year-old autistic girl put her head in her hands when she saw the amount of sums she would have to copy from the board. Simply giving her the sums already printed out to stick into her book would have made all the difference. And she would have got lots more work done. "

Claire

Always ask yourself one question: 'What is the aim of this task for this student?' Is it the skill of copying the sums from the board, or is it completing the sums? By giving her a print-out, you have removed any organizational difficulties, thus allowing the student to focus on the work itself.

- **Give your students a print-out** of any questions to stick into their copybooks instead of always expecting them to copy from the board.
- **Stick the printed-out learning objective directly into the copybook.** This can save time particularly when the student finds it difficult to copy from the board. To foster increased independence, draw an outline of a rectangle on the exercise

book page where the student can stick the cut-out learning objective. This simply gives her a visual guide which can be faded out eventually.

- **Pre-draw margins in the English copybooks and grids in the maths copybook** to help make it clear and keep the work very tidy. In a separate session, explicitly teach your student how to draw margins and grids in copybooks and give them time to practise this organizational skill. Use a class poster to show this skill too.

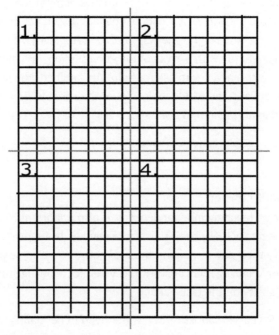

FIGURE 2.17 MATHS PAGE DIVIDED INTO CLEAR GRIDS

Frequently asked questions

Q: How can I manage or remember to write a task checklist for one student when there are so many other students who also need my help in different ways?

A: Why not write one up for the whole class on the board, and then ask another pupil to copy it down onto a mini whiteboard for your autistic student? After all, this is a great example of Universal Design for Learning.

Teach Me Ways to Cope with Anxiety

" The greater my stress or anxiety, the less my brain processing seems to work, and hence the less able I am to cope with things. "

Alis Rowe, autistic author and entrepreneur – founder of 'The Curly Hair Project' (Rowe 2013)

Autism and anxiety

Autistic author and animal scientist Temple Grandin has famously stated that 'fear is the main emotion in autism' (Grandin 2009).

- Anxiety is one of the most common mental health difficulties associated with autism, with 50 per cent of autistic children experiencing significant anxiety that impacts on their everyday lives (Rodgers et al. 2019).
- Autistic people can be more anxious than their typically developing peers, with 40 per cent of autistic people having an anxiety disorder at some point, compared to 10–15 per cent of the general population (van Steensel and Heeman 2017; Galanopoulos et al. 2014).
- Autistic adolescents who have a high cognitive ability may be at a higher risk for developing an anxiety disorder (van Steensel and Heeman 2017).

What can cause anxiety?

- Autistic people show differences in social interaction and communication, as well as sensory processing difficulties and cognitive inflexibility. These differences alone may cause an autistic child to feel more stressed at school compared to their non-autistic peers.
- Intolerance of uncertainty (IU) is also a key cause of anxiety in both non-autistic and autistic people. Simply put, IU is an adverse reaction to change and unpredictability, and a 'fear of the unknown'. It seems to be particularly salient as a cause of anxiety in autistic people (Rodgers et al. 2016).

Spending time teaching your students some useful strategies to help them cope with anxiety in primary school will make all the difference now, when they go to secondary school and when they go out and live independently in the big, bad anxiety-inducing world.

Anxiety at School

66 School was a very rowdy and quite hectic environment that wasn't really made for a neurodivergent individual. 99

Jack Welch, autistic advocate and campaigner, youth patron of Ambitious about Autism

Consider the school day. It is chock-a-block full of potentially anxiety-inducing moments. These include:

- transition from home to classroom
- transition from corridor into classroom
- free play
- carpet time
- talk partners
- group and individual work time
- playground time
- lunch time
- assembly
- tidy-up time
- walking to the hall to be collected by parents
- transition from school to home.

On Friday, the teacher told the class that they would be changing places on Monday. Laura, 8, felt such trepidation about where she would be sitting and who she would be sitting next to that she didn't sleep for the entire weekend.

Possible reasons
Laura felt worried because of the upcoming change. Suddenly, her world had become unbearably unpredictable.

What to do

- Tell Laura who she will be sitting next to, and where she will be sitting, in advance. Write this on a Post-it note so that she can check it over the weekend, whenever she feels worried.
- Give Laura a map of the classroom with her new seating arrangements clearly marked on it.
- Allow Laura to stay in the same place for longer periods, if appropriate.

Essential strategies to cope with anxiety during the school day

66 The thing to remember is that anxiety doesn't just go away. You have to use these basic strategies all the time, day in and day out. 99

Mother of a 9-year-old autistic girl

Using basic, tried-and-tested, autism-friendly strategies to help prevent or reduce anxiety in a whole-class setting is a very good start. These include:

- visual schedules
- pre-warning about upcoming change
- task checklists
- providing regular breaks
- use visual supports to enhance understanding around rules, games and upcoming events
- establish structured playground games
- sensory audit of the classroom.

A key way to decrease anxiety is to help your students to feel more in control of their lives. Insert structure and predictability throughout the school day.

Indeed, managing the school environment can go a long way towards preventing anxiety. But schools are dynamic and often-changing places, with visits, tours, science week, play practice, wet play times and staff changes. As much as staff try to manage the environment, it would be impossible to predict and pre-empt everything. What you can do is teach your students *coping strategies* to use whenever they feel anxious, both in school and beyond.

Ten Tips for a Calmer Day at School

" Training and playing matches gave me something to look forward to during the times in my life when I was struggling. Even today, when I'm feeling anxious, going to the gym or playing rugby helps me get out my hyperactivity. "

Tom Morgan, autistic rugby player and National Autistic Society (NAS) ambassador (Webster 2016, p.1)

 As well as using autism-friendly strategies at school, there are a variety of other ways to help autistic children cope with stress and anxiety. Often, these are similar to those used for non-autistic children. However, as always, approaches need to be adapted to suit the specific needs of autistic children by making them more visual and concrete. These include:

- **Cognitive behavioural therapy (CBT)** has been shown to have moderate effects on anxiety in autistic young people (Lang et al. 2010; Luxford, Hadwin and Kovshoff 2017; Rodgers et al. 2016). Cognitive behavioural/instructional strategies (CBIS) have been identified as an evidence-based practice for autistic children and young people (Steinbrenner et al. 2020). While CBT can only be carried out by trained clinicians, school staff can use some cognitive-based strategies as outlined below.
- **Mindfulness-based interventions and yoga** have been shown to help autistic people to self-regulate, decrease anxiety, increase well-being and manage co-morbid mental health problems (Cachia, Anderson and Moore 2016; Semple 2018; Singh et al. 2011; South and Rodgers 2017).
- **Physical exercise** has shown benefits for autistic youth (Healy et al. 2018; Sowa and Meulenbroek 2012). Exercise and movement (including physical exercise and mindful movement such as yoga) has been identified as an evidence-based practice for autistic children and young people (Steinbrenner et al. 2020).

By implementing these strategies, you are essentially trying to manage the contents of your students' 'stress buckets' throughout the day, so that they never have a chance to overflow.

1. **Ensure there is a clear daily routine in place and make plans for any upcoming changes.** This increases certainty and allows for structure, even during down time.

2. **Ask your student what he is worried about at the moment.** It could be school, the playground or something totally unrelated. By finding out, you can help him by sitting down together to talk about it and together come up with some useful strategies.

3. **Foster a flow state** by giving him lots of interesting and exciting activities to do. It is almost impossible to be anxious if you are in flow, which means being completely engaged and involved in an activity (Csikszentmihalyi 1990). This could include doing a crossword, painting, reading a book, writing, horse riding or anything that can totally engage your interest to the exclusion of anything else. Find out what your student's interests are and give him some activities related to these. Use a special interest, if appropriate.

4. **Ensure your student has a 'safe place and a friendly face' at school.** This could be a tent in the classroom, or a cosy corner containing books, headphones, music on an MP3 player. Ensure he knows who he can go to if he needs to chat. This is often a member of the support staff team or an in-class special needs assistant.

   Schedule exercise and calm sessions throughout the day. Don't be afraid to add in more, as and when needed. These include:
   - **Exercise:** sensory breaks, an obstacle course in the hall, tennis, ball games, running games, dancing, delivering a message, doing some 'heavy work' like pushing and pulling, whole-class dancing and lots of progressive muscle relaxation (PMR) activities.
   - **Calm:** breathing routines (rainbow breathing, square breathing, blowing bubbles), yoga, going to the cosy corner, tending to the school garden or taking regular breaks such as going for a walk, reading a favourite book or cycling on the school bikes.

5. **Have a 'take a break' system in place.** Use a secret signal (e.g. when he puts up his hand holding his red pencil) or a 'Take a Break' card so that the student can escape from a situation, as needed. Always allow the student to take a break, no matter what the class is currently doing. He may just need some quiet time to 'get back to green'. (See ⚷➼ 'Teach Me How to Recognize and Cope with My Emotions'.)

6. **Distract a child who is feeling worried** by changing the subject, finishing up the activity more quickly, offering a brand-new activity or offering a choice of two activities.

7. **Practice mindfulness** so that he can take a break from thinking with some mini moments of mindfulness throughout the school day. This could include mindful eating, colouring, walking, listening to music or a 30-second gong meditation, like below:
   - 'Sit at your desk, put two feet on the floor and close your eyes, or put your head down on the table and relax. I am going to play a gong sound on my

phone [using the free Mindfulness Bell app], and I want you to listen to it carefully. When you can no longer hear it, you can put up your hand silently. I'll tell you when I want you to open your eyes.'
- Repeat once more.

" Whenever I do this as a quick after-break, whole-class activity, all of the children appear visibly relaxed afterwards. When I ask them how many of them like having some peace and quiet during the school day, most of them put their hands up. "

Claire

8. **Practice progressive muscle relaxation** throughout the day. PMR is a relaxation technique designed to reduce arousal levels. It means tensing and releasing each muscle group in the body, one by one.

    Methodically work your way down the body. Make this more visual and autism-friendly by using a photograph or a body outline, or simply write the names of body parts on a blank track printed on a piece of paper, and work through each part to the end.

    Squeeze your face...and relax.

    Squeeze your shoulders...and relax.

    Squeeze your upper arms...and relax.

    When the body is tense, it sends a message to the brain that it is in danger and puts you in a state of high alert. When the body is relaxed, anxiety melts away and the brain can also relax. Practising muscle tense and release can really help your students to become used to the idea that they are in control of both their brain and their body.

    There are many readily available PMR activities and videos online. As always, making it really visual can help your students to understand it more readily and practice it in a systematic way every day.

9. **Use cognitive-based strategies** to help a child identify unhelpful thinking patterns or 'thinking traps'. These strategies will teach him new ways of looking at and dealing with a situation. These include:
    - **'Size of the problem' sheets or scales:** This can work so well to help students who have a tendency to catastrophize. Using humour here can really help children to see the funny side of life. For example, say 'Oh no, you forgot your homework. Is it a global emergency, or just a tiny glitch?'
    - **'What's in my control' and 'What's not in my control' sheets:** This can help a child to realize what he can actively control and what he needs to let go of.
    - **Emotions thermometer or scale:** This helps your students to better visualize and categorize their emotions.

    Teaching your students how to recognize and manage their emotions is another key anxiety management strategy. After all, if someone can recognize when he feels anxious, he can do something about it before it overwhelms him.

For further ideas and strategies to support your students with this, see 'Teach Me How to Recognize and Cope with My Emotions'.

Frequently asked questions

Q: I have an autistic boy in my class who is really anxious, but I don't have a huge amount of time. If you had to choose one thing to alleviate his anxiety, what would it be?

A: Keep it simple and start with the basics. Try to prevent anxiety from happening in the first place. For example, use a whole-class schedule, provide a tickable checklist for the lesson, print out his homework and ensure that you have prepared him for any changes. Do this first and see what happens. Then explore a variety of coping strategies with him and find what works for him.

Q: My class just won't concentrate enough to do a 20-minute meditation. What can I do?

A: Twenty minutes of meditation is just too much, too soon. Why not try a 30-second gong meditation with the class first? They'll all giggle at first but usually settle into it after a few sessions. Most children end up really liking it, saying that it helps them to relax.

Q: I'm not sure he's really anxious at all. I think he's just trying to get out of class.

A: It's worth giving him the benefit of the doubt. We know that autism and anxiety tend to go hand in hand. If you are worried he is missing out on his academic work, perhaps give him a timer to use for breaks. It is also worth observing in which parts of the day he usually takes a break, and what subject is happening at that time, as well as sitting down with him to find out if he is particularly worried about anything at the moment. In this way, you can then change the environmental stressor for him and he may not need to ask for as many breaks.

Teach Me How to Recognize and Cope with My Emotions

" A bird sitting on the branch of a tree is not afraid of the shaking branch, because its trust is not in the branch but in its wings. "

Anonymous

 Emotional literacy is one of the most important skills that any child can learn. It means that they can manage their own emotions by:

- recognizing when they feel happy/upset/angry/worried
- knowing how their body feels when they are happy/upset/angry/worried
- figuring out what strategies work to help them to relax
- recognizing, understanding and taking other people's feelings into account.

Many autistic children can find it difficult to recognize, name and understand their own emotions. Known as alexithymia, this is believed to occur in 40–65 per cent of autistic individuals and may also be related to the development of anxiety in autism (Griffin, Lombardo and Auyeung 2015).

Practically speaking, this means that your student may not realize *when* or *why* she feels anxious. For example, a younger student experiencing sensory overload from a flickering light or an overly loud maths game on the interactive whiteboard is unlikely to know how to help herself to feel better by asking for the volume to be turned down or going for a break. Instead, she might display some behaviours that may be perceived as challenging.

Teachers are often advised to 'work on emotions' with autistic students but are rarely shown how to actually do so. The following guides will outline a simple six-step progression for teaching autistic children about their emotions.

How to teach children about their emotions: A six-step progression

Emotions and younger students

1. Label my emotions for me.
2. Make me an emotions scrapbook.

Using an emotions thermometer

3. Teach me how to recognize my emotions (using an emotions thermometer).
4. Teach me how emotions make my body feel.
5. Teach me ways of coping with different emotions.

Generalizing

6. Help me to generalize what I have learned to other situations.

 Each child will move through each step at their own pace. For example:

- Younger children may focus on the first two steps over the course of a whole school year.
- Older students might start on step three and move through the steps more quickly, but will need daily and constant support to consolidate and generalize what they have learned.

🔊 Starting Out with Emotions

Step 1: Label my emotions for me

❝ When I first started teaching in a special school for autistic children, I used to walk around laden down by a heavy emotions key ring. It had lots of beautifully laminated symbols showing a variety of emotions, including 'happy', 'sad', 'surprised' and 'tired'. Whenever one of my students appeared anxious, I would hold the key ring up and ask 'How're you feeling?'

It took me a long time to realize that, often, a child doesn't have the words or the inclination to describe how he is feeling at that time.

I also used a Daily Feelings Board. It wasn't until years later that someone advised me to never ask a child to tell you how they are feeling, unless you are sure they are emotionally literate. Often the child will say 'happy' anyway, in a bid to encourage you to leave them alone. ❞

Claire

At first, keep it simple and begin with the three main emotions:

- happy
- sad
- upset/angry.

Label the child's emotions as they are happening

- 'I can see you are feeling happy because you're on the swings.'
- 'You're happy because you're eating a chocolate éclair.'
- 'You're a bit upset because you're going to assembly. Let's bring our First/Then Board and your Spider-Man toy to help you.'

This will help the student to relate his emotions to real world situations. He will start to associate a word with a feeling.

Show your student a picture of what 'happy' looks like, using either a photo of the child looking 'happy' or a symbol meaning 'happy'. Gradually compile an emotions key ring with a range of photos or symbols that you are certain the child understands.

However, remember that until you teach them explicitly, symbols will be largely meaningless to younger students, in particular.

Should you label strong emotions in real time? If a child is having a really difficult time, it is better to respond immediately by figuring out how to help the student to cope with the situation, rather than adding fuel to the fire by trying to label the emotions.

Depending on the age of the child, the teaching part can happen the following day, during a planned discussion. For example, you could say 'You were upset yesterday because swimming was cancelled.'

If appropriate, back this discussion up with written strategies or a story to read and remember for the next time this happens. For example, 'I will try to remember that it's okay when swimming is cancelled. I can do something different during that time, like drawing my favourite characters.'

Re-read this list of strategies or the story regularly as part of your student's daily work sessions so that he will begin to internalize the key messages and remember the strategies.

Step 2: Make me an emotions scrapbook

Once your student begins to associate the word with the feeling/situation, you can start to make an emotions scrapbook. Initial content will include pages for:

- happy
- sad
- upset/angry.

'Happy' pages

- Chat with your student about what makes him feel 'happy'.
- Discuss other words that mean 'happy' and write them down.
- Take photos of the student looking 'happy' – e.g. 'playing with Play-Doh, going on the swing in the playground, singing the days of the week song in class, playing with my friends' – and stick them in the scrapbook.
- Look at characters from their favourite books or movies who look happy and discuss what they are doing and stick these pictures into the scrapbook.
- Ask older students to list and draw/print pictures of what makes them happy.
- Re-read the scrapbook regularly and continue to add examples to the 'happy' pages.

Explore different emotions – *excited, delighted, surprised, shocked, worried* – depending on your student's age and ability. Teach the specific meaning of each different emotion, as outlined above.

Note: Avoid taking photos or videos of your student looking upset, sad or angry in real time. Instead, during story time, pick out characters that look upset, sad or angry and ask the child to mimic this facial expression. Stick in pictures of those characters from books or movies that look 'angry'.

Digital emotions scrapbook

As autistic children are often so highly motivated by technology, using apps like 'Book Creator' or 'My Story' provides an easy way of making a digital emotions scrapbook with both photos and video. Using technology also encourages children to re-watch or re-read the story, which helps them to internalize the information in the scrapbook.

 In order to help generalize these skills, make sure to re-read the emotions scrapbook during calm times and initially as part of your student's regular daily work, if possible.

Guide 18

Exploring Emotions Using an Emotions Thermometer

Why use emotions thermometers?

For many children, learning about different stages of emotions can be an abstract concept. Using an emotions thermometer can help to make emotions more visual and tangible.

Emotions thermometers (Figure 2.18):

- appeal to the visual processing strengths of autistic children
- make different *degrees* of emotion more obvious for your students.

An emotions thermometer scale is usually based on colours and/or numbers. This gives your students a common language, a short cut and a code that will let an adult know immediately how things are going in their world. Children very quickly become used to talking about emotions in this way.

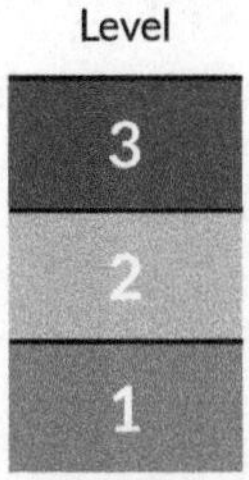

Level

FIGURE 2.18
EMOTIONS
THERMOMETER

> One 7-year-old boy used a green/yellow/red emotions thermometer regularly. 'I feel golden-green again now,' he said one afternoon, after taking a break from a noisy classroom. 'I felt a six out of ten yesterday because I missed out on the class prize because I was absent,' said another, confident that everyone would know what she was talking about.

Emotions thermometers can also be related to a favourite character or special interest. This can make learning about emotions far more interesting and relevant for certain students.

> One girl, 7, was particularly interested in the London Underground system, so her teacher devised an emotions scale based on train lines. When she felt angry, she was like the Central Line (red), when sluggish she was like the District Line (green) and when she felt great she was running smoothly, just like the Piccadilly Line (blue).

Step 3: Teach me how to recognize my emotions (using a green/yellow/red emotions thermometer)

Explore each colour on the scale over a number of sessions until your student is adept at telling you what green/yellow/red means and what makes them feel green/yellow/red.

- Green is *happy/fine/okay/chilled*.
- Yellow is *worried/rumbling/nervous*.
- Red is *angry/upset/shocked*.

Note: It is often useful to start with a three-point (rather than a five-point) colour thermometer, as it can be easier to understand. Using the phrase 'get back to green' (GBTG) throughout this process really helps children to understand their ultimate aim – that all roads must lead back to green.

Green

Can you think of any other words to describe 'happy'?

What makes you feel 'green'?

Let's draw pictures about what makes you feel 'green'.

Note: Being 'green' does not have to mean that a child feels ecstatically happy. It can simply mean that he feels calm and settled.

Step 4: Teach me how emotions make my body feel

Barry, 11, described his anxiety as feeling like he was 'going to have a heart attack'.

Stress can cause physical reactions in the body. One of the most important steps in helping your students to become emotionally literate is for them to recognize how different emotions can manifest in their bodies. Recognizing these body signals acts as an effective warning sign for children, helping them to figure out what is happening to them before the stronger emotions overtake them. They realize that they need to take a break and reconfigure.

Discuss how an emotion feels in the body once you have equated a colour to a feeling. For example:

- Green: *heart beating steadily, dry palms, steady legs, clear head.*
- Yellow: *heart beating more rapidly, butterflies in the stomach, clammy palms, headache.*

- Red: *heart beating very rapidly, pain in the stomach, sweaty palms, clenched fists, jelly legs, headache, I get sweaty, I run away.*

Draw their attention to the fact that body signals for 'red' can also mean really happy emotions like 'excitement' or 'looking forward to something'.

❝ It took me years to recognize that the place I feel anxiety most is in my stomach. Now whenever I feel worried, and feel my stomach beginning to do its familiar churn, I do some quick progressive muscle relaxation activities. They really help, and can be done anywhere, in the car before an appointment, at your desk or even during a staff meeting. ❞

Claire

Make this really visual by sticking a life-sized outline of a body onto the classroom wall. Put *butterflies* on the stomach area, *jelly* on the legs or *red dots* on the beating heart and the clammy palms.

The scientific approach to emotions

Using a scientific approach to emotions can really appeal to older students. Some children love learning that strong emotions can make you less intelligent. For example, stress can make your IQ decrease by 30 points, and anger can make it drop by 60 points (Attwood 2015).

They also tend to enjoy studying the science behind what happens to the brain when a person becomes angry and using words like 'amygdala' (the emotions area) and 'cerebral cortex' (the thinking and problem-solving area). Dan Siegel's (2010) hand model of the brain is a really useful analogy to help explain what happens when we 'flip our lid'.

❝ *What does anxiety or worry feel like to you?*

- 'I fiddle with things more and if I'm really anxious, I might tic.'
- 'I feel a bit sick and weird in my chest. Sometimes I struggle to breathe and notice my breathing more. I might start tapping or rocking very gently, almost unnoticeably. I might cover my face with my hair or put my head down.'
- 'Stomach-ache and shaking hands or legs.'
- 'My gut feels sore when I can't sleep with too much fear.'
- 'Fidgeting. Sick coming up.'
- 'I feel really cold and hot at the same time.' ❞

Year 9 students, Limpsfield Grange school for girls aged 11–16
with communication and interaction difficulties

Step 5: Teach me ways to cope with different emotions

Stress is not always a bad thing

Consider a pack of relaxed, grazing gazelles on an African prairie. When a lion suddenly appears, their adrenaline and stress kick in, giving them the ability to run away as fast as they can. Once the lion has captured one of them, the rest of them settle back into grazing patterns, as they were before. They have a superb ability to 'get back to green' almost immediately.

A certain amount of stress is important in our lives, as it helps us to escape if we need to, helps us cope with difficult events, prepares us to do things we may not really want to do and gets us out of our comfort zones.

However, what is important is that we know how to turn off this stress when we no longer need it. We need to teach our students how to 'get back to green', at first with help and then independently.

What to do

- Sit down together and compile a list of Get Back to Green activities with your student. Ensure they can be realistically done at school. While all GBTG strategies need be tailored to suit the individual needs of each student, some generic ones include:
  - Pop out to the toilet.
  - Take five deep, slow breaths.
  - Say 'I need a break' to teacher or use my 'Break' card.
  - Read a book in the cosy corner.
  - Check my emotions thermometer.
  - Go for a walk around school.
  - Do a progressive muscle relaxation activity.
  - Get my calm kit (a backpack containing Floam, bubbles, squeezy balls, ear defenders, a smell box or a favourite book).
  - Count to 50.
  - Draw or write about my feelings in my scrapbook.
- **Record the strategies on a list or board using pictures, words or photos** and stick it somewhere easily accessible, on the emotions thermometer or in the emotions scrapbook.
- **Practice this plan regularly**, particularly during calm moments. For example, 'We have some time. Let's choose an activity from your GBTG list.'
- **Whenever your student starts to feel** rumbly or 'yellow', point to the emotions

thermometer and say 'I think you're a bit yellow right now, let's try to get back to green'. Direct him to choose one of the Get Back to Green activities.

Your student now has a well-formed Get Back to Green plan that includes:

- becoming used to noticing and identifying his feelings throughout the day
- noticing and responding to how his body feels
- choosing from his list of ways of how to 'get back to green' at school.

66 *What strategies do you use to calm yourself down?*

- 'When I sing it makes me feel better when I am upset. That's why it is important, because as well as loving it, music calms me down.'
- 'Stroking animals, and thinking of something else.'
- 'I play or listen to music, create something, go on a walk, or see animals.'
- 'I focus on work, I fiddle with items or I listen to music.'
- 'Meditating.'
- 'I put my head down. I go completely silent. Water, fresh air and friends help.' 99

Year 9 students, Limpsfield Grange school for girls aged 11–16
with communication and interaction difficulties

Philip, 10, was really into the Horrid Henry series of books by Francesca Simon. His teacher made him a calm corner in the classroom with a sign stuck on it saying 'Horrid Henry's Hideaway', containing a selection of books and sensory toys that he liked to access whenever he felt worried.

Step 6: Help me to generalize my learning to other situations

66 How do you get to Carnegie Hall? Practice. 99

Anonymous

Working on emotions with autistic children is a lifelong conversation. By embedding this conversation about emotions into everyday life, it will enable your student to become comfortable and emotionally literate. As a result, instead of reacting to a situation in the moment, they can respond in a more planned, controlled way.

In order to generalize all of this new language and learning around emotions, it needs to be practised throughout the school day. You can do this in a number of ways:

1. **Model aloud how you are feeling every day** using a giant emotions thermometer stuck on the wall.

    For example, 'I'm feeling a bit yellowy today because I woke up late this morning and didn't have time to have my cup of coffee. How am I going to "get back to green"? I might sit down for a minute and relax.'

This helps your student to realize that:
- everyone else has strong feelings
- it's okay to have strong feelings
- the important thing is to focus on how to help yourself to feel better.

2. **Give your student his own mini, portable pocket emotions thermometer**, and have regular emotions check-ins with him at different times throughout the day. Carrying it around with him in his pocket or glued around his pencil will make this less of a one-off lesson on emotions and more of a way of life.

3. **Begin to generalize these skills** by asking your student to play 'Fastest Finger First' by putting his finger on the thermometer as you read out a variety of different scenarios:
- 'What colour would you be if pasta wasn't on the lunch menu?'
- 'What colour would you be if there was a substitute teacher in?'
- 'What colour would you be if the teacher gave everyone ice cream for a treat?'
- 'How might your body feel if you felt uncomfortable that there was a substitute teacher in?'
- How could you 'get back to green'?

Guide 19

The Get Back to Green Whole-Class Emotional Regulation Programme

'Getting back to green' for the whole class

66 'I get upset before a chess tournament', 'I am red before a football match', 'I feel it in my tummy', 'Yes, it's jelly legs, I know it!', 'I felt dark red when we lost the match'.

Often, at the end of training sessions about emotions, groups of children queue up to tell me, almost in wonder, that they too get 'that funny feeling in my tummy' when they're worried. It was as if they simply can't believe that other people feel this too, and until now had assumed they were wholly alone with this experience. 99

Claire

Often it can be logistically difficult for school staff to teach emotional regulation on a one-to-one basis. It may suit you better to do the Get Back to Green (GBTG) programme as part of your whole-class Social, Personal, Health and Economic education sessions.

Get Back to Green is a six-week emotional regulation programme designed to help children develop their emotional literacy. Based on a three-point colour emotions thermometer (green/yellow/red), the programme focuses on a different emotion/colour each session and centres around pupil discussion about their experiences.

66 I designed the Get Back to Green programme to teach and embed emotional literacy practices as a whole-class activity in mainstream schools. What I discovered is that, once given a chance and a common language to use, most children seem to love talking about their feelings. 99

Claire

Some advantages of whole-class teaching include:

- everyone can benefit from these important lessons, not just autistic students
- everyone can benefit from sharing their experiences and from hearing others' experiences
- everyone realizes that strong emotions are something common that all children feel regularly
- everyone figures out and shares ways to 'get back to green'.

Please see ⬇ Appendix 1 for a six-session outline of the Get Back to Green whole-class programme. Each session takes about 30–40 minutes.

❝ One teacher told me that teaching her whole class how to use the emotions thermometer helped all students to resolve conflict more easily, because they were able to communicate better using a shared language. ❞

Claire

Get Back to Green programme for the whole school

Why not become a Get Back to Green school? Having a whole-school approach to emotional literacy will ensure that these key lessons and strategies will be reinforced and carried forward with all students as they move up through the school.

You could do this in a number of ways:

- Create a Get Back to Green notice board in the main corridor.
- Stick giant emotions thermometers at different points around the school and ask staff to refer to these emotions thermometers when they are out and about with students.
- Have the whole school do the Get Back to Green six-week programme at the same time.
- Have a Get Back to Green assembly once a week for six weeks to consolidate learning from that week's session.
- Give everyone in the school a pocket emotions thermometer and refer to it during regular assemblies throughout the year.
- Make talking about your emotions an active part of your school day. For example, check in with the class emotions twice a day; ask the principal and other staff to pop into classrooms occasionally and tell the students how they are feeling. Explain why, and wonder aloud how they are going to 'get back to green'.
- Stick posters around the school with photos of your students holding mini whiteboards showing how they like to 'get back to green'.
- Stick posters around the school detailing anonymized reasons for 'What makes me feel green/yellow/red' – often children are fascinated by what their peers have said, and it really helps them to realize the universality of human experiences and emotions.
- Have a whole-school day celebrating different emotions with a variety of guest speakers, activities and workshops.

'Get back to green' at home

❝ I would have been able to mask no problem, and I kept myself together so much in school. I was neat and tidy, did my homework, and caused no trouble. I talked to everyone, the cool kids, the Goths and the nerds. But I was exhausted by the time I got home, and was often in bed by six thirty. It is only now, having been diagnosed with autism, that I look back that I realise why I was so tired. 〞

Lenore Good, autistic advocate, blogger and mother of six

Some autistic children can act very differently at home and at school. Holding in their anxiety all day at school, they often arrive home and simply burst from the stress of it all. They can spend hours talking to parents or guardians about perceived insults, or something that happened in the playground, or obsessively doing their homework to perfection.

The converse is also true, with some students only displaying behaviours that may challenge at school and being quite calm at home. It is often helpful for parents to know that this is a very common occurrence. After all, school can be a far more chaotic, noisy, demanding and unpredictable place compared to home.

〝 When my daughter comes home from school, she's at 3% battery power, and barely hanging on. We let her go upstairs and relax and when she's a bit more charged, at about 75%, she'll come downstairs and chat and there'll be a better flow in the house. 〞

Mother of an autistic 12-year-old girl

On the surface, Anthony, 12, was a quiet, content student. He did his work neatly, put up his hand in class, worked well in a group and played with others outside at lunch time. However, as soon as he arrived home every day, he would cry, slam doors, argue with his brothers and sisters and shut himself in his bedroom and would not want to leave the house again.

Possible reasons
Anthony was trying so hard and expending so much energy keeping it all together in school that he simply couldn't keep up the façade when he went home.

What to do
Build in some 'pressure valves' into Anthony's school day so that he can let off steam throughout the day instead of waiting until he gets home. These could include:

- ensuring that Anthony has some space to chat to an adult during the school day and offload any worries he may have
- adding more 'breaks' into Anthony's school day so he has more opportunities to let off steam
- ensuring that there is structure in place throughout the school day so that any stress arising out of intolerance of uncertainty can be easily mitigated.

> For example, by using a daily schedule and pre-warning Anthony of any upcoming changes
> - teaching Anthony how to use an emotions thermometer and how to 'get back to green'.

It is also really important to show parents how to embed Get Back to Green strategies at home.

- Send a large emotions thermometer home for parents to stick on the fridge, along with an explanation of how to use it.
- Encourage parents to refer to it daily for both themselves and the student. Let discussion about emotions and 'getting back to green' become part and parcel of the language of the household.

Once learned and understood, the phrase 'get back to green' often has the strange quality of being able to diffuse tension. This has also been described by Dan Siegel (Siegel and Bryson 2011) as the 'name it to tame it' technique.

> " One family did GBTG daily with their autistic 7-year-old. Whenever he was stressed out, they got the emotions thermometer that was Velcroed to the fridge, and simply said 'Peter, get back to green.' Eventually, after lots of teaching and practice, just saying the phrase was enough to help him to snap out of the 'red' wave that he was riding. He would seek out his 'green' spaces (the beanbag, or his bedroom) and begin to rally. "

Claire

Frequently asked questions

Q: I'm completely swamped. I've got a curriculum to teach, assessments to do and books to correct – I don't have time for all of that.

A: This is such a common issue in busy schools. It might work to match emotional literacy strategies to your whole-class Social, Personal, Health and Economic education targets and then teach it as a series of whole-class sessions. Have a look at the Get Back to Green programme for the whole-class – after teaching six sessions, it then only takes a few minutes every day to check in with students about their emotions or to do a quick Get Back to Green whole-class activity.

Q: Doing 'Go Noodle' (online movement and mindfulness activities for children) or PMR isn't going to help a child who's in the middle of a meltdown.

A: It probably won't help in that situation. But if the child has practised 'getting back to green' enough and is fluent in recognizing when his body feels anxious, and what to do when he feels like this, he will be less likely to reach the stage of meltdown or 'red'.

Q: It's hard to figure out when he's 'yellow'. He seems to ramp up to 100 miles per hour instantly, without any reason.

A: He might have been at 50 by the time he arrived at school and discovering that there was a supply teacher in stressed him out even further. Using a mixture of preventative and reactive (coping) strategies, as well as lots of ongoing work around emotions, should help him to get himself out of the situation or to 'get back to green' before he comes close to reaching a stress level of 100 miles per hour.

Q: I don't believe that children should have the expectation that they always have to be happy or on 'green'. It's just not realistic.

A: It's really important to remember that 'green' does not just mean 'happy' or that 'everything is perfect'. It also means 'calm', 'relaxed' or just 'okay'. While being permanently ecstatic certainly isn't possible or even desirable, what we do want is to teach our students ways to regain and maintain their equilibrium, and to stay on an even keel. Ultimately, that's what 'green' means.

Note: This chapter outlines strategies to try to reduce anxiety at school. However, if a student is displaying high levels of anxiety, we advise seeking input from professionals such as Child and Adolescent Mental Health Services (CAMHS).

Give Me a Break

 " I have always found all incoming sensations very intense. Sight, sound, touch, smell and taste are all too strong. As a young child I tried to avoid uncomfortable sensory bombardment or overload by spinning objects, watching predictable eye patterns or playing with sand and water which calmed me down. "

Tim Chan, autistic author

Autism and sensory differences

Have you ever seen an autistic child transfixed by the dust particles floating in the beam of light from a ceiling projector? Or someone who insists on wearing his jumper outside in the summer heat, who clamps her hands over her ears when the bell goes for lunch break or who refuses to go to the dinner hall because he cannot stand the smell of rice pudding?

We know that:

- Many autistic people have sensory difficulties.
- Autistic people can display more sensory difficulties than non-autistic people.
- As autistic children mature, sensory difficulties may decrease, or autistic people may be able to develop better coping strategies for them.

In 2013, sensory processing difficulties were included as part of the diagnostic criteria for autism in the newly revised DSM-5. In order to receive a diagnosis of autism, a person does not need to display sensory differences. However, research studies report unusual sensory responses in 42–88 per cent of older autistic children and higher overall rates of sensory symptoms in autistic children when compared to non-autistic children (Baranek et al. 2006; Baranek 2002).

" I think [sensory issues are] a huge part of autism. It is so intrinsically part of everything. "

Early intervention special class teacher

The eight sensory systems

Your body has eight sensory systems. These are vision, hearing, smell, taste, touch, proprioception (movement), vestibular sense (balance) and interoception (internal senses).

> **Proprioception:** This is the sense of where your body is in space, and also where your body parts are in relation to each other. Two ways to better understand proprioception are:
>
> - *Water cooler:* When using a water cooler, you instinctively know exactly how much pressure to exert in order to successfully fill a cup of water. An autistic child may not be able to figure out how much pressure to apply. He might hold the cup too lightly and drop it as it becomes heavy with water, or he might squeeze it too hard and spill it.
> - *Touch your nose:* Close your eyes right now. Touch your nose. How did you know where your nose was? Somebody with proprioceptive differences might not be able to do this.
>
> **Vestibular sense:** This is your sense of balance and movement and your ability to coordinate both. For example, being able to stand on one leg while getting dressed, stepping on and off curbs and riding a bike use your vestibular sense.
>
> **Interoception:** This refers to any internal senses, including hunger, thirst, the urge to go to the toilet, sleepiness, as well as the ability to recognize bodily signs related to emotions, and to regulate your own emotions, as a result.

What are sensory processing differences?

" I don't like lots of different noises all at once. I really hate people at school touching me. "

Year 9 student, Limpsfield Grange school for girls aged 11–16 with communication and interaction difficulties

> ### Key terms to think about
> **Sensory processing (or integration)** is the ability to coordinate and understand the information that goes between the body and the brain.
>
> When children have difficulties with sensory processing, it means that these body-to-brain pathways are not working as efficiently as they could be. The brain cannot process the endless information being thrown at it and becomes 'stuck in an endless rush-hour traffic jam' (Ayres 1972, p.7).

As a result, everything can feel too much (too tight, too hot, too loud, too bright), or not enough.

Sensory modulation refers to the way that the body can filter out extraneous stimuli in order to focus on the task at hand. It is like the body's in-built volume control that you can turn up or down throughout the day, as needed. Many autistic children can display poor sensory modulation, which can really impede focus and concentration in class.

Poor sensory modulation could mean difficulty when trying to focus on classwork when you can hear every pencil nib scribbling and every sniffle or cough, when the lights are flickering, the teacher is wearing sickly sweet perfume and your new woolly jumper has started to get itchy and sore at the neck.

Sensory Differences at School

> 66 I found noise really overwhelming, particularly the bustle of the playground, and group work and people talking over each other. I really struggled with school uniforms, and textures were difficult. I have great big issues with temperature regulation, I basically never wear jumpers as an adult. 99

Georgia Harper, autism advocate and Embracing Complexity lead at Autistica

At school, sensory differences can present in many different ways.

Some children can appear lethargic and *under-aroused*, while others can be super active and *over-aroused*. Autistic children are often described as being hypersensitive (oversensitive) or hyposensitive (under-sensitive).

- **Hypersensitive** children are oversensitive to stimuli. They are sensory avoiders. They want less.
- **Hyposensitive children** are under-sensitive to stimuli. They are sensory seekers. They want more.

	Hypersensitive (oversensitive) *I avoid*	Hyposensitive (under-sensitive) *I seek*
Smell	I can't stand the smell of Dettol in the hall so I can't go in there. Your perfume makes me want to vomit so I can't sit beside you.	I can't smell my own body odour. I love strong smells like curry. I like smelling unfamiliar people's hands.
Sound	I put my hands over my ears when I hear the lunch bell. I can't focus on my work in this noisy classroom.	I want the volume on the interactive whiteboard to be on the highest setting. I often shout when talking to you.
Sight	Bright lights hurt my eyes. I like to wear sunglasses outside, even in winter.	I want to stand here for a while, staring at the beam of light coming from the projector.
Taste	I'm a picky eater. I only eat dry foods like crackers and biscuits for lunch.	I like to eat the class Play-Doh. I love pickled onion crisps.
Touch	I prefer to wear my soft tracksuit to school daily as I can't bear the feeling of the scratchy uniform.	I want to sift lentils in my hands. I want to touch everything.

Proprioception	I may hold my pencil too lightly. I have difficulty holding a pencil. I hold my body in a slightly awkward position.	I may hold my pencil with excessive pressure and scribble firmly on the page. I often stand too close to my friends at school. I often bump into other children in the playground. I love getting squeezes from you. I love squeezing the top part of your arms when I'm happy. I drop things.
Vestibular	I get dizzy easily and often vomit when we go on bus trips at school. I don't like participating in some team sports. I go very slowly up the stairs at school.	I want to run, spin and hang upside-down on the playground apparatus. I often swing on or slide off my chair at school.
Interoception	I visit the toilet lots as I don't like the feeling of a full bladder.	I didn't react when I banged my head. I didn't think of wearing a coat over my T-shirt to play outside in the snow. I don't always know that I need to go to the toilet and can forget to go for an entire day. I never drink water at school as I rarely feel thirsty.

Note: Some children are hypersensitive with a passive behavioural response. This means that they may stay in situations that cause them distress. They may seem fine but eventually have behavioural outbursts apparently 'out of the blue' or go into 'shut down' or constantly suffer anxiety.

Other children are hyposensitive with a passive behavioural response. These are children who need more, but do not actively seek it out. They are the children who appear lethargic, slow to get going and not responsive to environmental cues. Often, these are the children who fly under the radar, as they don't cause as many behaviours that may challenge as sensory seekers or avoiders.

 It is important to remember that sensory sensitivities can fluctuate throughout the school day, depending on what is going on and how the child feels at that time.

Pip, 12, used to clamp his hands over his ears whenever the teacher played our morning meeting songs on the interactive whiteboard. However, whenever the other children were at assembly in the afternoon, Pip loved nothing more than to stay in the classroom on his own and listen to his favourite song at full volume.

The difference was that Pip was in control of both the music choice and volume in the afternoon. Often, when a child knows that they can control something, they may be more likely to be able to cope with it and tolerate it.

Using a special interest may even help an autistic child to overcome a sensory difficulty in that moment.

While out and about, Kevin, 7, used to put his hands over his ears if he even saw a police car in the distance, as he found the sound unbearable. However, when Kevin became obsessed with the movie *Madagascar 3: Europe's Most Wanted*, he was motivated to just about tolerate the sound of the siren in order to be able to quote his favourite line from the film (about the police) as the police car approached.

Autistic children can also demonstrate simultaneous hyposensitivities and hypersensitivities for different stimuli.

How to figure out what sensory input your students need

Before deciding on which sensory activities are best suited to your student, it is worth considering doing the following:

- **Sensory profile:** These tick lists guide healthcare professionals and teachers towards finding out as much as they can about a child's sensory preferences and dislikes through observation and by asking parents/the child. As a result, the environment can then be altered to suit the needs of the child.

    For example, if the child is noise-sensitive, let him leave the classroom five minutes before the home time rush, or allow him to wear headphones while working at his desk.
- **Sensory audit:** This is an audit of the school or classroom in a bid to make it more autism-friendly.

The main culprits are often noise, light or smells. Solutions usually involve fixing a flickering fluorescent classroom light, putting rubber feet on chairs, removing hand-dryers in toilets (or turning them off at the switch, as necessary) or even using foam dice for a quieter maths games session.

Sensory Breaks at School

❝ If I bring him out for ten minutes, I'll get an hour's work out of him afterwards. ❞

Teaching assistant, mainstream school

Regular sensory breaks are beneficial because they help your students to:

- avoid overload
- increase focus and motivation
- maintain or restore homeostasis, or the 'calm-alert' state, which is the optimum state for learning.

Structuring sensory breaks

Some students like to have sensory breaks scheduled throughout their school day. Others (particularly older students) prefer to be able to take a break as and when needed.

- 'Break' cards are often used with older primary school–aged children.
- Give a specific number of cards to a student to use throughout the day.
- Give the student an official 'Break' card that they can use whenever they need to. Print 'Break Ideas' on the back of this card to ensure the student remembers what her options are.

It is really important to always allow the student to go on a break when they present their 'Break' card.

Sam is taking a break. He can walk in the corridor outside the classroom.

This break card expires on 1st November 2020.

Signed: ms Daly

FIGURE 2.19 'BREAK' CARD

Initially, most children will take advantage of the break system and try to use as many breaks as possible. However, this usually settles down when they realize that they are allowed to access regular breaks.

What to do on a break

Outside the classroom:

- Take a message to another classroom. This could be a green folder that all teachers know means that someone is on a sensory break.
- Go for a walk around the school. Use a specific route.
- Go to the toilet (lots of students already use this as a self-directed sensory break system).
- Stick sensory walkways and activities around the school corridors. These could include signposts dotted around the school with relevant resources beside them.
- Do five wall push-ups.
- Jump on the hopscotch mat as you walk up the corridor.
- Do five jumping jacks.
- Set up circuits in the playground/hall. Ensure that each part of the circuit is finite and timed. For example, throw three beanbags into that basket, collect three hoops as you run between two points.
- Go on the swings for five minutes.
- Go to the sensory room. Consider not timetabling the sensory room for different classes, but rather ensuring that it is available as and when particular students need to access it.

Inside the classroom:

- Have a list of classroom jobs printed out and ask the child to choose from these jobs. This has the added bonus of boosting the child's self-esteem and gives him a break without it being too obvious. These could include sharpening ten pencils, emptying the bins, tidying the books in the library for five minutes or rubbing out the whiteboard.
- Whole-class movement breaks. These include 'Take Five', 'Go Noodle' or 'Stand Up and Stretch' at intervals.
- Perform Dough Disco Play-Doh and finger exercises in younger classes.
- A Move 'n' Sit cushion on a chair can help some children as it enables them to move while sitting still.
- Do chair and wall push-ups (stick handprints on the wall for a visual cue for where they need to place their hands).
- Sit on a peanut ball for a bounce break.
- Spend time in the quiet space, such as the library, cosy corner or pop-up tent.

Sometimes just knowing that there is a quiet space available is enough to help your students feel more relaxed.

- Rolling Blu Tack or playing with a fiddle toy can often help children feel more grounded.
- Scatter ear defenders around each group table so that anyone can take a break from the noise, as they need.
- Allow the student to get up and walk around as and when he needs to. Ensure that you have pre-taught the rules (e.g. allow others to do their work) and that staff are on board with this.
- Allow the student to access his water bottle as needed.
- Create a personalized sensory kit for your student, filled with items that either relax and soothe or energize her. This could include paintbrushes, different squares of fabric, a tissue with the student's favourite smell on it, light-up toys, headphones and a packet of salty, crunchy crackers in case of nausea on a bus.

Recording sensory breaks

On your planning documents, it's useful to record:

- why a student needs sensory breaks
- whether breaks are scheduled or ad hoc
- what kinds of breaks they access
- whether a teaching assistant supports them to access a sensory break.

Sensory diet: A sensory diet is a series of regular sensory breaks and activities inserted into a child's daily schedule.

Usually devised by an occupational therapist (OT) after observation and assessment, a sensory diet consists of different activities that address the particular needs of the child at particular times of day. This could include:

- **Morning:** Proprioceptive activities including deep pressure massages or heavy work such as hanging off monkey bars or doing wall push-ups. This may help a child to settle down more easily upon entering the classroom.
- **Mid-morning:** Alerting activities done before a work session, including drinking cold water or chewing on crunchy foods like raw carrots, crisps, crackers or apples to increase focus.
- **End of day:** Relaxing activities including listening to music on headphones in the cosy corner or reading a book.

With a 'diet' of applicable sensory activities inserted into the student's daily schedule, the student should ideally receive all the sensory input they need in order to stay calm-alert.

However, occupational therapists are in high demand. A regular schedule of generic sensory breaks can often be the best and only option for class staff.

If you are unsure as to the suitability of any sensory activities, do seek the advice of an OT.

Note: It is important to observe and notice how a particular activity affects your students. Sometimes a so-called calming activity can actually be alerting for particular students, and vice versa. Try to take note of how long the calming effect lasts after your student accesses different kinds of breaks.

Other Ideas to Help Children Cope with Sensory Differences

There are lots of other ways you can make life easier for the sensory sensitive children in your class. These include:

- Ask class staff to avoid wearing strong perfume or aftershave at work, if possible.
- Fix any flickering lights, or even turn off the classroom lights at times to give everyone a break.
- Allow a touch-sensitive child to participate in art or messy play activities by wearing plastic gloves or by putting the material in a clear, sealed plastic bag.
- Discuss what clothes to wear in winter and summer and write a social narrative for a child who chooses not to wear a coat outside in the snow outlining the reasons why it is important and offer a reward for when they do.
- Have regular, whole-class mini moments of mindfulness throughout the day to help everyone to have a break from the constant hustle and bustle at school.
- Introduce a menu of smells, sounds and touches either on a one-to-one basis, or as a whole-class strategy. Depending on the students' preferences, this could include:
  - a plug-in aromatherapy diffuser with essential oils (check with parents first if their child has any allergies)
  - a selection of soft brushes and creams for self-administered hand massages
  - relaxing music played during work time
  - zone different areas of the school by colour.

Could we colour-zone primary schools?
University College Cork has a colour-coded system throughout the university library.

- **Red:** Silent
- **Amber:** Quiet
- **Green:** Conversational

There is a general understanding in the library that some people simply need total silence when studying and others can tolerate more noise.
Obviously, in a busy primary school there would be less adherence to such

adult rules. However, would it be possible to establish a similar system in your playground, with colour denoting expected levels of noise or physical exertion?

- **Red:** Loud space
- **Green:** Calm and quiet space

This could be a useful system not only in the playground but throughout the entire school building.

 Get comfortable with silence

Staff members can often feel under pressure to constantly chat to students while out on a sensory break, in case it appears to other staff that they aren't doing their job.

I often advise them to relax, and get comfortable with silence, if that's what the student prefers. Sitting side by side on swings in a companionable silence, doing some quiet wall push-ups in a school corridor or gazing at the bubbles silently floating down the bubble tube in the sensory room can be blissful for some of our students who really need their sensory break.

Mention this plan in a staff meeting or in a memo so that all staff know that this is the plan for this particular student while out and about.

Take your direction from the student himself. *"*

Claire

Let's talk about stimming

" I still stim hundreds of times a day, but it will look like me tearing down the street or going on tiptoes indoors. "

Adam Harris, CEO and founder, AsIAm, Ireland's national autism charity (Harris 2019)

Stimming means 'self-stimulatory behaviour'. It could mean rocking, flapping, clapping, spinning books, tensing and releasing the whole body repeatedly, making patterns in the air with fingers or even reeling off lines from movies. Autistic adults have described how stimming can act as a release, blocking out the noise and chaos of the outside world.

We all stim. A woman beside me at the airport recently clapped her hands repeatedly in excitement when her toasted cheese sandwich and chips arrived at the table. Football stadiums are always full of people engaging in self-stimulatory behaviour. They jump, they clap, they punch the air, not to mention the manager who usually paces up and down the side-lines, energetically chewing gum to assuage his anxiety.

Staff often ask if they should allow a child to stim at school. If the stimming is not impinging on the child or his classmates in any way, then it is an easy way for autistic children to indulge in a self-directed sensory break from the world around them.

> 66 I think there's a stigma against stimming, or self-stimulatory behaviour – so hand flapping, pacing, going back and forth on tiptoes, those are quite common autistic traits that are picked up, and a lot of teachers try to pathologize this or tell us not to do it, whereas as long as it's not harmful to ourselves or others, it shouldn't be perceived as a problem. 99
>
> *Jack Welch, autistic advocate and campaigner, youth patron of Ambitious about Autism*

Teaching coping strategies for the real world

Of course, it is not always possible to change the environment for just one child. Throughout their lives, your students will face many undesirable sensory situations that are simply out of their control.

Examples include sitting beside someone eating a strong-smelling dinner on an underground train or putting up with someone sniffling noisily in a library while trying to study.

In fact, autistic author and journalist Laura James made herself a sensory kit to take with her whenever she left the house. It contained a soft coat, noise-cancelling headphones, sunglasses, a cashmere scarf and some of her favourite perfume kept in her bag at all times (James 2018).

Clearly, it would be really useful to work with your students to come up with similar strategies to cope in such situations.

You could teach a student to:

- escape to the toilet or go outside the door for a break when feeling overwhelmed in a noisy lunch hall
- mouth-breathe when confronted with a horrible smell in the classroom, or have a hanky with his favourite scent on it readily available in his pocket
- count in her head until the noise of the school bell has finished
- wear something nice and soft under a scratchy uniform.

As with everything, make this visual by discussing it, writing it down and re-reading it regularly with your student at a time when they are calm and relaxed.

And remember, have empathy for and try not to judge the parents or guardians of the child who brings in the same beige, crunchy lunch every day, who hasn't had a haircut all year or who wears worn-out tracksuit trousers that are almost too small. There is usually a sensory reason behind it, which could be:

- food sensitivities
- an aversion to going to the noisy hairdresser
- a preference for well-washed, worn clothes as they are softer.

Frequently asked questions

Q: What do I do if he is asking to go to the toilet for a break all day every day?

A: He clearly wants or needs a break. Timetable it so he has clear slots when he knows he can pop out. Sometimes just knowing you can have a break whenever you need it helps you to stay in the classroom for longer. Show him other options for taking a break too.

Q: I'm afraid that if we give him a 'Break' card, he'll be using it all day long and will miss out on his learning.

A: Every child will play the system initially. Allow it. Once they know that they can have a break whenever they want, they will stop using the 'Break' card as often.

You could also allocate five 'Break' cards that can be used throughout the day, as and when he needs them.

Q: I don't think it's very fair if she is out taking breaks all the time. She won't get this treatment in the real world.

A: She will. It's called nipping to the loo, making yourself a cup of coffee or staying in your classroom during lunch time to indulge in a spot of online shopping, rather than going to a noisy staff room.

As she gets older, she'll just have more autonomy in choosing what kind of break to take, and when to take it.

Q: I'm not sure that he is noise-sensitive at all. He was completely fine when watching a really loud movie on the interactive whiteboard today.

A: Remember, autistic children can fluctuate between being over- and under-sensitive throughout the day. Plus, if it was one of his favourite movies, perhaps he was just more able to handle that noise because he really, really wanted to focus on the movie.

Q: I feel sorry for the other children; they don't get any breaks during the day. It's not fair on them.

A: Most of the time, even without ever discussing it, the other children in the class intuitively understand that some children need breaks and others don't. It's often staff who feel a sense of injustice on behalf of the others. If in doubt, do more whole-class sensory breaks, or choose a lucky peer each day to pop out with the student who is taking a break. Most classrooms now do regular movement breaks throughout the day as a matter of routine, which is an excellent example of Universal Design for Learning

(UDL). (See 🔑 Guide 4: General Classroom Visuals That Work for Everyone for more information on UDL.)

Q: I'm not sure about using headphones – won't he just get too dependent on them and be unable to go anywhere without them?

A: That's a good point, as it's possible that your student may become too sensitive if he wears headphones all the time. However, do make them available so he can access them as and when he needs them. As with lots of things, simply knowing they are there can be comforting enough.

Help Me to Communicate

 Looking at social communication

Interacting, sharing, asking for information, chatting, socializing, flattering and persuading – we spend our lives engaged in communication with other people. Being able to communicate effectively ensures that you can function in the world, as well as giving you agency and choice. Thus, it is vital to help your students learn to communicate successfully, in ways that match their ability levels.

Differences in *social communication* are one of the key diagnostic criteria for autism. (See 🔑 Guide 1: Introduction to Autism: Six Key Points.)

Social communication is defined as 'the sharing of information, thoughts or ideas with another person' (Fuller and Kaiser 2019). This includes:

- understanding the point of communication, and that it is worth the effort
- producing and using words
- understanding other people's words
- understanding the subtle nuances of other people's words
- understanding non-verbal communication. This includes body language, gesture and tone of voice.

Being able to communicate effectively using an appropriate language system gives your students autonomy. It helps them to:

- express their wants and needs – 'I need to go to the toilet' or 'I am hungry'
- express opinions – 'I really love Shrek'
- make choices – 'I'd prefer to eat my biscuits right now'
- have needs met – 'I have a pain in my tummy, I need a drink of water'
- express emotion – 'I'd like to take a break'
- express uncertainty – 'I don't know what I am supposed to be doing'
- assert themselves – 'I don't want to do this right now'
- ask questions – 'Can you repeat what you just said?'

Ultimately, effective communication skills can help your students to show the world who they really are.

" I have always lacked the desire to speak to others – despite needing to, despite suffering due to it. I did not know what a word was or that it was a tool to communicate with others. "

Shanon B, autistic advocate and writer

Expressive and receptive language

Autistic children can have stronger expressive language skills than receptive language skills.

Expressive language is what you say and how you say it. It is how a person communicates using sign language, picture exchange symbols or words (see ⚿ Guide 24: It's Not Just About Talking: Alternative Ways to Communicate), as well as how they express themselves using facial expression, eye contact and tone of voice.

Some autistic children can have fantastic expressive language skills. They chat eloquently and at length, about a special interest or when reciting dialogue from their favourite book or movie. At times, this can mask difficulties with understanding or receptive language.

Edward, 10, really surprised everyone on his first visit to the local café for 'travel training' one day. Upon leaving, he said to the barista, 'Excellent meal, we are very pleased. I would like to thank the chef.' Staff were impressed with his out-of-character verbosity. However, for the next year, he repeated the same sentence to the barista every Tuesday. It turns out he had learned it from a favourite LEGO® YouTube clip about a café, and impressively, had pulled it from his store of phrases to use in a surprisingly appropriate context. The class staff's next job was to teach him a less formal way of saying thank you!

The above is an example of echolalia. Echolalia is when a child repeats speech previously heard, either immediately or later on. Sometimes it is used to comfort, other times to communicate or clarify and other times to express something that the child cannot yet generate their own words for, so the child instead uses learned phrases.

Once he had heard his mum saying the word 'aubergine', David, 9, started saying it over and over again. He always got the giggles by asking his little sister to shout the word in his ear.

When she was younger, Jane used to repeat the ends of words immediately after other people. If her dad said 'Let's go to the park later', Jane would say 'later, er, er, er, er'. Her family knew this meant she was a bit anxious about whatever was coming next.

" When stressed or tired, I will sometimes lose the ability to speak. It normally comes back soon enough. "

Jamie Knight, autistic research engineer, writer and podcaster

Sometimes, anxiety can cause someone to temporarily lose their expressive language skills, which can then lead to stress or embarrassment (Cummins, Pellicano and Crane 2020).

Receptive language is the ability to understand all forms of language, including words, pictures and sign language, as well as gesture, tone of voice and facial expression.

For many autistic people, language can be a slippery, unreliable thing, fleeting and easily misunderstood. It can be something that flies over their heads in millions of tiny pieces, like Mike Teavee in *Charlie and the Chocolate Factory*, before they have a chance to grasp it.

You might assume that your students understand everything that is going on in the classroom, but in reality they may be thinking:

- I don't know what's happening.
- I don't know where I'm going.
- I'm not sure what I'm supposed to do.
- I don't understand this story.

As a result, you will need some strategies to help your students grasp and tether all of this language before it floats away.

" I had auditory processing difficulties, and I was just very distracted by background noise. At school, I wondered 'How does everyone else know what to do? Where is everyone getting that information?' I realised that they heard it from the teacher and if they hadn't heard it from the teacher, they heard it from their friend. I didn't hear it from the teacher and I didn't hear it from a friend because I didn't have any. "

Paul Micallef, autistic advocate and founder of Autism Explained Online Summit https://paulmicallef.com.au

 In order to improve your students' communication skills, it is often useful to focus initially on two main questions. These are:

1. How do I support my student to communicate? (expressive language)
2. How do I support my student to understand what's going on? (receptive language)

Why not list and acknowledge the strategies you are already using, and then pick some further tips and ideas from the following guides?

Eight Ways to Support Your Students to Communicate With You

1. Label what I am doing

In order to be able to verbally communicate, your students need to hear and learn the words that describe their surroundings. Ask yourself the following questions:

- Does he know what his own name is?
- Does he know his teacher's and teaching assistant's names?
- Does he know the names of his classmates?
- Does he know the names of different places he visits in school (assembly hall, playground, sensory room, lunch hall, computer room)?

A good place to begin is by labelling what your student is doing at school. For example, start with saying 'Eating lunch', and then move on to 'I am eating my lunch' or 'Ricky is eating his lunch'.

Ensure all staff use identical phrases, so that your student will learn them more easily. It is a good idea to write down the phrases and stick them on a wall, so that staff can quickly check that they are using the correct phrase.

2. Make a photo book about me and my world

Make a photo book entitled, for example, *Ricky's Day at School*, with each picture showing a simple caption, and read it together daily.

Pages could include:

- I am playing with my Stickle Bricks.
- I am on the swings.
- I am doing work with Marie.
- I am eating my snack.
- I am drinking my orange juice.

Note: Some people prefer to teach students to use the child's name rather than the personal pronoun. For example, 'Ricky is playing on the swings.' If in doubt, consult your speech and language therapist, who will be able to advise on the most suitable language level for your student.

To increase motivation, use a talking photo book app such as 'Book Creator' or 'Our Story' and insert videos as well as text. For example:

- I am watching Jolly Phonics (and insert a video of his favourite songs).
- I am listening to 'Humpty Dumpty' (and insert video of the exact song he likes to watch).

3. Teach me some language by rote using 'My Info Book'

Another more interactive way of helping your student to hear and learn these words by rote is to make a 'My Info Book'. This is a simple, interactive photo book containing all of the information about their school world.

'My Info Book' can help minimally or pre-verbal children to get to grips with the language of the world around them. Used daily, 'My Info Book' encourages students to respond to class staff and learn responses to everyday questions. It allows your student to hear the same key language every day and to make connections between the photographs and the words.

The book consists of a ring binder of laminated pages with a selection of photographs to Velcro to the relevant pages.

There is a question and answer printed on each page, which ensures that all staff are consistent in the language they are using with the child. Through repeated readings, the student hears and learns the questions and answers by rote.

For example:

- **Adult:** 'What's your name?' and hands the photograph of the student to them.
- **Student:** 'My name is Bernie' or 'Bernie' and sticks the photograph onto the page.

If the child is reluctant to say anything, simply answer for him and encourage him to stick the photograph onto the page, or give him a verbal prompt by saying 'My name is B...'.

It is important to always encourage the use of natural language. For example, your student does not have to answer in full sentences such as 'I go to St Mary's Primary School.' Instead, allow them to simply say the name of their school, or respond by Velcroing the photo to the page.

'My Info Book' is a really useful starting point for your students because:

- It is all about themselves, their family, their school and their hobbies, so they are more likely to show an interest in it.
- There is something tangible to do on each page.
- It is a predictable part of the school day.
- It is finite. The end is always clearly in sight.

Fred, 12, didn't tend to use very much language. Staff read 'My Info Book' every single day with him, asking him the same questions, to which he replied in single-word answers. By the end of the year, he had not only learned the rote answers, but had started to generate his own, new sentences.

What to do

- Add one new laminated page per week to the book.
- Always have a task for your student to do on each page. For example, ask him to Velcro a photo or symbol to a page, or to match photos.
- To sustain your student's interest, use other media to accompany specific pages. For example:
  - Ask him to match and name photos of their favourite songs on a page. Then listen to one of these songs on the iPad.
  - After matching parts of the body, sing 'Head, Shoulders, Knees and Toes'.

Please see ⊕ Appendix 2 for a sample contents page for 'My Info Book'.

4. Teach me what words to use

" During my first year teaching a speech and language therapist advised me to 'Say it as he would if he could'. I have never forgotten this simple but very important tip when supporting the language skills of my students. "

Annelies

Simply model the correct language for your student. This can range from:

- A student who says 'pay', and staff then model the word 'play'.
- A student who says 'I go outside', and staff then model the sentence 'I want to go outside'.
- A student who says 'On Sunday I go to McDonald's', and staff then model the sentence 'On Sunday I went to McDonald's'.

It is usually best to avoid telling your student to 'Say "I go to McDonald's"', as he might then simply repeat the exact sentence – 'Say "I go to McDonald's"'.

Do not worry if your student does not repeat the exact language you have just modelled. Your focus here is on exposing him to the correct use of language.

Whenever staff asked Daniel, 11, to participate in P.E., he would usually shout 'I hate you'. What he really meant was 'I really don't want to do this because I find it so difficult.' While this was a very functional way for Daniel to get his message across, the class staff's job was to teach him a more socially acceptable way of communicating. At the same time, they were keen that he access at least some part of the P.E. session, as regular exercise was part of his Individual Education Plan (IEP).

What to do

- Staff modelled the correct language for Daniel every time.
- They wrote out a simple story describing alternative language that he could use to get this specific need met and read it daily with him.
- They tried to make P.E. sessions more appealing and manageable for Daniel by using a First/Then Board and by ensuring that visual supports were used throughout. For example, they used a mini schedule for P.E. so that Daniel knew exactly what activities he was doing, shortened particular activities for him and allowed him to read his favourite book on a bench at the end of the session for five minutes.
- They also re-jigged the timetable so that Daniel could exercise at other, quieter times of the day with a support staff member and another student.

5. Sabotage opportunities for language use

Once your student is confident with the new word, sign or symbol, provide ample opportunities throughout the school day to practice what they have learned.

'Sabotage' means to purposefully stage-managing situations throughout the day where your student has to initiate communication in order to get something they want or need. However, it is important to do this in a gentle manner that in no way causes even a soupçon of anxiety for the student.

- Pick two opportunities during the day where you will 'sabotage' a language opportunity for your student. For example:
  - Place a favourite toy in a closed cupboard so that the student has to initiate contact and communication with you in order to get the toy. Ensure that your student knows what it is called, or has a photo of the object, or can choose an image of the object that it is stuck on the cupboard door.
  - Give the student half of his cracker at lunch time so that he has to ask for 'more' (if you have already taught him this).
  - Hand out paper and paints to your child but absent-mindedly forget to give him the paintbrush so he has to ask for it.

You can also encourage verbal communication through play and playful use of language. This offers lots of opportunities for the student to hear and use natural language.

- Leave out the last word of familiar rhymes, poems and songs in order to encourage your student to say it.
- Make a mistake when reciting a rhyme and wait for him to correct you.
- Choose a story with lots of repetitive language, and after repeated readings, ask your student to fill in the key phrases.
- Model aloud the language of play, for example, 'Oh no, they crashed!' (when playing with cars) or 'It's going to fall down' (when building a tower).
- Use exciting cause-and-effect toys to encourage him to finish the phrase 'Ready, steady...GO' or 'One, two...THREE'.

Andy, 4, was using few words on arrival into his mainstream infant classroom. On discovering that he loved bubbles, staff began to take him on walks in the corridor outside the classroom, saying 'One, two, three, bubbles', and then blowing the bubbles for him. After two days of doing this, he began to respond with the word 'bubbles' after staff said 'one, two, three...'

A few days later, staff moved the goalposts very slightly again – in order to request bubbles, he had to say 'one, two, three, bubbles, Emma', which he managed admirably.

It is important to add a social interaction element to request-making by teaching your student to use your name whenever he requests something. For example:

- 'I want bubbles, Ms Murphy.'
- 'Mary, I want crackers.'

If you are using a picture exchange book, simply add in some photos of the staff members.

Mind your manners!

Autistic speaker Ros Blackburn has discussed the importance of manners in helping to overlook any social errors. She has also highlighted the value of teaching someone to say or sign 'Please' and 'Thank you' (Blackburn 2013). If you would like to teach the use of 'please' or 'thank you', simply add it onto the end of the sentence.

6. Offer me choices

Offering choices is a good way for your student to learn how useful communication skills can be. It also gives him a sense of control over both his environment and in his daily life.

Try to build in opportunities for choice throughout the day, using verbal language, visuals or signs. An easy way to do this is to offer your student choices about what activity they would like to do.

Create a Choice Board with two photographs or symbols of items. Categories could include:

- favourite lunch foods
- favourite toys
- favourite nursery rhymes.

If a student finds too much choice overwhelming, you could initially:

- offer just two choices
- offer a choice between a favourite toy and a less favoured one, to make it a bit easier.

“ In my special class, we used to play 'Songs' every single day after morning meeting. Sitting in a row in front of the interactive whiteboard, each student had a chance to choose their favourite song from a Choice Board that was passed around the group.

Children who were able to speak asked for their favourite song (from the selection that was on offer), while others pointed to pictures on the Choice Board.

As each child chose their song, we would then watch a video of that song on the whiteboard.

'Songs' enabled everyone to feel that they had agency. It was also an invaluable way of helping the students to learn the important skills of turn-taking and waiting. And they had the chance to listen to and watch a variety of songs at the same time. ”

Claire

 Use the snipping tool to snip the screenshot of the exact song that your student likes to watch, rather than a generic picture of it. In this way, your student can rest assured that he is choosing the song he really wants.

7. Explicitly teach me how language works

For a long time, autistic podcaster, advocate and research engineer Jamie Knight confused the concepts 'on' and 'in'. He had learned that when he was 'in a train', it was actually described as being 'on a train'. As a result, when the instructions on his microwave pizza box said to put it 'in the microwave', he put it on top of the microwave and turned the microwave on. For a while, he wondered why his pizzas remained so crunchy (Steward and Knight 2018).

As well as modelling language in a naturalistic way, it is also useful to begin using a structured teaching approach. The speech and language therapist will assess your student to highlight areas of language that he needs to work on. This may include teaching him basic language concepts.

Basic language concepts are 'words that a child needs to understand in order to perform everyday tasks like following directions, participating in classroom routines, and engaging in conversation' (Loraine 2008, p.1).

This could include:

- irregular plurals (man, men; fish, fish)
- question words (who, what, where, why, when, how)
- prepositions (in, on, under, over, off, on)
- colours
- shapes
- emotions words.

1. Start by teaching a single language concept. For example, the preposition 'on'. You could use your student's favourite toy or special interest to help to teach this point. For example, 'Buzz Lightyear is on the table', 'Buzz Lightyear is on the floor', 'Buzz Lightyear is on the climbing frame', 'Buzz Lightyear is on my head'. Ensure that you give him plenty of opportunities to practice placing objects on other objects and describing situations such as 'Buzz Lightyear is on the roof of the doll's house'.

Ketchup on Your Cornflakes? by Nick Sharratt is a lovely book for teaching the concept of 'on'. After reading and enjoying the book a few times, use a feely bag with a variety of props inside, e.g. plastic ice cubes, a woolly hat or a rubber duck, which your students can take turns to choose and put on their feet, toes or heads.

As a fun extension activity, make your own photo book or video montage of your students doing this, using a talking book app such as 'Book Creator' or 'Our Story'. Seeing themselves in the story often encourages repeated readings and thus increased exposure to the concept that you are trying to teach.

2. Teach the next language concept, for example, the preposition 'in', in a similarly fun and visual way.
3. Begin to mix both language concepts once your student is confident in identifying and naming objects located in these positions.
4. Practice generalization of these language concepts by using them in a variety of different situations. For example, in class say 'Please put your copybook on my desk', or during P.E. 'Look, Nellie is in the tunnel'.

Jordan always tended to use the pronoun 'he' when talking about both male and female friends. Staff always modelled the correct use of 'she', but Jordan just could not seem to remember this.

What to do

Jordan's teacher made a selection of resources. Initial activities included matching pictures of boys and girls and sorting pictures of familiar and unfamiliar boys and girls into two different boxes. She then used a three-step progression for Jordan. This was done by:

- using a feely bag containing only pictures of boys. Jordan chose one, and described what the person was doing, using the correct pronoun. Even though Jordan was successful at this as he was very familiar with the use of the pronoun 'he', staff reiterated each time that they were using 'he' because the subject was a boy.
- presenting Jordan with pictures of girls in different scenarios, e.g. playing, riding a bike and kicking a ball. Staff asked Jordan to describe what was happening in each picture. Initially he was inclined to use 'he' but with practice he started using the pronoun 'she'. Once Jordan was confident in using the pronoun 'she' when talking about girls, staff presented him with a mixture of photos depicting both girls and boys.
- asking Jordan to describe what different children and staff were doing throughout the day. This was done in a bid to help Jordan to generalize his learning. Staff also asked parents to do the same at home.

 For a list of further resources to teach your students about how language works, please see Appendix 3.

Don't forget to generalize these skills with regular practice throughout the day, inserting them naturally into work time as well as play time if possible.

8. Teach me essential conversation skills

66 During the coronavirus lockdowns in 2020 and 2021, I had multiple Zoom video calls with my friends, and sometimes friends of friends, usually at the weekend. I always found it really difficult to know how to leave a call. I found myself cueing up my departure with phrases like 'I'm only staying on for a bit tonight', and 'Girls, I'm going to head away now, have a lovely night', and pressing 'End Call' as fast as possible. It felt awkward to me every single time! 99

Claire

The ability to have a conversation is a highly nuanced skill. You need to know how to begin, how to maintain and how to finish in a natural, non-rushed way. This is something that many non-autistic people can also struggle with.

The elements of a conversation

Beginning: Greetings, looking in the person's direction, making initial small talk, knowing when and in what situation it is appropriate to start a conversation.

Maintaining: Allowing everyone to have a chance to talk, showing interest in what the other person is saying by looking in their direction and by asking follow-up questions about what they are saying, interrupting politely and knowing when it is okay to change topics.

Finishing: Leaving in a natural, non-abrupt way, coming up with an excuse (or a learned rote phrase) to leave if the conversation is uncomfortable in any way, showing that it's time to leave by looking at your watch, or doing up your coat, or pausing, or taking a step back and having an appropriate end phrase such as 'See you soon' or 'I better go'.

There are lots of commercially available social skills programmes that detail how to do each of the skills outlined above. (See ⊕ Appendix 3.) Pick the elements of each programme that best suit your student and use this as a foundation for your teaching. You may also choose to add in extra activities of your own, tailored to suit the needs of your student.

Lily and Joanne participated in 12 group sessions on conversation skills. Using both teacher-made tasks and commercially available social skills programmes, the progression of lessons included:

- looking at a person when you're talking to them (at their eyes or forehead if eye contact feels uncomfortable)
- greeting upon entering a room
- asking about the weekend on Monday mornings
- the elements of a successful conversation, e.g. good listening, turn-taking, greeting, maintaining and finishing.

In order to teach the targets, the support teacher:

- used puppets to dramatize examples of both 'successful' and 'not so successful' elements of conversation
- created home-made videos of fellow-teachers interacting in 'correct' and 'incorrect' ways
- enacted role-plays (with the students always role-playing the correct way of doing it)
- videoed the students themselves displaying good conversation skills
- modelled thinking aloud strategies daily whenever Lily asked her 'How was

your weekend?' by saying 'Oh, thanks for asking, that makes me feel that you're really interested in what I'm saying.'

By the end of the term, there was a marked difference in how both girls entered a room and greeted the support teacher in a far more confident way. The teacher really knew that they had taken the lessons on board when, out of the blue, Lily commented, 'You were a bit rude, just like Charlie [the puppet], because you walked off to put the paper in the bin when Joanne was in the middle of talking to you.'
Her awareness was now clearly switched on.

Below are some ideas for conversational scenarios that often crop up at school.

Greetings

Nine-year-old Jackie used few words during the school day and never greeted anyone as she arrived at school. In her autumn term IEP meeting, her mum identified that she would really like her to work on this basic communication skill, as she was now getting older.

What to do
- Class staff made a 'Hello Book' with each page featuring a photo of a staff member or a fellow student and a different greeting, e.g. 'Hi Sam', 'Good Morning Ms Smith', 'Hiya Alex'. Every morning staff read through the book with Jackie and practised the different ways of greeting people.
- Staff also asked Jackie to select one of the photos and go and greet that person in real life.
- In addition to this, they read *Hello!* by Janine Amos, a simple photo book detailing how a variety of people feel when you do and don't greet them.
- Staff planned to build on these skills by teaching Jackie that she only needed to greet someone once a day, and that if she walked past them more than once, a simple nod or smile would suffice.

Asking questions

During the Monday 'My News' class sessions, Harry, 7, usually listened quietly, but never participated in the questions and answers session after someone had finished speaking. He appeared disinterested in what his peers were saying, often preferring to talk about his own topic of interest. However, when Harry's teacher quizzed him about what his peers had said, he was always able to answer correctly.

She realized that he had actually taken in all of the information, but just didn't know how to ask follow-up questions.

What to do

Harry's teacher knew that most of the time, the children in her class usually told the same version of their news every week. She made a simple cheat sheet for Harry. She gave him a laminated A4 'Question' card with a question mark printed on the front. On the back of the card, she wrote a series of questions under the headings 'who', 'what', 'where', 'why' and 'when'. While Harry was listening to his classmate talking, he used a dry-wipe marker to underline the question that was most relevant to the topic, and then he asked it afterwards.

Questions included:

- 'What was your favourite part of the weekend?'
- 'What did you buy in the shop?'
- 'What did you do at the beach?'
- 'Who went to the beach with you?'

Continuing with a conversation

Although Alan, 8, really wanted to make friends at school, he often found it tricky to find common ground with his classmates. He had told his mum that he just wasn't sure what to say to other people.

What to do

Before the Year 3 class trip to *Matilda: The Musical*, Alan's teacher brainstormed some topics of discussion and questions he could ask his peers before and after the trip. She wrote them on a little index card for him and they practised them for a week.

Questions included:

- 'What's your favourite Roald Dahl book? Why?'
- Who's your favourite character in *Matilda*? Why?'

She likened it to pre-teaching essential elements of a maths lesson to a child who needs it, except this time, it was for conversation skills.

Monologues

Beatrice, 10, often talked at length about her special interest, which was horses. She never noticed her classmates becoming bored of the topic, and often got upset if they drifted off while she was still talking.

What to do

- Staff did some work around body language with Beatrice. They gave her cue cards to help her to learn about what people do during a conversation when they feel either bored or interested.

For example:

- Are they still looking at you? Or are they looking around the room?
- Are they nodding and smiling at you? Or are they yawning and straight-faced?

They role-played conversations where the staff member appeared either interested or bored and helped Beatrice to use the cue cards to notice how the other person felt.

- Staff practised ways in which Beatrice could include others in the conversation related to her special interest by asking them questions related to the topic. For example, 'Do you like horses?' or 'Do you have any pets?'
- Staff also wrote a social narrative for Beatrice detailing why it is a good idea to let other people chat in a conversation, too, and how people can feel if they do not get a chance to talk. They read this with her daily for a few weeks.
- In order to fulfill her desire to chat about horses, staff also offered Beatrice a designated ten-minute talking time every day where she could sit comfortably with them in the library corner and tell them everything she knew about the topic.

Boasting

When Dan, 8, came first in anything, from winning a board game to being first in the line, and from answering a question first to finishing a worksheet first, he talked about it incessantly for the rest of the day and often even into the next day. It annoyed his classmates, who usually told him to 'Be quiet' or simply avoided him.

What to do

- Staff let Dan know that there was no need to repeat a fact that everyone already knows.
- They filled out a 'Playback' form with him detailing how others think and feel when he starts to boast. (See 🔑 Guide 37: 'Playback' Forms.)
- They read some simple books about 'boasting' with him, including *Boris the Boastful Frog* by Karen J. Hodgson. While Dan didn't initially make any connection between himself and the boastful frog, staff simple nudged him in the right direction to make the link by saying 'Remember when Boris was boasting, do you think that's what you were doing just there? What could we do instead?'

'Think it' versus 'say it' comments

Whenever Julian, 7, received a present he didn't like at Christmas or his birthday, he would throw it on the ground, saying 'I already have this.'

In front of the whole class, Kieran, 9, asked his teacher if he could go to the toilet because he needed to pick his nose.

What to do

- Staff completed 'Playback' forms with the older students and outlined the reasons why it is not always a good idea to say what is on your mind, even if it is true, because it might be considered rude or too private. They discussed how others might think or feel.
- They discussed multiple scenarios with the students and asked them to identify in which scenarios they should 'think it' and in which they should 'say it'.
- They gave students lots of difficult scenarios and asked the students to decide what to say in those situations. For example, 'Your mum gets her hair cut and you think it's horrible and far too short. What could you say, if anything?'

Staying on topic

During a small social group, Ger, 10, would always change the subject and try to chat about lots of different ideas that came into his head. It derailed the conversation and left the other students bored and restless.

What to do

- Ms Joanna, the teaching assistant, devised a brilliant way of helping Ger to stay on topic. Knowing that he loved the movie *Cars 2*, she printed out a picture of a racetrack and Velcroed cut-out cars from the movie on it. Whenever Ger started to go off topic, she moved the car off the track and asked him to 'get back on track'. It was a very visual way of helping Ger to notice when he was taking over the conversation, and he found it very amusing.

 Don't forget – give me a reason to chat to other people

Of course, in order to have a conversation with someone, you will usually need to have a reason to talk to them. This can include:

- seeking information
- giving information
- asking a favour
- asking permission
- social conversation around shared interests.

In fact, autistic author and animal scientist, Temple Grandin, highlights the importance of shared interests for building friendships: 'You don't just socialise for chit-chat, you also do it to talk about things you like to talk about' (Grandin 2009).

Giving your students a reason to have a conversation will help them to practice and generalize these newly learned conversation skills in natural settings. This can be done via shared interest groups with other students (e.g. a Minecraft lunchtime club) or by organizing a group of students together for a common purpose (e.g. establishing an after-school movie or newspaper club to make an 'All About Our School' newsletter, or one-off photo or video montage).

In the movie *Life, Animated*, Owen Suskind, a 20-year-old autistic man, organized a group of students with different needs to get together regularly for 'Disney Club'. There, they watched parts of Disney movies and discussed them, and even invited special guest speakers from the movies. One young man even played along to the movie scores on his piano.

66 I started the Disney Club so I can get to know more people and they can be around me, so I can be more popular. It worked! 99

Owen Suskind, Life, Animated (Williams 2016)

It's Not Just About Talking: Alternative Ways to Communicate

Of course, talking is not the only way to communicate. For students who are not currently able to produce spoken language, the following systems are often used.

Picture exchange

Picture exchange is a commonly used way to help pre-verbal autistic students to communicate their needs by making requests using photographs or symbols. The core tenet of picture exchange systems is to help the child to realize that communication works and can be really effective.

> If I give you a picture, I will get something in return.

Picture exchange always starts with two adults and a child. The initial steps are as follows:

- Adult A stands behind the child who is sitting down.
- There is a photo of a toy train on the table in front of the child.
- Adult B sits on the other side of the table.
- Adult B is holding the toy train.
- Adult A silently places her hand over the child's hand and takes the photograph of the train and gives it to Adult B.
- Adult B says 'train' and immediately hands the toy to the child.

With repeated practice, the child soon learns that handing over a photograph of an object means that she will get the object.

The child becomes more independent as she moves through the different phases of the programme, eventually selecting a desired object from an increasingly greater number of visuals, spontaneously walking over to her teacher, gaining her attention and requesting something.

PECS (Picture Exchange Communication System) created by Pyramid Educational Consultants UK is the most widely used commercially available product. A speech and language therapist will be able to advise on staff training, as well as deciding what system would best suit your student and on what phase of the programme they should start.

However, if you are keen to get started on functional communication more immediately, it is useful to begin by creating a Basic Needs Board.

Basic Needs Board

FIGURE 2.20 BASIC NEEDS BOARD

- Make a list of the top six items or places that are important to your student (Figure 2.20).
  - These could include iPad, toilet, favourite toy.
  - You could equally begin with lunch items, as these are often something that students are highly motivated to request. For example, biscuits, Cheerios, milk.

FIGURE 2.21 ITEMS TO BE VELCROED TO THE BASIC NEEDS BOARD

- Photograph the items, laminate them and Velcro them to the Basic Needs Board (Figure 2.21).
- With another adult, model and teach your student how to request his item using these photographs, using the hand-over-hand method outlined above, if necessary.

- Ensure that you give the item to the student immediately, while saying the word at the same time.

Note: Some people prefer children to simply enjoy their food and spend time with their friends at lunch time, instead of having to complete a picture exchange for food items.

Signing

Two manual signing systems commonly used with autistic children are Makaton and Lámh.

- **Makaton** uses symbols and signs to support speech for children and adults (makaton.org).
- **Lámh** is a manual signing system used by children and adults with intellectual disability and communication needs in Ireland (lamh.org).

Both systems encourage teaching the signs in tandem with saying the words in order to facilitate better understanding and communication.

Using signing with your students

- List the top five items that your student tends to request.
- Learn the signs to go with each word.
- Create opportunities for both adults and children to use both the signs and the words throughout the day.

" In a special class for autistic students, we filmed a trained staff member doing one new Lámh sign a week, and then watched and learned the signs in these videos as a whole-class activity. We also turned it into a weekly game, where staff did the sign (this time, while mouthing the word) and the students had to guess what it was, which also enhanced listening and observation skills.

We emailed the videos to parents/guardians so that they could continue using the signs at home. "

Claire

 Your speech and language therapist will be able to identify what system best suits your students, as well as relevant training opportunities for staff.

Janet began to point to her stomach. This was a very functional way of saying she was hungry, and staff realized that this meant she wanted a cracker from her lunchbox.

What to do

Next steps include:

- Teach Janet to recognize a photo of a cracker.
- Teach Janet to give staff the photo of the cracker in return for a cracker.
- Offer Janet a Choice Board with a photo of crackers or a photo of her water bottle.

or

- Teach Janet the sign for 'cracker'.
- Teach Janet that signing 'cracker' means that an adult will give her a cracker.

There are lots of available apps to help students to communicate using a phone or tablet. Just remember to always have your devices charged.

Please see Appendix 3 for a selection of useful sign language video clips.

Home-school communication

If a student finds it difficult to communicate with you, it is important to have an easy channel of communication between staff and parents. This can be achieved by using:

- a home-school communication sheet or book
- a simple tick sheet with simple, tickable details e.g. 'Slept well/ate breakfast/ any other information'
- regular meetings
- communication via phone calls, email or ClassDojo.

This can really help both parents and staff to have all of the necessary information to ensure that their child's wants and needs are being met. It is often useful to manage parental expectations around home-school communication by setting boundaries such as having an email signature saying 'I will reply to emails within school hours or up until 4 p.m.'

Please see Guide 44: Communicating with Parents in Part 4 for further information on home-school communication diaries.

Four Ways to Support Your Student's Understanding in Class

1. Use clear language

" I often see people swooping in and chatting at length to autistic children. They're so used to doing it with non-autistic children, but what they may not realize is that they may be adding another level of noise and confusion for the child. "

Claire

Staff can increase comprehension of spoken language at school in the following ways:

1. Use reduced language.
   - Using reduced language means cutting out anything superfluous and speaking in short bullet points. Instead of flooding the child with language as soon as he enters the classroom, simplify your language completely, reducing it down to the bare minimum.
   - For example, instead of 'Hi John, how are you, take off your coat and hang up your bag and come to sit at the green table and take out your maths book', say 'Hi John' and wave.
   - Say 'Take coat off' and possibly use the sign for 'coat'.
   - Say 'Hang up bag' and possibly use the sign for 'bag'.
   - Say 'Sit at green table' and point to the green table.
   - Say 'Maths book' and hold up the maths book he needs to take out.
2. Be very clear and concise.
   - Ensure you gain your student's attention by saying their name before asking them a question.
   - Explain to your student that whole-class instructions are also directed at him, as some students simply do not realize this.
   - Tell the child exactly what you want them to do. Instead of saying 'Put the book over there please', say 'Put the book on the table beside the computer'.
   - Avoid using metaphors and idioms, at least initially.

2. Allow for some processing time: The eight-second rule

Some of your students may have language processing difficulties. As a result, it is important to give them some extra processing time whenever you ask her a question.

The recommended 'wait time' is up to eight seconds. Although this might initially feel unnatural, it will give your student a chance to get over the potentially overwhelming feeling of being asked, as well as to organize her thoughts.

If you need to repeat the question, do try to stick with your original wording. If you rephrase the original question, your student may well have to process this new language all over again.

Even though she was excellent at maths, Molly, 5, often appeared flummoxed whenever her teacher asked her a question during the group maths session. She would then get upset when she couldn't think of the answer on the spot, particularly when another student would often shout it out.

What to do
The class teacher:
- pre-warned Molly that she was going to ask her a question after the next student and told her what the question was going to be. This helped Molly to prepare her answer without any immediate social and communicative pressure.
- wrote down the sum on the interactive whiteboard or asked the support staff to write it on a mini whiteboard for Molly.
- counted to eight in her head every time she asked Molly a question during the group session. This gave Molly more time to gather her thoughts and to formulate her answer. She was usually able to give the correct answer by the seventh second.

3. Use visual supports around the school

Philip, 9, attended a literacy group in a mainstream primary school. The group was noisy, and Philip was often off task. Whenever the teacher asked him a question about the class novel they were reading, more often than not, he had his book open on an incorrect page and didn't know what she was talking about.

What to do
- The teacher wrote the page number of the book on a mini whiteboard so that Philip could double-check that he was on the right page at the start of the session, without needing to ask anyone.
- The teacher also wrote the question down on a piece of paper and gave it to Philip at the start of the session, so that he could work out the answer at his leisure.

As discussed in 🔑 'Make Everything Visual for Me' earlier in Part 2, using visual supports within the classroom will really help your students to understand what is going on.

Remember, using a signing system is also another way of making everything visual for your students. Using Makaton or Lámh has the added bonus of supporting spoken language by leaving a sign in the air for a few seconds, which remains as a brief subtitle after the spoken word has disappeared. It gives the child an extra chance to make sense of what you have just said.

4. Support a more nuanced understanding of literal language

Language can befuddle your students, as there are so many different ways of using it. They may take language literally, or at face value, and believe that everything you are saying is completely true. This can lead to misunderstandings and anxiety about what people are actually saying.

There are so many examples of autistic students taking language literally. These include:

- When the teacher said 'I've got eyes in the back of my head', and the student walked up and checked her head.
- When the teacher said 'See you later' on Friday afternoon, and the student said 'But I won't see you later.'
- When the teacher said 'Go and wash your hands in the toilet' and the student took this literally.
- When the teacher said 'Go over your spellings for homework' and the student asked 'What is go over?'

Idioms

❝ We used to teach 'Idiom of the Week' where we learned the meaning and drew pictures of various idioms. I was never sure of the value of this, as it seemed that there were just too many idioms to learn.

However, one day I counted the number of idioms I used in a single day, and was very surprised to count four, mainly while in conversation with adults. These were 'It's six of one, and half dozen of another', 'It's a day for ducks', 'Let's make hay while the sun shines' and 'Well, the ball is in your court now.' I realized how beneficial it was to teach at least a selection of these to my students. ❞

Claire

Actively teaching idioms is important as it gives your students a better chance to understand the language used around them. However, as well as teaching a random selection of traditional idioms, it is also important to identify colloquial idioms used by young people. Learning these will go some small way towards helping your students to navigate the social world, particularly in secondary school.

> **Colloquial idioms**
>
> **Cork, Ireland:** Contrary to what it sounds like, the phrase 'I will yeah' actually means 'No, I won't.'
>
> **London, UK:** Saying something is 'bare sick' has nothing to do with bear vomit. It simply means something that is 'cool' or 'great'.
>
> Someone asking 'You alright?' is not actually asking you how you are, but rather saying 'Hello' in an informal way.
>
> Of course, language is an ever-changing entity – what was cool last year may be passé now. Before teaching any of these phrases, check with a group of young teenagers what phrases and words they currently use, and make a list of them to use in your sessions.

Elroy, 13, was mocked by one of his fellow students when he started referring to his mum as 'my old doll'. He had simply misunderstood the phrase commonly used in his locality to refer to one's girlfriend. Once staff quickly explained the correct context, Elroy never used it incorrectly again.

Taking language literally

It is important to bear in mind also that misunderstandings may be subtler than someone simply taking idioms literally, like 'Pull up your socks' or 'It's raining cats and dogs'. Sometimes there is an implied meaning in words and phrases that some autistic people can miss.

Ros Blackburn described how, upon entering a school, she was asked by the secretary 'Would you like to sign the guest register?' Ros very politely said 'No, thank you' and walked on, whereby the secretary immediately called her back and told her it was mandatory.

Ros wondered why 'Would you like an ice-cream?' was considered a choice, whereas 'Would you like to sign the guest register' was most definitely not a choice' (Blackburn 2013).

In the brilliant graphic novel *La Différence Invisible*, the author Julie Dachez describes the autistic woman, Marguerite, at work. Her boss approaches her desk and asks her 'Do you have the Nung folder', to which Marguerite replies 'Yes' and keeps typing. She didn't realize that what her boss really meant was 'Please give me the Nung folder' (Dachez 2016).

Teaching Social Communication Skills: An Outline

Social communication skills assessment: What skills to target

Start by setting a baseline for your student's social skills ability. This can be done by:

- observing your student in a number of social settings over the course of a few weeks
- talking to other staff, parents and to the student himself to find out what social skills he would like to focus on
- completing a social communication skills assessment or checklist to find out where your student's strengths and needs lie in this area (see ⊕ Appendix 3)
- choosing which skills to prioritize, as a result.

Once you have identified what skills would be useful for your student to learn, use the six-step framework below to help you to teach the identified social communication skills.

Six steps to teach social communication skills

1. Give the students a clear rule.
2. Provide the students with a rationale for the rule – why do we do this?
3. Learn how to do the skill.
4. Role-play this skill.
5. Encourage generalization of this new skill by practising the skill in a variety of settings and situations.
6. Revisit this skill regularly throughout the year.

For example, when teaching the topic of giving compliments:

1. 'It is a nice thing to do if you give other people compliments when you first meet them.'
2. 'Other people feel good when you give them a compliment. They feel that you have noticed them.'
3. Brainstorm and record different types of compliments, or make video clips of staff members giving each other compliments.
4. Practise giving each other compliments, and use puppets if appropriate.

5. Give your student some homework practice in his 'Social Grids Book'. For example:
    - 'To tell mum that her hair looks lovely when she gets back from the hairdresser's.'
    - 'To tell my sister that she has nice handwriting when we are doing our homework at the kitchen table.'

Generalizing learned skills using social grids

The 'Social Grids Book' is a blank scrapbook that contains printed A5 pages of bingo or a 'Social Grids Book' page (see below). Each grid contains a list of tasks or missions to complete to fulfill a particular target. When all of the tasks or missions are complete (use a stamp or stickers), the student earns a pre-specified reward of his choice.

For example, the 'Looking at someone' 'Social Grids Book' page could include missions or tasks, as seen in Figure 2.22 below.

Focus: Looking in someone's direction when talking to them.		
To look at mum's nose when I say 'Hi' after school.	To look at Gran's forehead and say 'Hi' when I go to her house for tea on Tuesday.	To look at my sister's nose when we talk to each other while playing Connect 4.
Social Grids week beginning: 04.03.2020		

FIGURE 2.22 'SOCIAL GRIDS BOOK' PAGE

Using a 'Social Grids Book' will help your student to generalize the skills learned during one-to-one or group social and communication skills sessions.

Four Non-Verbal Communication Skills to Teach

Social communication skills also include the ability to recognize and understand non-verbal communication, such as gesture, eye contact and tone of voice.

1. Gesture

Gestures can be easily misconstrued, at times. Ros Blackburn described a situation where at the beginning of a talk, she was invited to sit down by the organizer, who gestured vaguely in the direction of a chair, saying 'Sit down here'. Misinterpreting the direction of the gesture and the words, Ros promptly sat on the floor (Blackburn 2013).

- Use fewer gestures until you are sure your students understand them.
- Use both gestures and words to show your students exactly what you would like them to do. For example, instead of saying 'Put the paint pots over there', say 'Put the paint pots on the shelf beside the sink' and point to show exactly where you mean.
- Explicitly teach gestures, include signs for 'Quiet', 'Stop', 'Come here' and 'Not now', and pointing to different items. This can be done through simple games. For example:
  - Make photos or video clips of a gesture and ask your students to guess the gesture, for example, stop, wait, go, come on, hurry up, I'm feeling impatient.
  - Play 'What am I pointing at?' (or what is the toy pilot/dog/cat/landmark pointing at) using a variety of engaging items or pictures dotted around the classroom.
  - Play 'What are you pointing at?' by whispering the name of an object to a child and asking him to point to it using a plastic pointer finger initially. The other students must guess what he is pointing at.

2. Looking in the direction of who you are talking to

Some autistic adults have explained how difficult it can be to make and maintain eye contact with someone else. It can be unbearably intense or can cause a person to lose track of a conversation because they are so focused on making appropriate eye contact.

66 You can have my eye contact or you can have my concentration. 99

Chris Bonnello, autistic speaker, advocate and educator

66 When I first started working with autistic children, we were told to 'teach eye contact'. We even had a basic computer programme featuring pixelated faces. The student had to look directly into the eyes before clicking through to the next face.

During social outings, some of my students used to tell me:

'It hurts to look at you.'

'I'm itching to look away from your eyes right now.'

Thankfully now we have a better understanding of just how uncomfortable it can be for some of our students. 99

Claire

While teaching eye contact is no longer considered necessary, it is, however, important to teach your student to look in the general direction of the person they are talking or listening to. Not doing so can make others think that the student is rude or disinterested in what the other person is saying.

- Teach your student the 'fake it 'til you make it' strategy, which means looking at a person's nose or forehead, instead of directly into their eyes, while talking to them.
- Using the class tablet, make simple videos of two adults talking to demonstrate different scenarios. These include:
  - a person not looking at someone else while talking to them
  - someone who stares intently without breaking eye contact
  - someone who does it just right, by both looking at the forehead or nose and by looking down every so often.

  By studying these videos, your student will very easily be able to see the optimum level of direction-looking required.
- Role-play different scenarios using puppets so that your students can choose which works better.
- Play a quick daily game during a student support session, where the adult and the student take turns to finish certain sentences while looking in each other's direction. For example:
  - 'I really like eating...'
  - 'I can see...'
  - 'I am looking forward to...'
- Practise, practise, practise. Draw attention to 'looking at me' when greeting your student upon arrival into the classroom and when saying goodbye in the afternoon. This will help him to generalize the new skills to different situations.
- Give your student some homework practice in his 'Social Grids Book'.

" Remember, not all autistic children have difficulties with eye contact. Some autistic children I have worked with have more direct eye-contact than non-autistic adults. "

Claire

3. Tone of voice

A group of 10-year-old students were supposed to be completing a group art project. Instead of working on the painting, they laughed and chatted, and one upturned the water pot all over the almost-finished painting. The teacher stopped the lesson, saying 'Well that's just great behaviour anyway.' When Michael, an autistic 10-year-old, said 'thanks', everyone laughed, and he got into trouble. He hadn't realized that the teacher was being sarcastic.

Some children can misunderstand tone of voice and get into trouble as a result. They can also be easily misunderstood by using a tone of voice that just does not match the situation. For example, a student who talks in a flat tone of voice with little facial expression can be misunderstood as being moody or sarcastic, when, in fact, she is simply being herself.

Ways to support your students

- Use an exaggerated tone of voice and facial expression when talking, to make your meaning really clear.
- Try to avoid using sarcasm altogether. Only use it if you are sure that the students will understand it or in order to teach them the meaning of sarcasm.
- Explicitly teach your students about different tones of voice when speaking. For example:
  - Write out flashcards containing different tones of voice, e.g. impatient, interested, disinterested, worried, sad, angry, annoyed, rude or polite. Each child selects one and has to say a pre-determined sentence in the tone of voice depicted by the picture. For example, say 'row, row, row your boat' in an 'angry' voice.
  - Play the 'What emoji?' game: Print out a selection of emoji pictures or special interest characters. Spread the emoji cards face up on the table in front of your students. Say a sentence in a particular tone and ask the students to choose the correct picture to match your tone of voice.

- Play 'tone of voice bingo': The bingo caller reads out a sentence in a specific tone of voice and the students mark off the corresponding emoji picture or word on their bingo card.
- Discuss and practise the correct tone of voice in simple familiar scenarios. For example, when saying 'Hello' to the principal, or to your friends on the football pitch.

66 As is the case with everything, there is no one size fits all with autism. I know an autistic little boy who adores, understands and gets a great kick out of sarcasm. However, these are usually well-worn jokes and phrases used at home by his family. He is comfortable with the jokes because they have been used many times before. 99

Claire

4. Language register

Language register refers to the level of formality that you use when speaking to different types of people. Some children may not understand that there is a need to vary the type of language and tone used according to whether they are speaking to a peer, a parent, a teacher or the principal.

Greg, 11, used an over-formal and stilted register with his friends. Whenever they asked him to join them in a game or offered him a chocolate, he said 'No, thank you', which marked him out as being a bit conversationally stiff. Staff highlighted this to Greg and showed him that, often, a more casual 'No, thanks' was sufficient when chatting to his peers.

Ways to support your students

- Play 'Who would you say this to?': Print out pictures of friends, the principal, a teacher and Mum. Make a list of different scenarios and ask your student to pick one and match it to the most suitable person. For example:
  - 'Good afternoon.'
  - 'Hiya.'
  - 'School is so boring.'
  - 'I feel sick.'
- Other categories include:
  - **'Greetings':** How would you greet the Principal, your friend, your granny?
  - **'Complaints':** If you had a complaint about school, who would you go to, what would you say and how would you say it to each of these people?

- **'Chit-chat'**: What kinds of things would you tell your principal, your friend, your granny about?

Conclusion: Don't forget double empathy

While it is important to help your students to build their communicative repertoire if they so desire, it is also equally important to educate society about autism, and about how autistic people communicate. This comes back to the double empathy problem (Milton 2012) where both autistic and non-autistic people need to focus on understanding each other. (See 🔑 'Help Me to Navigate the Social World of School' later in Part 2.)

'Double empathy' can help with communication

Cummins, Pellicano and Crane (2020) interviewed 18 autistic adults to find out their views on their own communication skills and needs. The participants noted the importance of communication for expressing emotions, making friends and increasing feelings of social connectedness.

While they acknowledged difficulties with communication skills (particularly around anxiety, generalizing learned skills, and initiating and continuing conversation), some of the participants also noted that it was helpful when other people:

- understood and recognized their differences
- understood that any apparent lack of attention did not necessarily mean they were not listening.
- clarified and repeated information for them.

Some participants also found it easier to communicate with autistic adults than with non-autistic adults.

Help Me to Navigate the Social World of School

❝ I didn't mix with my peers, but that's not to say I didn't want to mix with my peers. ❞

Adam Harris, CEO and founder, AsIAm, Ireland's national autism charity (Harris 2019)

 ## Introduction

Schools are social places. From the time your students arrive in the morning to when they leave in the afternoon, they interact with numerous peers and adults, participate in class, form and maintain friendships, contribute to group work and navigate the playground.

Many non-autistic children pick up social skills as if by osmosis. They seem to automatically know how to join a ball game, when to give others a chance to talk or how much physical space to leave between themselves and other children when chatting. This does not always happen for autistic people. One of the core diagnostic criteria for autism is differences in social interaction and social communication (APA 2013). As a result, many autistic children can really struggle to figure out the subtle nuances of the social world at school.

The 'hidden curriculum'

The 'hidden curriculum' consists of all the unwritten social rules that many people simply pick up as they go along. For autistic children, studying the elements of this hidden curriculum can play an important role in helping them to succeed socially at school.

In many ways, developing social skills and understanding in the primary school years is just as important as learning to read and write. Part of the hidden curriculum, these skills have to be learned, practised and generalized in order to be fully embedded.

The guides that follow will provide a roadmap for teaching your students about the hidden curriculum. Pick and choose what is relevant for your students at this time.

In this section, we will look at teaching social skills (including play skills) and increasing social understanding.

Social skills are the skills used to communicate and interact with others. They include looking at someone while talking to them, knowing when to join and leave conversations and participate in games as well as successfully regulating emotions.

Social understanding is an awareness and understanding of the reasons behind why people act the way they do and knowing why and when certain social skills may be needed.

The double empathy problem

While teaching social and communication skills is important, it is crucial to ensure that the impetus is never solely on the autistic child to change how they act in order to fit more neatly into the so-called neurotypical world. Increased understanding needs to come from both sides, both autistic and non-autistic.

Damian Milton (2012) describes the 'double empathy problem', where both autistic and non-autistic people say to each other:

- I don't understand you.
- You don't understand me.

Both groups must make an effort to understand each other further, through education and interaction.

 See Part 3: Being Inclusive.

Ultimately, self-esteem and happiness are more important for your student than understanding and abiding by every single social rule.

Why can autistic children show differences in social interaction?

Below are some of the reasons why autistic people may struggle with social interaction:

Theory of mind: Autistic children may have an underdeveloped 'theory of mind'. This is the ability to mind-read in social situations and to see situations from other people's point of view. Most non-autistic children develop a theory of mind aged about four (Peterson, Wellman and Slaughter 2012).

Context blindness: Autistic people may have just as much social knowledge as non-autistic people. They simply may not know *how to adapt these skills* to use them in a variety of different contexts (Vermeulen 2012).

Deep Dive into Theory of Mind

Director of the Autism Research Centre at the University of Cambridge, Simon Baron-Cohen proposed that autistic people may have an underdeveloped theory of mind (ToM) (Baron-Cohen, Leslie and Frith 1985).

> **Theory of mind:** This is your 'social sense'. It gives you the ability to put yourself in someone else's shoes, and to know that other people think and feel differently to you.

Also known as 'mentalizing' (Frith and Frith 2003), ToM is the ability to guess the invisible mental states of other people based on their behaviour and act accordingly.

It means that you can:

- imagine how your words or actions can affect others
- guess how someone else is feeling
- have a good chance at predicting what people are going to do next
- take other people's points of view into account
- figure out what makes people tick.

CONSIDER YOUR OWN THEORY OF MIND

Sarah arrives into work on the first day after the summer holidays. All she wants is a quick cup of coffee before she heads to teach her first class. At the entrance to the staff room, she meets a colleague, Tina, who has spent the summer touring Australia. When Sarah asks her how the holiday went, Tina pulls out her phone and starts scrolling through photos, showing her all the different places she visited. Sarah nods and makes all the right noises of appreciation, her heart sinking slowly as she realizes she won't get that coffee until later on.

Clearly, Sarah understands the rules of social interaction, and is displaying sound ToM here. She does not want to hurt her colleague's feelings by appearing disinterested in what she is saying. She knows how she would feel if the shoe was on the other foot and Tina looked bored by what Sarah herself was saying.

Tina, on the other hand, has not picked up on the subtle signals Sarah has sent out (walking backward, the empty travel mug and her quiet air of desperation) and is displaying poor ToM.

A note on the concept of empathy

Note: The word 'empathy' is often wrongly equated with the ability to care or to feel emotions. Autistic people are not lacking in either of these skills. Some people have explained how they can feel heightened emotions at the plight of others. Autistic writer and speaker, Pete Wharmby, has described how he can at times find it hard to understand why people may feel the way they do.

> 66 As for empathy – we can identify whether you're sad or angry or happy. Of course we can, and I think this is true of many autistic people. I'm a slave to the general ambience of a room, hugely affected by the prevailing mood, so empathy isn't a problem. But I'm not sure I can pinpoint why you may be feeling the way you do… I may also struggle to join you fully in your emotions, even if I recognise them. For example, you may be sad but it could take me a while (or absolutely ages) to realise you need a hug. Instead, I'll just sit there, feeling sad for you but not having a clue what to say. 99

Pete Wharmby

Theory of mind at school (ToM)

At school, an underdeveloped ToM can lead to difficulties with friendships and miscommunications with staff that manifests in a variety of ways.

ToM is not simply about being able to understand others. It can also influence:

- **Literal thinking:** 'I believe what you said because we all think the same way.'

Ms Smith, the class teacher was writing something on the board. Hearing some whispering behind her, she said 'Keep working. I've got eyes in the back of my head', and an autistic student, Kelly, 10, came up to the board and checked the back of her head. Everyone laughed thinking Kelly was trying to be funny, but Ms Smith gave Kelly extra homework because she thought she was being rude.

- **Over-honesty:** 'I find it hard to predict how overly honest words or actions will make you feel.'

'I could explain my project in more detail to you, but it's complicated and I know you just wouldn't understand', said one 13-year-old girl to her classmates while giving a presentation.

'Was I rude?' asked Alan, 9, after being sent out of class for telling his peer that her story was 'boring'. After all, he had just told the truth.

- **Different communication style:** 'I didn't realize I needed to explain my actions because I assumed you already knew why I did that.'

When Grace, 11, had finished her maths, she took out her notepad and started to colour. Her teacher told her off because Grace hadn't thought to tell anyone that she was finished, assuming that because she knew, they would automatically know too.

- **Social naivety:** 'I believe that people always mean what they say.'

Jackie, 7, was an autistic student in a mainstream school. At Christmas, one girl brought in chocolate Santas for some of the girls in her friendship group, and didn't include Jackie. She told Jackie that she had left Jackie's chocolate Santa at home and would bring it in the next day. Jackie took her at face value and asked the girl about it every day for the next two weeks.

- **A different understanding of character motivation and development in stories or films, at times:** 'I'm not sure why people are acting this way.'

Temple Grandin has said that she prefers action movies like Wallace and Gromit to 'relationship kind of movies' which she finds 'very boring' (BBC Two – Horizon 2006). She prefers magazines about business or science to women's magazines because she is not interested in cooking or the reasons why someone's marriage may have broken up.

Ultimately, the world must feel very daunting for someone who finds it difficult to predict or even guess what others are about to do. Autistic author and speaker Ros Blackburn has described how 'threatening and frightening' this feels (Wood, Littleton and Sheehy 2006, p.149).

To help someone to better understand how other people are thinking and feeling, you can use a variety of methods. These include social narratives and Social Stories™, 'Playback' forms and thinking aloud about social situations. Please see ⊙➥ Guides 37–39 for more information on each of these.

The Importance of Play

Why is play important?

66 September is for assessment, observation and play – my only agenda is that my students think school is the best place in the world, and they want to come back to this party tomorrow! 99

Mary McKenna, teacher, lecturer and founder of the first early intervention class for autistic children in Ireland in 1999

Do you remember the last time you had fun?

- What were you doing?
- Who were you with?
- What made it funny?

66 When it started lashing rain while we were in town, and we ran through the empty streets with newspapers on our heads, and we just looked at the ridiculousness of each other and just couldn't stop laughing. 99

66 Watching my dogs run and bark and jump around in the woods. 99

66 Yesterday, when we three were shaking with silent laughter while sitting in front of our computers in the office because Janet had just told a story about a famous singer and got the name totally wrong. 99

Fun is important because it helps us to:

- relax
- release stress
- take a break from the humdrum of everyday life
- be in the present moment, without worrying about the past or the future.

Just like anyone else, autistic children also need to relax, socialize and have fun. However, as they may not naturally pick up all the skills needed to play successfully, they need to be taught explicitly in a step-by-step way.

By teaching your autistic students some skills to be used during leisure time in the classroom, the playground, the hall or the playing pitch, you can:

- help them to find a natural way of releasing stress and tension
- help them to practice socializing in natural settings, with their peers, rather than in a one-to-one setting with an adult
- broaden their horizons to find new hobbies and interests that they may develop further as teenagers and adults.

“ It's wrong to say autistic people don't know how to play – if you were to observe me playing when I was a young child, I spent hours lining things up or setting things up in a particular way – I wasn't setting things up to play, setting up was the game. ”

Adam Harris, CEO and founder, AsIAm, Ireland's national autism charity (Harris 2019)

While they play and socialize, children develop vital skills and dispositions. These include:

- communication
- language skills
- problem-solving
- gross and fine motor skills
- creativity
- imagination
- risk taking
- exploration.

Autism and play

Autistic children can often find play difficult. This can arise as a result of differences in social interaction and communication, as well as lack of flexibility of thinking and underdeveloped joint attention skills.

Because of this, they can miss out on all the benefits and rich learning that tends to happen vicariously through play. Jung and Sainato (2013) found that improvements in play skills increase positive social interactions and decrease behaviour that may be considered to be challenging. That's why it is so important for school staff to find ways to help their younger autistic students to discover play activities and toys that they are interested in, to expand these interests and to engage in play experiences with other students, as appropriate.

Assessment and observation

Mikey, 5, was playing at a table beside two other boys. While he wordlessly whizzed his LEGO® aeroplane around his personal orbit, the two other boys crashed their

LEGO® cars into each other, narrating every second of their own play. Mikey just didn't seem to realize yet that he could involve the other boys in his play.

Observe your student and see what makes him tick. Ask questions such as:

- Does he tend to play alone or with others?
- Who does he play with?
- What toys or activities does she like to use?
- Does he repeat or act out recognizable play sequences from cartoons or movies?
- What does she like playing with at home?

You could also use a commercial play observation form or assessment, including, for example, 'The Social Play Record' by Chris White.

Stages of play

Following observation and assessment, make note of where your student is currently at in the developmental stages of play and where you would like him to progress to.

Parten's six stages of play

Parten (1932) identified six stages of play progression. These are:

1. **Unoccupied:** Not engaged with toys or playing with others.
2. **Solitary:** The child entertains herself.
3. **Observer-onlooker:** Watches other children but does not join in.
4. **Parallel:** Plays alongside other children but does not really engage with them.
5. **Associative:** Begins to notice and engage with the other children.
6. **Co-operative:** Plays with others in games with rules and teams. Conflict can often arise during co-operative play. Group and friendship skills are developed from here.

 Rather than overly focusing on age-related expectations, look at where your student is developmentally, and use this as a starting point for developing strategies and ideas.

Joint attention

A really important first step for younger children is to develop their joint attention (JA) skills. Many autistic children have difficulties with joint attention.

Joint attention is the ability to share a single focus with another person.

It can involve sharing attention with someone, following the attention of another person or directing them to attend to what you want to show them.

For example, joint attention happens when an adult points at an object and the child looks at the object. Both people share an experience of looking at the object together.

JA plays a key role in the development of language and communication skills, which in turn facilitates social skills development (Dawson et al. 2004; Kasari et al. 2010; Murza et al. 2016). It is also linked to symbolic play skills, as well as associative and co-operative play skills.

Joint attention can be developed in a variety of ways.

- **Make yourself the most amazing and fun person in the room:** Over-exaggerate your facial expressions, act like everything is amazing and as a result, let your students catch your enthusiasm for any activity. For example, close the jack-in-the-box and together wait for it to jump up; sing 'Humpty Dumpty' with a real egg and a wall made from boxes and wait with bated breath before you drop the egg from a height; play suspense or waiting games such as 'peek-a boo!'
- **Cause and effect:** Blow bubbles and ask your student to pop them; throw a ball and let your student catch it; act out a scene in character and ask your student to mirror it; play a tug of war or together try to pull a Stretch Armstrong toy as tight as you can go; play on a see-saw together.
- **Hide and point:** Hide a really enticing object and point to where it could be. In the beginning, always leave part of it visible.
- **Shared activities:** Paint a picture of a favourite character together; complete a jigsaw based on a favourite movie together; keep a ball jumping on a shared parachute; dance to a favourite song.

Gina Davies' (2014) 'Attention Autism' programme is a useful way to begin to develop joint attention skills. The programme's ethos is built on the premise that if you create activities that are irresistible enough, children will spontaneously and genuinely want to attend to and engage with these activities.

Types of play

Many autistic children have more difficulties with symbolic play than they do with functional play skills. In fact, the development of symbolic play skills is highly linked to a child's non-verbal cognitive and language skills (Jung and Sainato 2013; Kossyvaki and Papoudi 2016).

Functional play: Using toys according to their particular function. For example, pushing a train around a track.

Symbolic play: Using objects, actions or ideas to represent other objects, actions or ideas. For example, a banana becomes a phone, or a wooden block becomes an aeroplane. Symbolic play also involves being able to pretend that something is happening (pretending that the aeroplane is crashing) and imagining that something is there (flying past an imaginary air traffic control tower).

With play interventions and support, autistic children can learn to enjoy playing in a variety of different ways both with peers and on their own.

Ten Ways to Inspire Children to Play

1. Meet your student where he is, and take your direction from him for a while

> Katie, 4, seemed to prefer doing her own thing rather than interacting with any of the adults or students. One day, the class special needs assistant simply sat on the ground beside Katie, who was moving toy figures inside a toy castle. After sitting and watching for some time, he began to copy what Katie was doing, both her sounds and movements. Gradually, Katie started to look at him, and then made some sounds, and looked back and forth at him as he copied her.

Sit beside the child and let her become used to your presence. Let her lead the play. Copy her actions, sounds and words.

For example, if a child loves sifting sand through his hands at the sand tray, sit beside him and begin to silently sift the sand yourself. Gradually, begin to borrow one of his containers to sift your sand, or sift some sand onto his hand.

This is an informal type of 'intensive interaction'. Based on the psychological principle of imitation, *intensive interaction* starts from infant–mother interactions, where the infant makes a sound or a movement and the mother imitates it, thereby facilitating a communication with her baby (Caldwell 2011). Intensive interaction is often used with autistic children as a way of becoming part of their world.

This is an easy way for the child to have a positive interaction with you and to see that you are a benign being in their universe, who is not going to interfere too much. It also marks the beginning of developing joint attention.

2. Help your student to expand on his play

Some children tend to play in the same way with the same toy or activity. This could include running a car around a mat repetitively, or repeatedly acting out a scene from a cartoon with a plastic dinosaur.

Although it may appear as though the child is playing with a toy, he may simply be re-enacting a favourite cartoon in his head and using the car as a prop. This is a form of stimming, which can be a very relaxing activity for the child. However, it is also important to introduce him to new ways of playing.

After watching your student play for a while, slowly but surely begin to introduce him to new ways of playing with his toys. For example:

- **Cars:** Show him how to wash the car at the car wash, drive the car into a cardboard garage, have races with a few different cars and crash cars into each other, exclaiming 'Crashhhh!'
- **Dinosaurs:** Make play really visual and literal by using a giant playmat scene of mountains, lakes and forest. Show him how to make the dinosaur fly, let it drink from a lake or walk it up a mountain on the dinosaur playmat.

This approach is based on the principles of DIRFloortime® and can be done over a number of sessions. DIRFloortime® is an intervention aimed at fostering interaction and communication skills. The adult and the child literally get down on the floor during one-to-one play-based interactions. These sessions initially focus on shared attention, moving towards two-way purposeful interactions and reflective thinking.

If the child is not ready yet for expanding her play, it is often useful to move the activity to a more sociable place, so that she is learning to accept others and experience sociability.

For students who are just beginning to interact with others, introduce play between staff and the student beginning with big bulky objects such as a trampoline, peanut ball, blanket or parachute, and play peek-a-boo!-type of games, such as jumping on the trampoline while singing a song or counting. Or you can sing 'Humpty Dumpty' while bouncing on the peanut ball, pushing the child gently off when you say the word 'fall' and waiting for him to climb up again. The main idea is that you are trying to elicit eye contact (or looking in your general direction), gesture, a vocalization or a verbalization.

3. Pick a weekly or fortnightly theme for play and toys

An easy way of teaching all the children in your class about how to play with particular toys is to pick weekly or fortnightly themes for toys. For example, during train week, show the children a different way of playing with the trains every day. This includes:

- driving the train around the track while singing 'I've Been Working on the Railroad' or 'The Little Train'
- going through a tunnel
- saying 'choo-choo' really softly and getting louder as the train gains momentum and gets faster around the track
- screeching to a sudden halt at a stop light
- going over obstacles (teddies, pieces of LEGO®, blocks) on the track
- starting to build the track in a different direction.

You can also introduce new toys into your student's repertoire in a controlled way. For example, one teacher in an early intervention setting puts a limited number of toys on the toy trolley and changes them every two weeks. In this way, every child learns a variety of different ways to play with specific toys before moving onto a new set.

4. Help your student to move on to playing with something else

Some children can become stuck on only playing with one particular toy or activity. This activity may feel safe and predictable, and they can disappear into their own world while playing with it. They may not realize yet that there is so much fun to be had with all of the other toys around them. You can broaden their horizons, help them to step outside of this choice and experience and introduce them to a whole new world of fun!

- Take a photograph of the toy or activity you want to introduce the student to.
- Show him how to play with the toy or do the activity. Make it look like the best fun ever!
- Give him time playing with his favourite toy. Set a timer and show him a photograph or present him with the new toy when the timer beeps.

5. Make play instructions visual

Some children find it hard to know what to do with unfamiliar toys or scenarios. You can show them exactly what to do in a number of ways. This includes:

- modelling the play, using live or video modelling
- putting photographs at different areas with photographs of children doing a variety of play tasks. For example, a child pouring the tea out of the teapot in the kitchen, with a speech bubble saying 'time for tea'
- making a photo book of all the different activities you can do in the home corner. For example, making the bed, pouring the tea, making dinner
- providing a photograph of the completed activity or of the steps to get to the finished product, e.g. a completed Mr. Potato Head or a photo of the LEGO® piece you want to build
- putting iPads at different areas with videos of staff or other children showing what to do there
- using picture scripts or play scripts.

Picture scripts can be really useful to show a child all the different ways of playing with one toy. This can also give a child confidence, as it makes everything more predictable.

- Show the child the picture of a tower made from five bricks. Build this together.
- Once the child has mastered this picture script, move on to a new picture script of someone knocking the tower down, saying 'Crashhhh'.

Write the language you are using on the back of the picture script. Whoever carries out the activity with the child says the same words, making it easier for the child. As your students master each picture script, add more language in order to extend the interaction.

In this way, your student will learn different ways of playing with toys and will build up a repertoire of ways to play with his peers for different themes. Picture scripts can also act as an aide-memoire, increasing independence for the child. They can be faded out over time as the child learns different ways to play with the toys.

Play scripts are used to explicitly teach the language or sentences needed in different play areas of the classroom. This could include learning how to buy something in the class shop or how to answer or talk on the toy phone.

For example:

Shopkeeper: Hello! How are you today?
Customer: I'm good, thanks!
Shopkeeper: What would you like?
Customer: I would like a kite and a skipping rope, please.
Shopkeeper: Here you go. That's €10 please.
Customer: Thank you. [Hands over money.]
Shopkeeper: Here's your change.
Customer: Thanks. [Reaches hand out.] Bye!
Shopkeeper: Bye!

It would be very easy to video these short vignettes on the class tablet and allow your students to re-watch them.

6. Structure play

For younger children, it is often recommended that play is child-centred and child-led. However, many autistic children prefer some of their play experiences to be more structured. They often need to know 'What's expected of me in this moment, in this place?'

Why not introduce specific times during the school day where play is more structured? This can be done by:

- giving your student a mini play schedule using photographs or symbols. For example, 'blocks/trains/bikes/finish'
- using a timer. Once the timer beeps, give him a few moments to finish up and get used to the idea of moving onto the next activity. Show him the photo of his new activity
- giving him a ziplock bag containing

- a photo of what you want him to build, and the exact number of LEGO® bricks inside
- a photo of the Play-Doh spider you want him to make, along with black Play-Doh, eight pipe cleaners and two googly eyes
- ensuring play activities are closed-ended or finite and are not too long. For example:
  - give me five cars to push down the car park ramp
  - put five marbles to roll down the marble run
  - put five shapes in the wooden shapes box
  - sing 'Row, Row, Row, Your Boat' as you push a boat through the water in the tray. When the song is over, the play activity is over.

Repeat these activities over a number of weeks and extend them each week to incorporate more elements. For example, spend more time at the activity, or do it with another student and an adult.

7. Show your student exactly what to do at freeflow activity stations

In 🔑 Guide 12: Three More Great Ways to Motivate, we discussed how some autistic children can find freeflow activity stations difficult to manage.

You can make any child-led play activity area more accessible by making it more structured and predictable, as outlined in '6. Structure play for me' above. Some further ideas include:

- **Dress-up area:** Put photos of what the children can dress up as at the dress-up station.
- **Play-Doh and LEGO® areas:** Provide mats with outlines that they simply have to fill in with Play-Doh.
- **Tuff trays (sandpit, sensory):** Find five items in the sandpit. Place them on a sheet of paper divided into five squares. When there is an item in each square, the task is over.
- **Home corner:** Practice simple scripts and stick them in the home corner so that the child knows exactly what he is expected to do there. For example, 'How to use the toy phone'. In many ways, you are simply pre-teaching the skills needed for whatever theme the home corner is each fortnight. This includes the post office, the shop, the library or the airport.

◉ Of course, doing all of this will require staff supervision in order to teach the child what to do in each area. However, if you try to *keep the general structure of tasks at some areas the same*, you can then simply change the activity to match the fortnightly theme. For example:
- LEGO® table: During the Christmas theme, have a photo of a LEGO® Santa for

them to make, and during the post office theme, have a photo of a LEGO® post office building for them to make. Once the child has been taught and is sure of what to do at each area, you will be able to gradually fade back on staff support.

8. Offer some choice

Use a Choice Board to offer your student a selection of toys, songs or play activities. Offer just two options initially, as too much choice can be overwhelming. If you want to encourage your student to choose something different, simply remove his usual choice from the board before you show it to him.

9. Use his special interests

Researchers have found that embedding a child's interest into games can help them to participate in reciprocal play with their peers or siblings, and these social skills can then be generalized to other unrelated games or play activities (Baker, Koegel and Koegel 1998).

Find out what kinds of activities your student loves and what really engages him. This can be done through observation or by asking parents and the child himself. Then make a list of five toys, cartoons, games and songs that your student loves. Create activities based around these interests. Embed these interests into games to play alone and with peers.

10. Don't forget fun!

It goes without saying that your students will be more motivated and engaged if you introduce any new activity or game in a fun and playful way.

Be silly, sing songs, and over-exaggerate your facial expressions. Act super surprised, happy, amazed or astounded – anything to help them to be in the moment with you and to focus on the task at hand.

The Playground

 " Over the years, I have observed many autistic children in the playground. Some had great fun playing with their friends, and others had that one special friend who they depended on. Some wandered the periphery of the playground, trying to look busy until the bell rang, while others ran super fast around the playground on their own. Some tried to join in games but things went awry, and in the end, sometimes the other children just didn't want to play with them. "

Claire

Many autistic children can find playground time difficult. Often, this is the most unstructured and unpredictable part of their day and depends completely on their ability to socialize effectively.

Your student might wonder:

- **What** am I supposed to do out here?
- **Who** am I supposed to play with?
- **How** can I ask someone to join in a game?
- **Why** did everyone change the rules of the game just now?
- **How long** will this game last?
- **How** can I learn the rules of this new game?

Other factors that can make the playground difficult for your students include:

- **Sensory differences:** An aversion to being touched, unexpected noises, smells, bright sunshine, different temperatures, a feeling of unpredictability in a wide-open space.
- **Proprioceptive differences:** Being unintentionally rough or not knowing their own strength when playing group games.
- **Cognitive inflexibility:** An inability to go with the flow when the rules of the game change; desire to always be first; desire to win every time.
- **Gross motor skills:** An inability to participate in some games or to keep up with others.

As a result, students often seek a *playground anchor* in the form of a special friend, an adult or a particular solitary routine.

During play time, Billy, 7, loved running from one end of the playground to another, apparently at random. However, when staff observed him, it was clear he was following the same route every time, tipping the wall with his left hand, then twirling and touching the goalpost on the way back. In a bid to make playground time more predictable for himself, he had created a routine for himself.

Do autistic children want to play?

At first glance, it may seem that your students prefer to be on their own in the playground. They can walk around the perimeter of the playground fence, run about trying to look busy or link arms with the supervising staff.

In fact, autistic children can 'share many of the same desires and capacity for play, friendship and peer-group acceptance as typically developing children' (Wolfberg, Bottema-Beutel and DeWitt 2012, p.58). They simply may not know the best way to go about it, or they may have had so many unsuccessful or negative experiences that they decide that it is easier to simply opt out.

The special needs assistant on duty asked a little boy, who was always on his own in the playground, if he would like to play a game. His face lit up, and he suggested playing hide and seek. They had great fun until he just left the game and returned the climbing frame while the special needs assistant was still hiding. He just hadn't realized that he was supposed to tell her he was no longer playing.

What skills are needed for the playground?

In order to participate in playground games, children need a variety of skills. These include how to:

- understand the rules of a variety of games
- take turns
- wait
- be a gracious winner and loser
- join a game
- leave a game
- go with the flow and accept that the rules of games can often change at any time.

Jojo, 7, tried to get involved in a game of catch that was being played by three other children. But instead of asking to join in, he darted into the circle, took the ball and ran off, looking behind him for their reaction. Unimpressed, they shouted at him to give the ball back.

Think of the playground as an extension of your classroom – what do you need to teach your students so that they can have fun out there?

Planning for Success in the Playground: The Five Ps

1. **Plan for success by observing your student** in the playground and see what she needs.
   - What is she doing?
   - Who is she playing with?

   Ask your student how he feels about the playground.
   - Is there anything he finds difficult about the playground?
   - Are there any games or activities he would like to do in the playground?

2. **Prepare staff, students, peers and the playground** by setting up resources and structures to ensure success. This includes:
   - explicitly teaching them the rules of the games
   - buying new playground equipment, if needed
   - organizing staff rotas for games days
   - printing out laminated games lists
   - learning about winning and losing.

   ### How to explicitly teach the rules of games
   Sometimes, games can be easier to learn and generalize than other play skills:

   - Have a whole-class discussion about what games are popular in the playground.
   - Make a list of these games and discuss their rules.
   - Explicitly teach your student these rules in order to increase their play repertoire.
   - Take pictures of or make videos about these games.
   - Make a scrapbook about playground games and their rules. Send this home too, so that parents and guardians can also practise the rules of the games with their child.
   - Discuss winning and losing, as well as role-playing and reading stories about this, if needed.

3. **Practise the games**, initially with a support adult, then a peer and finally a group of peers.

4. **Play the now familiar games** in the playground in a structured and organized way. For example, ask staff to lead a particular game on a particular day each week.

5. **Put play into perspective.** Celebrate successes and/or help your students to figure out where things might have gone awry and how they can prevent or manage this in the future.

⚷ See Guide 37: 'Playback' Forms.

Eight Ideas for the Playground

" You can't make someone enjoy socialising, but what you can do is create the environment for that to work. "

Adam Harris, CEO and founder, AsIAm, Ireland's national autism charity (Middletown Centre for Autism 2017, p.6)

1. Organize staff-led games

Sometimes, games can be easier to learn and generalize than other play skills. Make a list of easy playground games that can be played with minimal equipment. These include:

- duck, duck, goose
- ball games
- the beans game
- parachute games
- Simon says
- 'What time is it Mr Wolf?'
- traffic lights game
- chasing
- keep fit activities.

Designate a specific area of the playground for organized games so your students always know where to go.

Ask staff members to take turns being in charge of organizing these games.

Velcro a laminated list of games to the back of a door leading to the playground so that on-duty staff can access it easily, to avoid the need to come up with new ideas daily. Alternatively, give staff laminated playground key rings with games lists or icons printed on them.

Make it visual: Staff holds up pictures of the games to show the students what game they will be playing each day.

Some schools have a designated game for each day of the week. The weekly timetable is stuck prominently in the playground for all to see, as well as being emailed to classes every week. For example:

Monday	Tuesday	Wednesday	Thursday	Friday
Ball	Champ	Skipping	The beans game	Hula hoops

FIGURE 2.23 WEEKLY GAMES TIMETABLE

Make it visual: Ensure your student has access to this visual games timetable and knows what he is going to do in the playground every day.

Of course, it is not always logistically easy to organize games in the playground. Even aiming to have structured games for ten minutes three times a week is a great start.

2. Establish student-led activity stations

One 8-year-old boy got on brilliantly at break time when there were organized ball games – he simply lined up, shot the ball at the hoop and returned to the end of the line. At lunch time, however, during free play, he tended to get into trouble, often saying the wrong thing to classmates or getting upset when he had no one to play with.

Alternatively, ask older students to take charge of the organized lunch time games. This could involve letting them out of class ten minutes early to lay out equipment, as well as:

- taking charge of one game or station each
- helping the younger students to play appropriately at each station
- tidying up at the end.

Often, the selected students feel a sense of pride and responsibility in being in charge, and they tend to enjoy the excitement of leaving class ten minutes early to set up in the playground. Organized games also have the added bonus of making play time calmer for all students. Activity station ideas include:

- hula hoops
- skipping ropes
- ball games
- hopscotch
- champ
- basketball net.

To ensure that every student has some time to play and relax themselves, assign different older students to take charge of this a few times a week, or rotate the responsibility between all senior classes.

3. Set up a friendship bench

" I was always wary of the idea of a 'friendship bench', considering it to be more aspirational than realistic. After all, who wants to be that person, sitting at the edge of the playground, friendless and waiting to be rescued?

However, one support staff member pointed out that it can be useful simply because it gives aimless children a set point to congregate and be together as a group if they have nothing else to do. Give them some resources and you have an easy common interest for anyone who wants to join in. "

Claire

Friendship benches work best when children are explicitly taught how to use them, and if there is an emphasis placed on:

- kindness and empathy for children who have no one to play with
- always asking someone to play if that person is sitting at the friendship bench.

Providing a box of resources (toys and books) at the friendship bench may also spark conversation about shared interests. Even better if you can include some resources linked to your student's special interest, such as a pile of Minecraft annuals, that may also attract other children with similar interests.

" There is absolutely no substitute for a real friend. The best thing an adult can do is to set up people through special interests. We bond through special interests. "

Paul Micallef, autistic advocate and founder of Autism Explained
Online Summit https://paulmicallef.com.au

When 10-year-old Gary's special interest was pilots, he often found it hard to find a common ground with his peers. However, once he started watching the Harry Potter series of movies, he was delighted to find that he suddenly had a way to interact with others. He spent one magical afternoon at a party with his friends re-enacting scenes from Harry Potter, casting spells and discussing favourite parts of the movies.

4. Establish playground zones

A great way of providing structure for autistic children who struggle with free play is the creation of zoned playgrounds. Playgrounds are divided into different activity zones, including physical games, as detailed above, as well as quieter zones in covered areas. These include:

- LEGO® table
- drawing area
- chatting area.

Make it visual: Provide a map of the playground with designated areas marked in. Support your student to choose what she is going to do, who she is going to play with and what specific areas she is allowed to access before she goes out every day.

Having this playground plan will give her something to do and a reason to be in the playground, thus making this unstructured time feel more manageable and predictable.

5. Create playground jobs

Give your student a playground job to complete with a peer. This could include helping younger students, collecting equipment or ringing the bell at the start and finish of play time. This may also give them status amongst the other students.

Make it visual: Create a weekly schedule of jobs with the name or photograph of who is going to accompany your student.

6. Don't forget free time

66 Because of my social problems, I didn't enjoy [the playground] so much at the time. I kind of felt like the teaching assistants were forcing me to partake. No doubt they were doing it for my own good. 99

Michael, teenager on the spectrum

It is important to strike the right balance between organized fun and letting your students relax and do their own thing. Being allowed to go to the library or to the computer room with a friend on certain days may also be worth thinking about as an option for older students.

7. Daily check-in

66 I have a limited supply of 'social calories' that I can either use up gradually in extended, relaxed social activities, or burn rapidly in high-pressure social settings, after which I need some time alone to recover. 99

Stuart Neilson, autistic author (Neilson 2019b)

At times, being in the playground can be exhausting and stressful for your autistic students. A fifteen-minute post-playground daily check-in with an adult can act as a pressure valve for your student to:

- offload about anything that happened
- release any pent-up anxiety
- take a break
- clear up any misconceptions
- make a plan for what to do in the future.

Information gathered in these short sessions can also provide content for the next social skills or social understanding lesson with the support teacher.

🔑 A 'Playback' form could be used here. See Guide 37.

10-year-old Elodie spent much of her playground time walking around alone. Every time a classmate approached, she looked up hopefully and then bowed her head again as they ran past. She always stayed in the busiest part of the playground, despite there being an option to go to a quieter area. She had always shown particular kindness and skills with the younger students whenever she did reading buddies with them in their classroom.

Possible reasons
Elodie clearly wanted to join in with her classmates in some way, but was unsure as to how to join in.

What to do

- As Elodie loves horses, staff bought some horse books and annuals for her to take out to the playground for something to do. At the same time, they designated a summer reading bench for everyone to use and put a box of mixed books out there. This was a stop-gap measure while they figured out what she might like to do in the playground.
- Staff organized daily structured games for younger students, and asked Elodie if she would like to be in charge of these games.

- Staff presented a series of autism peer awareness sessions for the whole class, without ever discussing Elodie or any other student by name. They simply highlighted the importance of looking out for classmates who may not feel sure about how to play with others.

8. Provide playground training for staff

Often, there is a core group of staff who manage the playground every single day. Training these staff members about autism, finding out their ideas about what works and what does not work and ensuring they know who the autistic children are in the playground will go a long way towards ensuring a successful playground time for your students.

Kretzmann, Shih and Kasari (2014) trained school staff to support autistic students in the playground and found that engagement between autistic children and their peers almost doubled after the ten-week intervention. Their intervention included:

- delivering a one-hour training session to staff about autism and social interaction differences
- observing autistic students in the playground
- helping staff to choose and implement a variety of games
- helping staff to decide when to jump in and when to fade out support.

Indoor Games

Autistic author and animal scientist Temple Grandin has highlighted the importance of practising turn-taking with children. As a child growing up in the 1950s, she learned how to take turns through playing regular board games and card games at home with her family (Grandin 2009).

Play games with a clear end

The easiest games to begin with include those which are naturally finite, including:

- Pop-Up Pirate
- Buckaroo!
- snap
- go fish.

With these games, your student knows for certain that the game is over when the pirate or horse pops up, or when all the cards have been taken by the players.

Make any game autism-friendly

With a bit of lateral thinking, you can make almost any game autism-friendly. For example:

BINGO				
4	15	21	16	2
11	40	34	57	78
66	52	14	22	40
3	18	32	82	13
97	79	8	50	26

- **Hot potato:** Play with a timer to signify the end.
- **Connect 4 and bingo:** Define how many rounds you will play before you start by drawing boxes on a mini whiteboard and ticking them off as each round is completed.
- **Five-Second Rule, Junior Version:** Assign an adult to be the question master to differentiate questions given to children of different abilities.
- **Dobble:** This game can really appeal to the visual strengths of autistic children. Often, the only adaptation needed is to ensure the rules are really clear by writing them out and revising them before each game.
- **Blurt!:** Use a turn-taking system instead of allowing everyone to shout out their answers. This can decrease unpredictability and anxiety.

Teach the hidden skills for playing games

During your social skills sessions, teach the hidden skills for these games.

- Role-play skills such as *turn-taking* and *waiting*. Practise these skills during indoor games time.
- Tuck a simple story about winning and losing inside the box of each game. Read the story every time you play the game, in addition to working on these skills during one-to-one social skills sessions.
- Model aloud how you feel when you lose a turn or slide down a snake in snakes and ladders. For example, say 'Oh no, I'm going down a snake back to two. I'm so upset but I might get lucky with a six on my next go.'

In the beginning, choose predictable, quick-play games. If a board game is too unpredictable and anxiety-inducing for your students, simply shelve it for the time being and work on other, simpler games.

Cater to a special interest

Make games more appealing and encourage your students to participate by using their special interests. For example:

- **Go fish:** Make cards using a student's favourite movie or book characters, or using letters and numbers.
- **Snakes and ladders:** Stick favourite cartoon villains on the 'snakes' and heroes on the 'ladders'.
- **Card games related to a special interest:** For example, for someone with a special interest in air travel, make a set of 'Would you rather...?' index cards bearing the names of different airlines. 'Would you rather travel with American Airlines or Wizz Air? Why?'

Jack, 7, was very interested in the London Underground, and learned the fundamentals of card games by first playing the 'Mind the Gap' matching card game. He then moved onto Uno, which was very visually attractive, and relatively quick to play, and is now beginning to play snap using a pack of traditional playing cards.

 Technology

Whenever children play together on the class computer or tablet, make sure to specify:

- how long each player has

or

- how *many* rounds each player can play.

Velcro an electronic timer to the wall behind the computer or set the timer app on an iPad to manage how long each child uses it for. When the timer goes off, the iPad locks to the home screen.

Make it visual

- **Turn-Taking Board:** A mini whiteboard with a line drawn down the middle, with each child's name or photograph stuck on it. As a child has his turn, put a tick under his name.
- **Timers.**
- **Tick boxes** on a mini whiteboard to specify how many rounds of the game you will be playing, ticking one off as each round is over.

Golden time

Sometimes golden time can be difficult for your students. It is often useful to give a student a written choice of four activities to do during golden time and ask him to choose two. Write these in the order he would like to do them and tick them off as he goes along. For example, 'Jenga – one round' followed by 'Reading for ten minutes'.

Rosie, 11, didn't want to participate in any of the golden time games. However, once prepped by class staff, she was more than happy to be the quizmaster for Blurt!, calling out the questions and generally managing the game. In this way, she was fully part of the group in a way that suited her best at that time.

Frequently asked questions

Q: I don't think he has any problems with playing, he seems to be very sociable.

A: Some of our students can play appropriately and have no difficulties in the playground. It may well be that he feels comfortable in the playground because you have structured it so well, or because he has a particular friend or group of friends.

However, it might be worth observing him in the playground one day to gauge whether he is actually involved in the game, or simply existing alongside other children.

Q: She's very good, she links my arm and we walk around the playground.

A: Some autistic children choose to chat with the adults in the playground, as it is often easier than interacting with their peers. It would be really useful also to facilitate some peer interaction. Would you be able to organize a game once a week and encourage other students to participate so that she is also getting practice in playing with her peers? Think about what is possible for you logistically.

Q: I feel that he needs that time in the playground to relax and do his own thing.

A: Absolutely, he does. But why not gently offer him a menu of predictable, practised activities and see if he begins to like any of these?

Q: He seems to really like being on his own. Shouldn't we just let him be?

A: Perhaps he does. It would be useful to ask him, too, and double check that he really is content on his own in the playground.

Social Skills

" As soon as I learned the social 'rules', it became easy to trick people into thinking I am just like them. If the other person likes to talk, it's easy. I just have to ask them a bit about themselves, they talk and I just go along with it. "

Alis Rowe, autistic author and entrepreneur – founder of 'The Curly Hair Project'

 Basic social skills are important because they enable everyone to fit in, if they so wish, and to adapt their behaviours to suit different situations. Some autistic people may not know intuitively how to act or what to say in social situations. Best-selling author and salesman Dale Carnegie boiled down successful social interactions to some key points in his book *How to Win Friends and Influence People* (Carnegie 1936/2009). Tips included:

- smiling at other people
- remembering their names
- asking other people questions about their own lives.

Teaching your students some simple social tips could make all the difference to their lives and friendships both at school and throughout adulthood.

However, teaching social skills is not simply about starting at the beginning of a social skills programme and working through it from cover to cover. It is about figuring out where your student is at and working from there.

Guide 34

Social Skills: Five Things to Consider

1. Social skills assessment: What skills to target

Start by setting a baseline for your student's social skills ability. This can be done by:

- observing your student in a number of social settings over the course of a few weeks
- talking to other staff and parents and to the student himself to find out what social skills they would like to focus on
- completing a social skills assessment or checklist to find out where your students' strengths and needs lie in this area
- choosing which skills to prioritize, as a result.

Doing both a pre- and post-programme assessment will also help you to show progress in social skills learning, as well as providing the all-important rationale to school management for the continuation of such interventions.

2. Social skills programmes: How to teach these skills

There are many commercially available social skills programmes available that lay out assessment, progression for teaching and lively, interesting ways to teach these skills. Steps usually include:

- Identify the goal.
- Teach the necessary skills, ensuring that you explain 'why' it is done like this.
- Notice what both successful and unsuccessful social skills look like, using puppets, role-play, video clips and video modelling.
- Practise in a variety of different scenarios.
- Generalize to other situations.

Once you have identified what targets you are going to work on, choose key lessons from a social skills programme and tailor them to suit the needs of your student, adding and deleting parts as necessary.

Please see Appendix 3 for a list of well-known social skills programmes.

3. Peer-mediated interventions (PMI)

Although social skills are often taught by school staff in one-to-one or group settings, it is important to note that studies have shown peer-mediated interventions to be very effective in improving the social skills and peer acceptance of autistic children at school (Kasari et al. 2012; Płatos and Wojaczek 2017).

Peer-based instruction and intervention (PBII) were found to be evidence-based practices (EBP) by the NCAEP (Steinbrenner et al. 2020).

Peer-mediated intervention usually involves teaching non-autistic students how to interact with their autistic peers in a planned way in order to increase social skills, interaction, engagement and social networks. An obvious advantage of PMI is increased opportunities to practise in day-to-day settings, thus aiding generalization of skills (Watkins et al. 2015).

This is done by:

- teaching peers about autism
- explaining to peers about what the target child needs to learn
- using role-plays, visual aids and modelling, peers are taught how to engage with the child, how to prompt the child to play or how to elicit the learned script from the child, as well as how to respond positively through praise
- providing feedback to the peers once the programme/sessions are complete.

(adapted from Chang and Locke 2016; Watkins et al. 2015)

PMI is often done via Circle of Friends sessions, playground buddies or social clubs, which can be based around the target child's particular interest.

Examples of PMI include:

- asking someone to play in the playground
- showing someone how to play with certain toys. For example, how to play in the toy kitchen, or how to build blocks, or modelling how to respond when you lose a board game
- eliciting a learned response. For example, greeting the target child every morning, or asking them a pre-planned question and responding positively.

4. Focus on the 'why'

It is really important to explain the reasons behind using a particular skill. After all, if you know why you are being asked to do something, you are more likely to continue doing it.

❝ For example, when the sign at my local pond simply stated 'No Fishing', few people took any notice. However, when it was changed to 'No Fishing Due to CEV virus', people started to heed the warning, as they now knew the reason why. ❞

Claire

Understanding the 'why' is often a catalyst towards your students actually using a newly learned social skill.

❝ Of course, it's helpful to know what the norm is that people are expecting of you. But what happens then if you don't fit the norm? That little bit of 'social skills' knowledge doesn't help beyond a superficial level. That's why the 'how' and the 'why' are really important. For example, learning to say 'hello' to someone. If you understand the purpose of it, then you can deliberately use it to achieve something. You can get a lot of resistance against a solution if somebody doesn't know the reason behind why they are being asked to do something. ❞

Paul Micallef, autistic advocate and founder of Autism Explained Online Summit https://paulmicallef.com.au

5. Generalize learning to other situations

Participating in a weekly social skills session will only teach your student how to use the skill in that particular setting. He will need many more opportunities to practise these skills with other people outside of the classroom, either in semi-structured settings like a games club or in natural settings like the playground, the park and at home.

In fact, Bellini et al. (2007) found that the success of a social skills programme depended on the extent to which skills could be generalized across multiple settings and people.

> **Generalization** means transferring skills learned in one setting to another setting. See ⊶ Guide 54: Tailoring the Curriculum.
>
> For example, if you attend a weekly adult night class to learn Spanish, but never visit Spain or practise outside of the class, then it is unlikely you will ever become fluent. On the other hand, if you go to Spain on holidays, and order in Spanish from a restaurant menu every night for a week, it is likely that you will at least learn and remember a few key words and phrases because you have learned in a natural and functional way.
>
> Similarly, if you teach a child to greet you by saying 'Hi' when he arrives into your classroom, this skill then needs to be generalized to greeting classmates at a group table, greeting the principal at the school door and greeting relatives who come to visit during holidays.

Many autistic children can find it hard to generalize learning done in one setting to another. In order to help your students to generalize learned skills, you can:

1. **Brainstorm and practise ways to generalize a learned skill** to another setting in a way that suits the setting. For example, 'How would you ask to join in a game in the park at the weekend? What could you say?'
2. **Choose a lunch time or after-school club** as a key time to practise a social skills target. For example, 'Ask a friend if you can borrow a pen during homework club today. Make sure to look in their direction when you ask.'
3. **Give a simple Social Grids Board** for homework to practise at home for a period of time, based on his current target. ➤ See Guide 26: Teaching Social Communication Skills: An Outline.

🧠 Don't Forget Social Media!

Autism and the internet

Social media platforms such as TikTok, Snapchat and Instagram have become a major part of socializing for many young people. Such platforms can be a way to make friends and communicate with other people from the comfort and safety of one's own homes. Particular advantages for an autistic person include:

- less pressure than in face-to-face interactions
- little or no need to focus on eye contact
- more time to formulate answers without being put on the spot
- more opportunities to meet people who have similar interests, for example, Minecraft or special interest forums
- greater level of control – a person can begin or end the social interaction with the push of a button.

Autistic adults and social media
- Many autistic adults use social networking sites, with the majority reporting that they use them for social engagement and connection (Mazurek 2013).
- Autistic adults and adolescents who use social media may benefit in terms of better friendship quality, happiness or well-being (Van Schalkwyk et al. 2017; Ward, Dill-Shackleford and Mazurek 2018).
- While it is no doubt beneficial to connect with people online, it is also important to note that Mazurek (2013) found that it was offline friendships that resulted in decreased loneliness for one group of autistic adults.

❝ Social media can be a good entry point for some people socially because it's easy to find other people who like the same things as you – you can interact in the way you want to interact. However, I only use it because I have to. I don't enjoy it at all. It's not a real connection to me, it's a really superficial connection that will likely never develop any further. ❞

Paul Micallef, autistic advocate and founder of Autism Explained
Online Summit https://paulmicallef.com.au

Social media use in primary school

" A significant proportion of primary school-age children have their own social media profile. "

(Ofcom 2019)

A 2019 Ofcom survey of children aged 5–15 found that:

- 45% of 5–15-year-olds own a smartphone.
- 59% of 5–15-year-olds play games online.

With regards to social media profiles:

- 21% of 8–11-year-old online users have a social media profile.
- 71% of 12–15-year-old online users have a social media profile.

Even though it may be less stressful than face-to-face interactions, the online world can be a potential minefield of misused emojis, unanswered text messages and compliments gone wrong.

In a study of autistic adults' views of their own communication skills and needs, one participant discussed the difficulty around ending a lengthy text message conversation. They concluded that sometimes the only solution is 'to turn off your phone, or take out the SIM card' (Cummins, Pellicano and Crane 2020, p.683).

Think about your own social media use. Did anyone explicitly teach you that:

- the 'crying laughing' emoji can be a polite way to acknowledge someone's joke, without getting into a prolonged conversation
- if someone replies to your texts with one-word answers, it probably means they are not in the mood for a chat right now
- you can respond with 'xxx' to friends' texts, but you probably would not use it to reply to your boss.

Although autistic children typically spend less time using social media than their non-autistic peers (Mazurek and Wenstrup 2013), it is also true that older primary-aged children often begin to dabble in social media. As a result, teaching autistic children and teenagers how to communicate effectively and safely online is now as important as learning how to manage social interactions in real life.

A social media curriculum could include the following objectives:

- How to start, maintain and end a conversation on WhatsApp/Snapchat/Discord.
- How to understand when someone does not want to message anymore.

- Understanding emojis in text messages.
- What types of comments to make on social media.
- How to tell white lies on social media and why this is important.
- How to differentiate between real and superficial friends on social media.
- Ground rules for commenting on social media, for example, 'If it's not kind, don't post it.'

Linda, 12, had fallen out with some of her classmates as she had posted overly honest comments underneath their online photos. Staff pointed out the hidden rules of social media, which dictate that either staying silent or telling white lies may be the best approach when commenting on photographs of friends.

Practical general social media strategies

- Discuss what social media platforms your students use.
- Take screenshots of carefully chosen relevant social media posts or create your own. Study these posts and discuss effective and non-effective comments and interactions.
- Discuss what to do when a friend posts an unflattering picture online, or how many comments to post underneath the picture.
- Create a series of WhatsApp conversations detailing effective and non-effective conversation starters and finishers. Screenshot these and print them out to discuss with your students.
- Discuss the implications of posting a picture online. Make it really concrete – would you be prepared for your photograph to be beamed onto the front of your school building?
- Play games to understand emoji use. For example, get to know the different emojis through playing 'emoji snap', or call out different scenarios and ask your student to pick the most appropriate emoji to respond with. Discuss what emojis to use in particular contexts. For example, 'Heart-eyes can be used to say that you really like a photograph that someone has posted.'

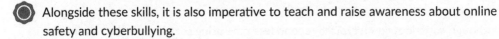 Alongside these skills, it is also imperative to teach and raise awareness about online safety and cyberbullying.

❝ In a class, there are lots of cues to figure out what the other people are doing. None of that exists online. The potential for bullying is there. It's like closing the door and putting all the kids in there. People can be talking and laughing about you and everyone knows except you. There is no way to police that. ❞

Paul Micallef, autistic advocate and founder of Autism Explained
Online Summit https://paulmicallef.com.au

'My Personal School Handbook'

Autistic author Jennifer Cook O'Toole has said that she wished she had a 'secret rule book' when she was younger that explained all the unwritten social rules of life (Cook O'Toole 2013).

A 'My Personal School Handbook' created for a specific student details expected behaviour in different situations across the school day. This blueprint will enable your student to adapt better to any school situation because he will know exactly what is expected of him.

Staff can:

1. Make a list of different school scenarios and occasions. These include:
    - assembly
    - carpet time
    - arriving into school in the morning
    - doing work at my table
    - in the playground
    - dinner time
    - music time.
2. Discuss the rules and options with your student for each section. Either type or write in the information and ask the student to illustrate each page.
3. Remember to help your student to understand why they must behave in certain ways. For example, discuss why it's important to notice what everyone else is doing in assembly.

Menita, 11, used to over-react in certain situations. For example, during assembly, she whooped and threw her hands in the air when someone got a prize, while everyone else clapped quietly.

While staff did not want to quash Menita's lovely enthusiasm, they decided that it was important to teach her to look around in assembly, to notice how others are responding and to adapt her reactions accordingly. They created an 'assembly' page for her personal school handbook.

Assembly

This is what you can do during assembly:

- Sit on the floor in the same row as your class.
- Look around and notice what most of the other students in the assembly hall are doing – are they clapping quietly or loudly?
  - If they are clapping loudly, you can clap loudly.
  - If they are clapping quietly, you can clap quietly.
  - If they are cheering loudly, you can cheer loudly.
  - If they are cheering quietly, you can cheer quietly.
- When a teacher asks a question, put your hand up to answer it if you know the answer. Wait for a little while because he might not see you immediately. If you don't get called on, put your hand down again. And don't worry, you will get a chance to answer another time. There are 300 students in assembly, so the teacher can't call on everyone.

 Instead of having loose pages in a binder, scrapbooks are handy because they lend themselves to being re-read, like a storybook. And re-reading means over-learning and hopefully, generalizing to different situations.

Social Understanding

" In primary school, I had a lot of wonderful time by myself, and probably enjoyed spending time by myself, but was also quite miffed about how my peers managed to have closer friendships or relationships with one another, and how they kept them quite consistently throughout the years... I definitely struggled there, just in terms of keeping friendships and maintaining them, but also knowing who was actually a friend, and who was just somebody who I see around school and maybe say 'Hi' to. "

Sam Ahern, artist, autistic advocate and Barbican Young
Visual Arts Group Member 2019–2020

Turning up social awareness

A key part of social skills development lies in helping your students to notice and be more aware of:

- how others are feeling
- why people act the way they do
- what is really happening behind the scenes in their daily social interactions
- how their behaviour and actions can affect other people.

Pointing the social attention spotlight

You can help your students to further understand people by switching on or turning up their social awareness. This can be done by pointing a social attention spotlight on different parts of social situations that they may never even have considered before. After all, when your attention is drawn to something, you start to become more aware of it. This often helps students to realize what is happening and to have an 'aha moment'.

The frequency illusion

Think about buying a new car. After much deliberation, you choose a red Fiat. Almost as soon as you drive out of the showroom, you start to notice red Fiats everywhere.

This is known as the frequency illusion. You think you're seeing more red Fiats than usual, but your awareness of them has simply been switched on.

GETTING TO THE 'AHA MOMENT'

Alan, 9, had shouted at his teacher in front of the whole class. When the special education teacher sat down with him to discuss the moment and help him to figure out what the teacher may have been feeling (embarrassment), he had the 'aha moment'. He simply hadn't ever really stopped to think about it in this way.

Julie, 10, hadn't realized that the abrupt and quiet way she greeted and left conversations made people think she was rude. Once it was pointed out to her and different skills were practised over a series of lessons, she continued to use these skill appropriately. She just hadn't known this before.

Marcie, 12, didn't realize that, after saying hello to someone, she immediately looked at the ground, which made the other person feel as though she wasn't interested in what they were saying. When staff pointed this out to her, she made an effort to change this seemingly small gesture, which made a big difference to how other people responded to her socially.

By alerting your students to the different facets of social interaction, they will then become more attuned to social nuances and become more used to interpreting social situations as a result.

Strategies include using:

1. **'Playback' forms** to help your student see the situation from another person's perspective. See Guide 37: 'Playback' Forms.
2. **Social Narratives** to increase learned social awareness and teach different ways of acting. See Guide 38: Social Narratives.
3. **Social rules and 'Power' cards** to help explain appropriate social behaviours for younger students. See Guide 39: Using Social Rules, 'Power' Cards, Thinking Out Loud and Relationship Circles.
4. **Thinking out loud about social situations**, for example, saying 'When you ask me about my weekend, it makes me feel really good. It lets me know that you are interested in what I am saying.' See Guide 39: Using Social Rules, 'Power' Cards, Thinking Out Loud and Relationship Circles.

Guide 37

'Playback' Forms

'Playback' forms can help your students to analyze social situations in a very concrete and visual way.

This is done by:

- writing and/or drawing out exactly what happened
- paying attention to what both the student and the other person was thinking and feeling
- making a plan for what to do the next time.

Staff can:

- **fill out the 'Playback'** form with the student (see ⬇ Appendices 4 and 5)
- **scribe for the student**, if necessary. The focus here is on social understanding, not handwriting
- **practise the habit of perspective taking**, using a variety of different scenarios. For example, 'How would you feel if she called your art "ugly"?'
- **collect completed forms** in a folder or scrapbook to re-read sporadically throughout the year.

Remember to:

- **celebrate successful social interactions using 'Playback' forms too**, so you are not simply collating a record of past mistakes. No student wants to read back over that!
- **catch your student being successfully social**, for example, you could say 'Becky was really grateful when you loaned her a pen earlier'
- **'strike while the iron is cold.'** The best time to analyze an event in a calm manner is later on or the following day, after the dust has settled
- **ensure that all staff are clear about the reasons for using 'Playback' forms.** Some schools use similar forms for all students as a type of restorative justice. It is really important that your students never interpret filling out these forms as a type of punishment.

'Playback' form

What happened?

I didn't get off the computer when Majella asked me to. I shouted at her. I was sent to Mr Browne's office.

What did I say or do?

Noooo! I'm not doing it!

What did I think?

I really, really just want to finish this level on my game.

_____
Me

What did they say or do?

Time to get off the computer. Time for lunch!

What did they think?

I think he's being a bit rude for shouting at me.

_____
Other person

My new plan is:

If I don't want to do something, I can say:
Can you wait a minute please?
Can I have I more minute to finish this level?
Can I check my schedule please?

What can I say or do?

Please give me 5 more minutes just to finish this level?

What will I think?

I'd love 5 more minutes and so I'm going to ask nicely. If she says 'no', that's okay. Check the schedule.

_____
Me

What can they say or do?

Okay, 5 more minutes to finish the level. I'll set the timer now.

What will they think?

Oh, he's been really polite and asked for more time. That's fair enough.

_____
Other person

Guide 38

Social Narratives

Autistic author Laura James has described how she finds it difficult to pick up skills such as 'how to shop, catch a bus, cook, clean or manage money' simply by osmosis. Instead she describes how she needs 'a book, a video or someone to explain and show [her] how to do them' (James 2018).

 Social narratives (also known as Social Stories™) are stories (written and with pictures) that explain situations to your students and give them strategies to cope with those scenarios. They show your students how other people may feel and give clear suggestions for appropriate behaviour.

Devised by Carol Gray (Gray 1993), Social Stories™, under the more general heading of *social narratives*, are considered to be one of the 28 evidence-based practices for autistic children and young people (Steinbrenner et al. 2020).

In order to write an effective Social Story™, Gray recommends following a specific set of criteria. Training on Social Stories™ is often available via local education centres and outreach teams.

Once you have written a Social Story™ for your student, it is helpful to remember to:

- read it together at a time when your student is relaxed, and not directly after something upsetting has happened
- only focus on one story at a time
- read it daily with your student until he understands it (this could take up to three weeks).

Story topics that often arise in primary school include:

- Why I can't always be first in line.
- Why do I have to come to school?
- What to do when I arrive at school.
- Making mistakes is not a big deal.
- Why it's okay to stop work before I have actually finished it.
- Asking for help in class.
- Asking for a break in class.
- What to do when teacher is absent.
- Who's collecting me today?
- What to do when I hear the fire alarm.
- Winning and losing.

- Sharing and turn-taking.
- Personal space.
- Why it's sometimes okay to tell white lies.
- Hygiene: Why I must blow my nose into a tissue; Why I must close the bathroom door.

⚙ Generic stories

Individualized Social Stories™ are the most effective to use, as they are tailored to suit the individual needs of each child. However, if you have not yet managed to access official Social Stories™ training, it is also possible to buy or download generic stories and tailor them to suit your student's needs. There are also books that describe responses to a variety of different social situations.

⬇ See Appendix 3 for a selection of children's photo and story books that outline responses to a variety of different social situations.

Carol Gray also devised comic strip conversations. Similar to Social Stories™, these are individualized comic strips that outline what to do in different social situations, as well as detailing how others are thinking and feeling.

Using Social Rules, 'Power' Cards, Thinking Out Loud and Relationship Circles

Social rules

Social rules are shorter than stories. They are often used with students who do not yet have the capacity or the patience to read through and understand a social narrative. They give a quick reminder about what to do instead (Figure 2.24).

Hands down, squeeze your Koosh ball

FIGURE 2.24 'SOCIAL RULES' CARD

'Isn't it ironic?': The white bear problem

 'Whatever you do, don't think of a white bear. Go on, close your eyes, relax, but don't think of a white bear.'

So, what happened? Most likely you were overwhelmed by thoughts of a white bear. Deliberately trying to suppress a thought about something can actually make you think about it even more. As a result, when teaching your students about different ways to act in social situations, it is vital to teach them *what to do*, instead of only teaching them what *not* to do.

So instead of 'no kicking', use 'legs down, let's go for a walk'.

Or instead of 'no shouting', use 'quiet talking, say "teacher, I need a break"'.

 Velcro social rules to a wall or to a desk so that you or your student can easily access them as needed.

'Power' cards

'Power' cards involve using a child's special interest in order to further familiarize them with a variety of social rules and conventions (Gagnon and Smith-Myles 2016).

For example, the Power Card on the following page might work well for a child who likes Sonic the Hedgehog.

Just like Sonic!

Sonic the Hedgehog always washes his hands after going to the toilet.

He knows that hands have invisible germs on them after using the toilet.

He washes his hands with soap and water.

He dries them with some tissue or with the hand-dryer.

That's what Sonic does!

Thinking out loud about social situations

Of course, it would be impossible to create a written resource for every social situation that happens during the school day. Instead, insert teachable moments during the school day, explaining what happened, what to do and the reasoning behind why you would like them to take this course of action.

For example:

- saying: 'When you complimented me on my new haircut, it made me feel really good.'
- explaining: 'The reason that we have to wait here for so long is that there is someone in the principal's office and their meeting has gone on too long. Let's count backward from 100 and see if they are out before we reach the end.'
- noticing: 'Did you notice that Marie was cross when she lost the game, but she managed to say "well done"? That was really polite of her and showed everyone she's a good sport.'
- correcting (gently): 'When you say "I must be off" so abruptly in conversation, it sometimes makes the other person feel uncomfortable. Let's think of a better phrase we could use in future.'

Vermeulen (2019) describes this as 'giving subtitles' to explain what is happening in different situations. This includes telling someone what they need to do and why they need to do it.

Considering context

Vermeulen (2019) considers that teaching someone to take context into consideration is often more important than thinking about social skills differences in autistic people. He posits that many autistic people have 'context blindness', where, instead of having social interaction differences, they have actually not managed to process the situation in context. He emphasizes the importance of 'pushing the context button' to help your students to notice and understand how context can influence the way they perceive a situation or how they should act.

For example, if somebody is crying, does it always mean that they feel sad? If two people are hugging at a funeral, it probably means they are sad. If two people are hugging at an airport arrivals gate, it probably means they are happy.

In other words, instead of making hard-and-fast rules for social situations, it is important to look at each social situation in context.

Ted, 11, loved to play by the rules. However, whenever somebody bent the rules slightly, he would tell on them, even if it was his friend. One day, he told the teacher that his friend had brought some chocolate in his lunchbox, because it broke the 'healthy lunch' policy at school.

What to do

Staff worked with Ted to help him to understand the grey areas about when and when not to tell tales specifically at school. They discussed rules such as 'Are you in danger? Tell an adult', 'Is someone else in danger? Tell an adult', and 'If not, there is no need to tell your teacher about what your friend is doing in class.'

At the same time, they worked on a personal safety programme, where Ted learned that if he felt uneasy in any situation, he should 'get away and tell an adult'.

Relationship Circles

Relationship Circles can help to clarify context for a number of different scenarios. For example:

Nicola, 9, was a very tactile and friendly girl who always hugged everyone she met, including any unknown adults and teachers who came into the classroom. Staff felt that as Nicola was now getting older, they needed to help her to understand who she could and couldn't hug.

What to do

Staff drew up a Relationship Circles diagram with Nicola, discussing different ways of greeting different people. It included:

- parents and siblings: hug and kiss
- Auntie Marie: hug
- friends in my class: high-five
- friends in other classes: high-five

- teachers: say 'hello' or 'hi' and using their name
- strangers on the street: not saying 'hello' because you don't know them at all.

Conclusion
'Live and let live': Let everyone pick what they want from the menu

Remember, there is a fine line between developing social understanding and causing your student to overthink every social interaction and develop 'paralysis by analysis' as a result.

Together with your student, pick one focus (for example, greetings) to work on over a period of time or choose just a few teachable moments sporadically throughout the week to work on with your student.

Your ultimate aim is to provide your students with a menu of social skills and social understanding strategies from which they can pick and choose as they wish. At the end of the day, it is more beneficial for them to have this social knowledge than not to have it – as knowledge will give them choice and power.

❝ You need to learn the [social] rules, before you're allowed to break them. ❞

Paul Micallef, autistic advocate and founder of Autism Explained
Online Summit https://paulmicallef.com.au

Part 3

Being Inclusive

Introduction

❝ We, as a collective (the neurotypicals and the neurodiverse) have to work together as a whole; in a way that binds our strengths together and supports our weaknesses, to bring knowledge and understanding to the world we live in. ❞

Erin Davidson, autistic advocate and narrator of 'Walk in My Shoes' (Donaldson Trust 2020a)

A school principal who gives a high five to an autistic little girl and stoops down in a corridor to chat to her at length – that's inclusion. A teenage boy who feels confident to share some information with his classmates about his autism diagnosis – that's inclusion. And an autistic girl who is given a central role in a class assembly, even though her teachers know that she might decide to opt out at the last minute – that's inclusion, too.

The majority of autistic children are now educated in mainstream schools both in the UK (70%) (Department for Education 2014) and Ireland (65%) (AsIAm 2019). As a result, it is highly likely that all teachers will work with an autistic child or children at some point in their career. This means that school staff will need to have a clear understanding of what meaningful inclusion is and what it might look like, as well as being aware of some practical strategies in order to implement it successfully.

Inclusion: Barriers and benefits

Some of the benefits include:

- **Students with disabilities** can experience less bullying in inclusive schools, do better academically, display better social skills and can be more likely to belong to groups at school or in the community.
- **Typically developing peers** can experience positive effects on their academic development, as well as learning to understand and become more accepting of difference.
- **Staff** can become more attuned to recognizing the strengths and needs of every student and become used to differentiating for all students.

(based on Grindal et al. 2016)

Many school staff support the idea of inclusion and are keen to include children with different needs. However, some of the barriers (as outlined by teachers themselves) include:

- lack of knowledge and training regarding teaching children with special educational needs
- lack of funding for resources
- little time to differentiate lesson content or to work on a one-to-one basis with students
- little time to co-ordinate and plan with other staff.

(based on Young, Mannix McNamara and Coughlan 2017)

Teachers also identified a lack of training around special educational needs, particularly during initial teacher education. In fact, newly qualified teachers acknowledged that doing their placement in a special school, class or with a special education team during initial teacher training was particularly helpful in preparing them for meaningful inclusion in the classroom and school (NCSE 2019a).

Note: While this chapter focuses on the concept of inclusion of autistic students within a mainstream school, it is important to note that currently there is no definitive conclusion from the research literature that supports one type of educational placement over another for children and young people with special educational needs (NCSE 2019b).

66 We have seen autistic students thrive in both mainstream and special schools, and think that the best school is the one that the child is best suited to and will best meet his or her needs. 99

Claire and Annelies

Two questions to consider about inclusion

1. What is the difference between *integration* and *inclusion*?

Despite having very different meanings, the terms 'inclusion' and 'integration' are often used interchangeably.

Integration is more like the medical model of disability. See ⚷ Guide 2: Ten Things Every Teacher Should Know About Autism.

It means:

- You will have to adapt to make this work.
- We will help you to make the changes you need to fit in.
- You have to follow our school rules and our behaviour policies.
- You will have to abide by the rules of this classroom.
- We are inflexible.

Inclusion is more like the social model of disability.

It means:

- We will all have to adapt to make this work.
- We will adapt the environment (by increasing staff and student understanding and adjust tasks, policies and even the school building, if needed) to suit you.
- We will change the rules, if we need to, to acknowledge and accommodate your needs.
- We are flexible.

2. What does meaningful or authentic inclusion look like?

❝ Ultimately, inclusion means 'understanding' and being flexible enough not only to accommodate but to celebrate a diverse student population. In many ways, it is more about attitude than it is about action or strategies. ❞

Claire

Creating a 'one classroom for everyone' education system is a noble ambition. However, it is important to consider what meaningful inclusion really entails, and to stop and reflect on whether, at times, teachers are under pressure to pay lip service to the notion of inclusion, without ever really being fully trained, supported or prepared for it.

Consider the case studies below. Which do you consider to be the better example of meaningful inclusion?

CASE STUDY: ALAN

Alan, 8, attends a special class for autistic students attached to a mainstream school. He goes to the mainstream class every afternoon for an hour of History and Geography, where he sits at the front of the classroom, often drawing or doing his own thing. He doesn't really understand what's going on, and some of his mainstream peers don't know his name. The class teacher feels guilty because he doesn't think that Alan is learning as much as he could, but the principal is happy because Alan's parents wanted him to have more time in the mainstream class.

CASE STUDY: LUCINDA

Lucinda, 12, attends a mainstream school. She can find it hard to focus on classwork at times, so her teacher has given her permission to get up and walk around the class whenever she feels like it during written work time, as long as she doesn't interrupt anyone else on her travels. Staff have written down these guidelines for Lucinda, with pictures to support her understanding, and read this with her regularly. They also set up a cosy corner for her in the class library containing books, music and headphones, for times when she needs to take a longer break.

Case study: Alan is an example of lip-service inclusion. There is no doubt that Alan exists physically alongside his peers in a mainstream classroom, but his levels of interaction and learning are negligible.

Case study: Lucinda is an example of 'meaningful inclusion' because Lucinda's support is centred around her specific needs, rather than trying to make her fit into the existing systems and routines, or catering only to the needs of her parents. Lucinda is a fully paid-up member of the class, in whatever way, shape or form this takes.

Is it time to re-frame your notion of inclusion?

School staff and parents often have to completely re-frame their notion of what inclusion actually means in order to ensure that school is as worthwhile as possible for the student. This involves thinking about how to include a student more fully in a lesson, as well as having the confidence to make the decision that he may be better served by *not* participating in a particular lesson, and by doing something else entirely.

> 66 I observed a 10-year-old autistic girl in a mainstream classroom during carpet time. The support staff member felt under huge pressure to help her to sit still on the ground like all the other students, and so kept showing her the 'quiet legs' picture

whenever she stretched out her legs. The girl put her hand up a few times during the session, but for the most part, her questions and comments had little to do with the task at hand.

Teaching a child how to sit still for 50 minutes in silence in class, and pretend that she understands everything that's going on, is not inclusion. It's worth considering whether this student would be better off to have a layered carpet time, where she spends some time with the whole class and then accesses some one-to-one support from a teaching assistant on either the same topic or a different topic, works on an individual project or goes for a sensory break instead. 〞

Claire

Key questions

- What lessons does your student excel in?
- What lessons does your student find difficult to participate in?
- Is there anything you can do to enhance his understanding in lessons he finds difficult?
- Are there any key times in the day when your student might benefit more from doing something else?

Guide 40

Creating an Inclusive, Autism-Friendly School

" The best bit about school is the teachers understanding you. "

Year 9 student, Limpsfield Grange school for girls aged 11–16
with communication and interaction difficulties

Morewood, Humphrey and Symes (2011, p.64) described how any school aiming to become autism-friendly needs to be 'saturated in autism understanding and awareness'. In this section, we will outline ways of *saturating* our schools in autism understanding, by educating staff and students alike.

Of course, creating an autism-friendly school also involves adapting lessons and activities to suit the needs of the students, as well as adapting the physical building, for example, the classroom, playground, assembly hall and toilets. Strategies for this are covered extensively in Part 2 and elsewhere throughout the book.

Autism-friendly schools in practice

Of the six years Claire spent visiting mostly mainstream primary and secondary schools to support the inclusion of autistic students, the most inclusive schools tended to share some similar practices. These included:

Leadership

- **Senior management**, particularly the principal, actively promote inclusion.
- **There is an autism expert or champion**, usually a special educational needs coordinator, in the school, who is part of the senior management team. Being on the leadership team gives them some clout to affect change within a school.

Core staff

- **Staff participate in whole-staff autism training.** This includes teachers, teaching assistants and the board of governors, as well as the school secretary and caretaker, cooks, cleaners and bus and taxi escorts and drivers.

- **Staff know which students have received a diagnosis of autism.** This is particularly important at secondary school, as often students do not have a central class or teacher as they do in primary school.
- **Most classrooms have basic autism-friendly strategies** in place as general good practice. For example, staff use a daily schedule and understand the advantages of this.
- **Staff have access to excellent and up-to-date special education needs** resources to use with their students.
- **Teachers are given time** to meet with other professionals and to prepare for such meetings.
- **Staff feel empowered through training and are confident to try new strategies.** For example, at any one time, two students might be outside having a quick game of tennis in the playground with a special needs assistant, one boy might be relaxing in a classroom cosy corner and another student might be happily completing an adapted worksheet with a timer beside her.

Students

- **The different skills and abilities of all students are celebrated** throughout the school via assemblies and whole-class lessons.
- **Students participate in assemblies** to learn more about autism.
- **Students participate in autism peer awareness training** in smaller group settings.

“ One of the most inclusive settings I ever worked in was a mainstream school with a number of special autism classes attached to it. I think what really worked was that, over the years, lots of the staff had had a chance to work in the special classes as a special class teacher, on a one-to-one or small group basis as a special education teacher in the mainstream school and in the mainstream classes. As a result, there was a school-wide understanding and awareness of autism. Staff were so empathetic to the needs of their autistic students. This, more so than using the latest resources or strategies, created such a lovely atmosphere throughout. ”

Claire

Key question: What do you currently do to help staff and students to better understand autism?

Guide 41

Increasing Staff Understanding

66 Having one good teacher in your life can have such an impact. 99

Jacinta, mother of Michael

66 Teaching Assistants were the saviours in terms of ensuring that my experience at primary and secondary school were much more bearable. 99

Jack Welch, autistic advocate and campaigner, youth patron of Ambitious about Autism

School staff play an intrinsic role in helping their autistic students to have a happy school experience. A secure understanding of autism and why some children act the way they do is far more valuable than an endless list of strategies, which often fall by the wayside if results are not immediately obvious.

Using first-person accounts written by autistic people can be particularly illuminating to help staff to better understand autism. Before accumulating strategies, it is worth spending some time reading, watching or listening to a selection of autistic people describing their lives, each from their own unique perspective.

⊕ See Appendix 3 for further resources.

After all, using first-person accounts written by autistic people can be particularly illuminating to help staff to better understand autism.

66 I was training a group of school staff once on the benefits of using visuals for older autistic students. Some weren't convinced that writing things down helped as much as I suggested. It wasn't until I mentioned autistic journalist Laura James, who used to stick a Post-it note on her bathroom mirror to remind herself to brush her teeth and to cleanse, tone and moisturize, that the penny dropped.

They realized that if this highly competent journalist needs visual supports, then their primary-aged students definitely do too. 99

Claire

Other ways to increase staff knowledge and understanding about autism include:

- **Choose a block of time to focus on autism awareness at school and in staff meetings.** An ideal time to increase awareness in a general way is during World Autism Awareness Week, which takes place every year in March. The National Autistic Society (NAS) and Irish charity AsIAm publish autism awareness packs every year ahead of World Autism Awareness Week.

- **Harness the expertise** of the staff themselves. Ask them to share their top tips in staff meetings.
- **Invite an autistic speaker to talk to staff.**
- **Organize professional training sessions for staff** and find out beforehand what staff want to know about autism via a quick Google Forms survey or a simple question box in the staff room.
- ⬇ **Hold in-school training** using our free, downloadable 'All About Autism' Staff Training Pack in Appendix 6. This contains:
  - links to our ten short video clips (1–3 minutes each) detailing 'What is autism?' and including a range of autistic voices. They also outline five key strategies for staff to try in mainstream classrooms
  - coaching cards to accompany five of the video clips, to stimulate discussion amongst staff
  - weekly step-by-step outlines for three 30-minute staff meetings about autism
  - the Quick Reference Guide to Better Understanding Autism (a curated list of autism resources for staff to dip in and out of).

Guide 42

Increasing Peer Knowledge and Understanding About Autism

❝ If two brains run on a different operating system, well then let's meet each other halfway, and learn from each other's operating system. ❞

Dr Peter Vermeulen, autism advocate, trainer and author
(www.petervermeulen.be) (Vermeulen 2019)

According to Lindsay and Edwards (2013), almost 50 per cent of children with disabilities described that 'they do not belong within their class' and felt 'lonely, isolated and unsafe'.

Just being in the mainstream classroom does not necessarily guarantee that an autistic child will feel included and part of their class. In fact, it can be the opposite, with autistic students being significantly more likely to be bullied than their non-autistic peers (Altomare et al. 2017; Humphrey and Symes 2010; Sterzing et al. 2012). This can include physical bullying, as well as social isolation.

> **Bullying at school**
> When Little (2002) interviewed 411 mothers of autistic children or children with other non-verbal learning disorders in the US, aged between 4 and 17 years, she found that:
>
> - 94 per cent said that their child had experienced bullying at least once in the previous year.
> - One third reported that their children experienced indirect bullying, such as not being invited to a friends' party, being picked last for teams and being excluded from daily school lunch groups.

Bullying can also continue into secondary school with autistic adolescents more likely to be bullied and experience more social isolation than their neurotypical peers (Kloosterman et al. 2013; Wainscot et al. 2008).

❝ I really hated secondary school. I was bullied for being so quiet. I'm still traumatised by the mockery of my peers. Some of the children used to jump out at me and shout 'speak' as if I were their pet dog. ❞

Alis Rowe, autistic author and entrepreneur – founder of 'The Curly Hair Project'

Disability peer awareness programmes may help to reduce bullying

It is clear that being bullied and victimized are serious problems for autistic students, both in primary and secondary schools. However, educating peers about disabilities can lead to decreased bullying and more positive relationships. As school staff, we have an opportunity to stand in the middle and help autistic children and their non-autistic peers to come together in mutual understanding and acceptance.

- Providing non-autistic peers with training about a disability can change attitudes and influence relationships towards those with disabilities (Lindsay and Edwards 2013).
- Positive relationships with peers are a significant factor in protecting autistic students from bullying (Hebron and Humphrey 2014).

One way of doing this is by using disability awareness programmes that celebrate diversity, and, more specifically, by educating peers about different types of disabilities. As a general rule:

- **younger students:** focus on celebrating difference
- **middle and older students:** focus on introducing them to the facts about autism, as well as listening to a host of autistic people telling their stories via books, video clips or podcasts.

Autism peer awareness programme

One way to educate peers about autism is to roll out an autism peer awareness (APA) programme across the school. This can be done via one-off assemblies, by providing access to books, video clips and games, as well as by doing a formal project about autism.

World Autism Awareness Week, which takes place annually in March, can be a good time to do work around autism peer awareness.

CASE STUDY: FIVE-WEEK AUTISM PEER AWARENESS PROJECT

'Autism is where children or adults get very angry and violent', wrote one 9-year-old student. 'It's when a person holds a lot of anger and can't keep it inside', wrote another.

When asked 'What is autism?', a group of Year 4 children had some interesting answers. We weren't surprised. These students' only experience of autism was with a highly anxious peer who had frequent meltdowns in class. But would their opinions change after completing a five-week APA programme?

With 70 per cent of autistic students being educated in mainstream schools in the UK, we knew that we needed to spread awareness about this 'hidden' disability.

Our aim at the Bridge London Trust Outreach Team was to create a series of lesson plans specifically about autism that would encompass the best of all the available programmes, as detailed by Lindsay and Edwards (2013) in their systematic review of disability awareness programmes.

We developed a five-session autism peer awareness programme to roll out to 9- and 10-year-old students in mainstream classes. This included:

- Two class-based sessions, including discussions about how we are all different; visible and hidden disabilities; a case study about Ravi, a fictional boy with autism; celebrating the strengths of autistic people; highlighting well-known autistic people; and learning to use Makaton and Picture Exchange Communication System (PECS).
- A visit for ten students to the Bridge Primary School, a special school for students aged 2 to 19 years with severe or profound learning difficulties and/or autism, to interact with the school cohort.
- A class presentation or an assembly to the whole school about what they had learned.

All participating students answered a 15-question pre- and post-programme questionnaire. Out of 23 students in the class discussed above, 12 mentioned 'anger' when asked 'What is autism?' At the end of the programme, only two mentioned it. Most responses also displayed a greater understanding of autism e.g. 'It is a hidden disability', 'It is when they have trouble with their senses' and 'When they can't make friends easily'.

The teacher commented that reading the story about an autistic boy of a similar age to the students particularly clarified what it was like to be autistic: 'It was like a light bulb went off when they saw Ravi', she said.

The autistic child's answers had also changed by the end of the programme. When initially he wrote that autism was 'When everything is really loud and you can't look at people', his answer afterwards was 'It's how minds think differently'.

Lindsay and Edwards (2013) identified the key elements of effective disability awareness programmes, which include multiple sessions, class-based activities and direct social experiences with pupils with disabilities. They also concluded that a whole-school approach to disability awareness (including the head teacher, governors and teaching staff as well as pupils) is more powerful than involving just one class.

With the numbers of children being diagnosed with autism increasing, and with evidence that increased knowledge about disability can influence pupils' attitudes towards their peers with disabilities, it is vital to keep doing these programmes.

Especially when they stimulate answers like this: 'True or False: Children with autism can become doctors or teachers when they are older'. 'True', circled one student, with the addendum, 'If you believe you can do something, you can achieve' written in a childish scribble (Droney 2017).

This article first appeared in *Impact: Interim Issue, Journal of the Chartered College of Teaching* on 17 May 2017. This has been re-published with permission from the Chartered College of Teaching.

Guide 43 contains some other simple ways to raise pupil awareness about autism in your school or classroom.

Eight Simple Ways to Celebrate Diversity and Teach Your Students About Autism

1. **Celebrate difference by reading books about difference.** This is an excellent starting point for a discussion or project about autism, or indeed about any disability, and will help every child to feel accepted for who they are.

⊕ See Appendix 6: 'All About Autism' Staff Training Pack for a list of relevant books and video clips.

2. **Create a whole-class/whole-school video montage or poster wall** about celebrating difference at school with the title 'It's okay to be different'.

   For example, 'It's okay to wear glasses', 'It's okay to use a wheelchair', 'It's okay to dislike maths', 'It's okay to like dancing'.

   Ask each child to identify something they are proud of, or that is unique to them. Ask teaching and support staff to participate too, if they like.

3. **Play games** to highlight how different and unique all children are. The very simple aim is for your students to realize that:
   - we are all different
   - we all like different things
   - if we all liked the same things, life would be very dull and boring.

   For example:
   - **'Thumbs up, thumbs down':** Show pictures on a slide, or call out a range of different foods – for example, olives, hummus, chocolate, pizza, gherkins – and ask the students to put their thumbs up if they like the food and thumbs down if they do not. Repeat for other categories including singers, sports, games, clothing or drinks.
   - **'Tell me about':** Prepare some cards or slides with one category word on each – for example, singer, occupations, food. Ask a student to pick a card/ slide, and share with the group who her favourite singer is, or what she wants to be when she grows up, and why. Record on a chart and ask other members of the class to share their own preferences.

4. **Discuss 'visible' and 'invisible' disabilities.**
   - **Visible disabilities** include being deaf, visually impaired or a wheelchair user. Discuss how people with visible disabilities manage in their daily lives. For example, visually impaired people can wear glasses, use white

canes or technology such as Microsoft Seeing AI, deaf people can use sign language and wheelchair users can use ramps on buses and trains to travel independently.

- **Invisible disabilities** include dyslexia, dyscalculia and autism. Highlight that autism is an invisible disability, because you cannot tell just by looking at someone that they are autistic.

5. **Introduce children to the concept of a spectrum** by playing the 'sliding scale' game. Call out sentences and ask the students to line up wordlessly in order from the most to the least. Designate one side of the classroom with signs saying 'I agree', on the other side saying 'I disagree' and 'I'm not sure' in the middle.

For example, 'I love hockey', 'I love cats', 'I love P.E.', 'I love dancing', 'I love writing stories'.

6. **De-mystify autism by introducing children to a variety of autistic people via books and video clips.**

⬇ See Appendix 6: 'All About Autism' Staff Training Pack for a list of relevant books and video clips.

7. **Celebrate the strengths associated with autism** (Figure 3.1) by introducing your students to a host of famous and ordinary autistic people.

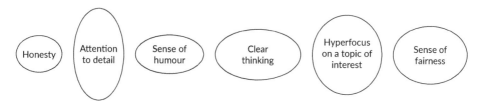

FIGURE 3.1 STRENGTHS OF AUTISM

Highlight that the strengths associated with autism may be the reason or one of the reasons that these people are so successful in their field. Their unique autistic brains allow them to see the world in many different ways, to focus on their passions and in some cases, to devote their lives to these passions.

- **Aoife Dooley** is an artist, cartoon creator and comedian. She has great visual strengths, and a unique and humorous way of looking at the world.
- **Greta Thunberg** is an environmental activist. She has used her special interest, the environment, to raise awareness of climate change on a global scale.
- **Clay Marzo** is a world-famous surfer. His intense focus on swimming and surfing enabled him to start winning national competitions from just 11 years of age.

- **Charlotte Amelia Poe** is an autistic author who says their hyperfocus helped them to write 20,000 words a day for their book.
- **Stephen Wiltshire** is an artist who draws detailed cityscapes. He often flies in a helicopter over a city, observes it briefly and draws it in detail after landing. His autism has given him an ability to pay attention to detail, and great visual skills.
- **Temple Grandin** is an animal scientist. She developed her special interest in cattle at 15 years old and has used this to become an expert on developing more humane ways to slaughter livestock.
- **Chris Packham** is a television presenter. His special interest has always been nature and the natural world, and he has channelled that into working on TV programme 'Naturewatch'.
- **Alan Gardner** is an award-winning gardener who won a silver medal at the RHS Chelsea Flower Show in 2015. He has loved gardening since he was 15 years old.
- **Alis Rowe** is an autistic author and entrepreneur. Her focus and discipline allows her to create books, videos and songs about autism awareness, as well as manage her web development company for vets.
- **Jack Monroe** is a chef and writer. She can create inspiring dishes from any ingredients, and likens her mind to a 'pocket calculator' when it comes to menu planning.
- **Naoise Dolan** is the Irish best-selling author of *Exciting Times*, who was diagnosed with autism at 27.
- **Hannah Gadsby** is a comedian, writer, actress and television presenter.

There are a whole host of autistic young people vlogging, Snapchatting or podcasting about their lives. Introduce your students to these, and to other ordinary autistic people who are simply getting on with their lives just like everybody else. Make autism even more relevant by inviting an older student to come and present to the children about his or her diagnosis.

Deep dive: Autistic strengths – A focus on details

Children love hearing about Dr Uta Frith's 'Where's Wally' experiment. Frith showed a small picture of Wally to a group of autistic people, and to one non-autistic man. She then asked them to locate Wally on a blown-up, highly-detailed poster taken directly from a 'Where's Wally' book. As predicted, the autistic people found Wally almost immediately, while the man struggled on until Frith eventually pointed him in the right direction (BBC Two – Horizon 2013–2014).

This detail-focused orientation can be a strength for many autistic people. However, it may also mean that autistic people can spend too long focusing on tiny details and miss the bigger picture altogether. This is known as the 'weak central coherence' theory (Frith 1989), which is another theory posited to explain autistic differences.

Central coherence: If you look at a picture with lots of tiny details (such as an image that contains shops, traffic, a zebra crossing, people, a lollipop lady, a group of children and a school in the background), you can usually form a general overall sense of the picture. You can get the gist of it; for example, it's going to be a story about a school set in a city.

Having central coherence means that you can quickly make sense of something, read a situation and judge the emotional tone of a room and are able to add up all the elements of a situation, and rapidly generalize to figure out what's going on. You can contextualize a situation.

However, an autistic person may zoom in on the tiniest, most irrelevant detail, and miss the key message (for example, by focusing on the lollipop lady because that is a current area of interest).

Weak central coherence: a tendency to focus on small details at the expense of seeing the bigger picture. Without the skill of being able to focus on the bigger picture, every new situation requires new thinking, there is less generalization and life can become exhausting.

In practical terms, this means that your autistic student may be over-focused on a tiny detail and miss out on what you are trying to teach them. They may find it difficult to:

- generalize what they have learned to different situations
- summarize a story
- focus on a lesson
- self-motivate
- prioritize what is important
- socialize
- have an overview of anything
- discern subtle nuances (if all of your energy is focused on generalizing and pulling the bigger picture together from tiny details, then there is no time for philosophizing)
- think in an abstract way.

But, of course, it all depends on what you are looking for. If someone is working in a job that needs local processing, rather than global processing, and a focus on the finer details, then this attention to detail is seen as a huge strength. Make sure to highlight and celebrate your student's detailed-focused skills by:

- praising them for their ability to focus at length on a topic

- showing their work to the class.

Some ways to support your student to more fully understand a task include:

- using a task checklist
- ensuring they know the lesson objective
- offering a smaller choice
- pointing out links between topics to aid generalization.

Support understanding of stories/narratives by:

- sequencing pictures of a story
- summarizing (e.g. by using 'spidergrams' or using the 'Instacollage' app on the iPad)
- repetition and over-learning of the story (e.g. read the story, watch it on YouTube, re-enact it as a puppet show, do 'Reader's Theatre' and choral reading)
- highlighting pronouns in a bid to help students know which pronouns refer to each character in the story (this is known as anaphoric cueing)
- underlining relevant information and picking out salient facts.

8. **Set up a 'school links' programme** with a special school or an autism class in your school, where small groups of students visit each other's school or classes to participate in an organized classroom or playground activity.

" Two mothers I met described how their daughters' schools had done some autism awareness work. Both daughters had arrived home after the sessions and said 'Mum, I think I might have autism'. They were grateful to school staff for opening up what was going to be a lifelong conversation about autism. "

Claire

Key points to note before doing any autism awareness work:
- Send a note or email to all parents outlining what material you will be covering.
- Send home links to video clips and information, if relevant.
- Check with the parents of your autistic students whether they would like their child to be part of the class session. Emphasize that you will never identify anyone in the class as being autistic, and that it is simply a generalized whole-school or whole-class awareness programme.
- Ensure your students who are aware of their diagnosis know that these autism awareness sessions will be taking place. Check with them if they would prefer to remain in the classroom, participate in the lesson or leave the classroom while the lesson or project is ongoing.

- Tell all students that this lesson or project is not about any student in particular, and that you will not be discussing or naming any child in the school. At the same time, be prepared for someone to put up their hand and tell everyone that they, or someone else, is autistic. If this happens, thank the student, and simply repeat the rules you outlined at the beginning of the session: 'Remember, we are not discussing anyone in this class or this school. We are talking about autism in general.'

Part 4

The Art of Communication

Communicating with Parents

> ❝ It's about the parent and teacher working well together to do their best for the child. We are all rowing the same boat. ❞

Jacinta, mother of Michael

 Parents love getting information about what their child is doing in class, as their child might not always communicate this to them. Open communication fosters a mutually supportive environment for the children and bridges the gap between home and school life. With the proliferation of modern technology, there are many methods you can use to communicate with parents. Whatever method of communication you use, always inform parents how and how often you intend to communicate with them. Figure 4.1 provides some insight into both teachers and parents' perspectives about communicating with one another.

You have to be able to tell parents difficult things regardless of what they are going to think of you. You have to gauge what is the best way to talk to some parents. It depends on personalities.

Maria, special class teacher

I spend a lot of time and energy building up a relationship of trust with parents in the beginning of the school year. I think it's totally worth it, as once you have their trust, you can do miracles.

Special class teacher

The backwards-forwards relationship between the teacher and myself made me realize how important it was what we were doing at home because it was a reinforcement of what was being done all day.

Parent

Communication varies upon the individual you are communicating with. At times it was easier. It depends on who you are dealing with.

Parent

FIGURE 4.1 QUOTES FROM TEACHERS AND PARENTS ABOUT
COMMUNICATING WITH EACH OTHER

Written communication
Regular notes or emails

" Two-way communication, daily or every second day, especially when they are young, is vital. "

Parent

 Home–school communication books or email are a suitable means of communication to keep the parents informed of:

- general practicalities
- small 'victories' and anecdotes from class, for example if the student particularly enjoyed an activity or was especially good at something
- the general demeanour of the student, in particular if it was out of the ordinary
- well-being-related issues and updates on the student's health, such as if the student hurt himself or appeared tired.

Tips when communicating with parents

- Before you decide to communicate via email, check if the parents are reading their emails regularly.
- Always email from your school email rather than a personal email account.
- Avoid educational jargon at all times.
- Ensure that there is a balance between practical messages, positive news and notes that might be perceived as more negative.
- Avoid writing sentences such as 'Johnny disrupted Circle Time.' If you really want to communicate this to Johnny's parents, write: 'Johnny sat for five minutes during Circle Time and then attempted to climb onto the windowsill.'
- Aim to be honest, objective and diplomatic at the same time. Be explicit and describe behaviour in specific terms rather than writing vague descriptions.

" Instead of writing a note that says 'Angela was in good form today', I always try to describe why a student was in good form: 'Angela sang along during Circle Time. She sat down for 20 minutes while completing her work and she laughed when a staff member mispronounced a word.' "

Annelies

- Have a sheet of paper on your desk and jot down some anecdotes about what happened during the day. This makes writing a note much easier as you have the information at hand when you sit down to write notes.
- Remember that most notes are written at the end of the day when you are,

more than likely, tired. If you are not sure about the tone of your note, read it aloud to a colleague who can give you some feedback about the clarity and feel of your note.

Weekly plan

You can give parents a general idea of what their child is doing in class in a simple but efficient way. Send home a brief weekly plan with subjects or activities that apply to every student. This avoids the need to write multiple notes about general class activities such as Art, Music, or Story Time (see Table 4.1). This weekly plan can be tied in with the home–school communication sheet mentioned in the next paragraph.

Table 4.1 Brief weekly plan for parents

Theme: The farm	
Story book	The Little Red Hen
Dance	'I've got the wiggles' 'Wag your tail'
Songs and rhymes	'Old MacDonald' 'The Animals on the Farm' 'Five Little Ducks'
Oral language	Farm animals and their young: horse/foal, pig/piglet, duck/duckling cow/calf, cat/kitten, dog/puppy, goose/gosling, etc. Farm vocabulary: field, hay, gate, tractor, trailer
Art	Paste animal figures onto template Paint a pig in the mud
Sensory play in tuff tray	Farm set sensory tray with seeds, soil, farm animals, tractors and diggers

Home–school communication sheet

A home–school communication sheet, also called home–school visual bridge (Figure 4.2), is a sheet of paper with pictures of activities the student completed in school. It is particularly useful for students who find it hard to communicate about what they did in school. Use the following steps to create the communication sheet:

1. Print out a single A4 sheet showing a variety of different activities that your students participate in throughout the school day. Ideally use images from your visual timetable as the students will be familiar with these. Store this sheet in a plastic pocket.

2. At the end of the day staff, possibly in cooperation with the students, use a whiteboard marker to circle activities done during the day.
3. The student then shows the communication sheet to his parents. Some students will use the sheet to further elaborate about their day, while others might simply point at the pictures. Each day you can wipe away the previous day's activities and reuse the sheet again.

When the home–school communication sheet and weekly plan are used together, parents have much more information about what is happening in class and they will be able to ask their child more specific questions about their day. For example, when story time is marked on the communication sheet, parents can cross-check this with the weekly plan and identify that the story in question was called *The Little Red Hen*. They can then talk to their child about this book or read the story with them at home.

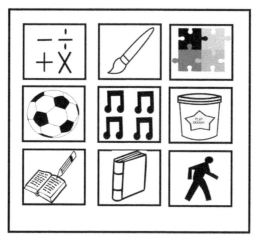

FIGURE 4.2 HOME–SCHOOL COMMUNICATION SHEET

Digital portfolios and class blogs

Many schools compile hard copy portfolios that contain samples of students' work throughout the year, which are then sent home at the end of the year. A digital portfolio is exactly the same, but stores photos in online applications such as Dropbox, Google Drive, Seesaw or ClassDojo. A digital portfolio has many advantages:

- Parents receive regular updates of their child's work rather than receiving one paper portfolio at the end of the year.
- It is particularly useful for students who might not have a lot of written work.
- It is environmentally friendly as it reduces the amount of printing.

- You can easily top up your students' portfolios by regularly uploading photos or you can teach your students how to do this under your supervision.

Class blogs go a step further as they have the possibility to connect the class with the wider world. Not only do students develop a wider range of IT skills, but a class blog can also help them to learn about responsible digital citizenship.

 Check with parents if they are happy that their child features in a photo that is shared with other parents. Also ensure that you follow the data protection laws of your country and region.

Leaflet

Providing parents with an information booklet or leaflet about the school and the class in particular can be very helpful. An A to Z format provides a structured and nice layout while acquainting parents with the routines of the class and school. (See Appendix 7 for an A to Z information leaflet template for parents.)

Verbal communication

66 I remember that one day I collected Ben and he had a bit of a moment. I remember his teacher saying 'Ben this is not how we speak. We cannot help you until you calm down.' It was the tone and the language she used... I learned that I can do this at home too. I used that exact same sentence the next time it happened and it worked. We were so afraid of pushing him too far. I was really thinking: 'Are we being unfair? Are we expecting too much from him?' It was brilliant to see someone who had a bit of expertise in the area to see what he could do and then I thought: 'I can do this.' 99

Parent of Ben

Information evening

Providing parents with information about how the classroom is organized and what strategies are used helps them to become part of the school community and ensures that they can support their children through their school days. The best way for parents to get to know what happens in class is to simply show them. During an information evening, include a slideshow with photos and video clips of students engaged in classroom activities.

Note: Seek parental permission before taking and showing any videos or photos of your students, and make sure to follow data protection laws.

Voice messages

Voice notes are a great way to send brief messages to parents and save an incredible amount of time. Using a voice recording app on your phone or the class iPad allows you to send practical reminders and short anecdotes about the day in a fast and efficient way.

Phone calls

Lately, Josh, 10, was reluctant to do any work or activity in school. The class teacher had mentioned this a few times in the home–school communication sheet. However, he had not received a response from Josh's parents in relation to this issue. He decided to phone Josh's mother and he found out that Josh had been having sleep difficulties over the past few weeks. Just before going to bed, Josh was re-hashing anything that had gone wrong for him during the day. The class teacher suggested that Josh's parents could discuss his day with him straight after dinner. He suggested that they stick to a bed-time routine and possibly read a story before bed to distract Josh from over-focusing on things that went wrong earlier that day. He told them he would contact them again in a week's time and discussed the possibility of a meeting to further discuss this issue.

When an issue is of a more sensitive nature, making a phone call to parents is always preferable. Because of their two-way nature, phone calls have the following advantages:

- You immediately get a better picture of what is happening at home.
- Actively engaging in a dialogue with parents helps you to find a solution together.
- You prevent any possible miscommunication and find a solution faster rather than waiting for a scheduled meeting.

" If possible, I prefer speaking to parents face-to-face rather than making a phone call. If it's only something small, I try to have a quick chat with them when they are collecting their child at home time. "

Jessica, special class teacher

Meetings

Please see Guide 45: Meetings for more specifics.

Apart from planned IEP meetings (Guide 51: Individual Education Plans goes into more depth on these) you might need to organize additional meetings if your previous methods of communication have not been successful in solving a specific situation with a student. If you have concerns that there might be a misunderstanding or need to exchange ideas and perspectives, organize a meeting straight away.

A face-to-face meeting provides plenty of opportunities for discussion and brainstorming. Following a meeting to discuss a difficult situation, always plan a follow-up meeting to report progress and good news.

Guide 45

Meetings

Meetings are a fantastic opportunity for parents and teachers to exchange information, concerns and ideas. A well-planned meeting can provide a safe and respectful platform for both the teacher and parents to work together to prioritize the needs of the child. An NCSE research report revealed that newly qualified teachers felt underprepared for working collaboratively with parents (NCSE 2019a).

Preparing for a meeting

" It would really help if parents could get an agenda before the meeting. It gives them the chance to prepare for the meeting. "

Aoife, parent

- Before the meeting takes place, spend some time thinking about what might happen in the meeting and anticipate what questions and key issues might come up.
- Create an agenda with points you would like to discuss and send this agenda to parents and other participants a few days before the meeting.
- Ask your principal, another teacher or classroom staff to accompany you if you would like to be supported during a meeting. If necessary, organize someone to take minutes of the meeting.
- Meet somewhere comfortable, for example in your principal's office. If you have the meeting in your classroom, have adult-sized chairs and tables.
- If possible, have some biscuits, coffee, tea or water in the room.
- Write down a few anecdotes that illustrate your observations about the student. Bring some work samples too, if relevant.

During the meeting
Start of the meeting

" I suffer from massive anxiety and nervousness, at the thought of going into school to discuss anything about my child. I feel the same anxiety that someone would feel going for a first interview in five years. "

Parent

- Greet everybody and shake hands.
- Put a time limit on the meeting. After greetings, say 'We have until about 12 p.m. today, which should give us plenty of time.'
- Start the meeting by discussing the child's strengths, or tell a funny anecdote. This will help to put everyone at ease.
- Ensure that you check in with parents throughout the meeting and ask for their thoughts about key points. O'Byrne (2018) found that at times, teachers tend to talk more during parent–teacher meetings, leaving less time for parental input.

Self-awareness

❝ I think that teachers need to have a sense of their own issues. They need to have an idea of who they are themselves, so they don't react when parents are having a meltdown and respond in the same way. ❞

Jacinta, mother of Michael

Be aware of how you are feeling in the moment and how you respond to parents' questions or statements. As well as being in charge of what will be discussed during the meeting, you might also need to be prepared to deal with conflict if it arises.

Awareness of parents' perspective

It is important to consider how parents feel about attending meetings (see Figure 4.3).

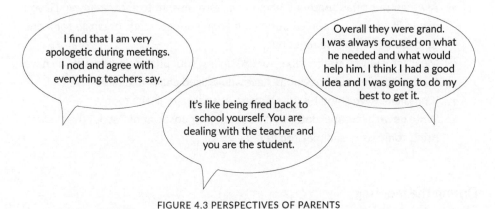

FIGURE 4.3 PERSPECTIVES OF PARENTS

- Be friendly and warm but professional at the same time. Parents often prefer a 'personal touch' rather than a professional–client relationship (Lindl 1989).
- Avoid using jargon and explain any necessary terminology such as sensory needs, reward system, TEACCH®, IEP or work basket system.

- Be aware that parents might be nervous about meeting you or be influenced by their own past school experiences. They might be frustrated about a previous, completely unrelated encounter, or they may be afraid of not being heard. All of these external factors can influence the way they communicate with you.
- Be aware that the student you are discussing, analyzing and commenting on is their child.
- Try to find a way to praise parents for all of their effort and hard work. It is usually much appreciated.
- Be aware that how you are feeling can show through in your body language. Try to insert some humour if appropriate.
- Demonstrate to parents that you understand their child, you are trying your very best for their child and that you are going to work together to come up with some new strategies for their child.

Having productive meetings

- Try to stick to the agenda. If things are veering off topic, gently steer everyone back by referring to the agenda.
- Allow time for parents to provide you with information or ask questions. Check in regularly with parents throughout the meeting and ask them open questions to bridge any reluctance they might have to talk. Avoid waiting until the end to ask parents about their perspectives, as you might run out of time.
- If you cannot think of an answer immediately simply say 'I'll have to check that and get back to you.'
- Only promise what you can deliver and what is in your power to control.
- Generate an action plan as a result of the meeting with clear, achievable targets. Ensure everybody knows who is responsible for each part of the plan.
- Set a date for a review meeting. This can be very reassuring for parents and shows your clear commitment to progressing with the action plan.

Having difficult conversations

Remember that some conversations are difficult for both the teacher and the parent. You might be feeling nervous or, due to a variety of reasons, a parent can arrive stressed, tired or frustrated. By keeping the following tips in mind, an otherwise difficult conversation can actually turn into a constructive discussion about the student.

'If you want the parent to listen to you, begin by listening to him. If you want him to acknowledge your point, acknowledge his first' (Ury 1991 in Gorman 2004, p.57).

- Try to think about the possible emotions in the room; stress, fear, exhaustion, defensiveness, exasperation and frustration with the system may all be present.
- Stay calm, be kind, remain positive and demonstrate active listening skills.
- Take deep breaths and take your time answering any difficult questions.
- Try not to take anything personally. Avoid picking up on the energy of the other person if they are feeling upset. Make an effort to remain as calm as possible.
- Stay focused on the issue being discussed rather than allowing the conversation to digress into unrelated points.
- Involve parents in coming up with solutions.
- Sometimes it is useful to suggest to take a quick break or to simply move on from a particular point by saying 'I think we should move on to the next point, but I will be sure to consider this and get back to you about it at a later stage.'

Displaying active listening skills

Use the SOLER technique (O'Brien 2016) to ensure parents are put at ease by your body language and by demonstrating active listening skills. SOLER is a technique that is used frequently by counsellors and social workers when talking to clients. It stands for:

- **S**quare posture: Your way of sitting should always show active involvement, whether you choose to sit square across from a parent or slightly angled.
- **O**pen position: Display openness through your posture and avoid crossed arms, as this comes across as defensive.
- **L**ean in: Slightly leaning towards the other person communicates interest and empathy.
- **E**ye contact: Maintaining a healthy and appropriate level eye contact shows that you are listening and attentive.
- **R**elax: Appearing relaxed makes the parent immediately more comfortable.

After the meeting

" There have been times that I went home after a meeting and cried about it. I was angry with myself for having said something and not having said something else. "

Parent

- Avoid focusing on the one critical question that parents might have asked you (Delaney 2017). Remind yourself that a parent is the primary caregiver of their child and that it is part of their duty to advocate for their child, raise concerns or ask questions when they are worried.

- Take some time for yourself after the meeting if you need it. Pop out to the toilet or to the staff room if it is quiet. After work, try to put aside what happened and do something relaxing (See ⚷ Guide 65: Three Things Staff Can Do After an Event for more ideas on this.)
- Follow up on any key points. Send the action plan and promised resources to parents, share the new strategies and ideas with your class team and make the relevant resources and begin to use them as soon as possible.

Guide 46

Staff Working Together

66 Alone we can do so little, together we can do so much. 99

Helen Keller

 Inevitably, when people are working together, there are differences of opinion, differences in personality or approach and errors in communication. Having a strong team in which every member of staff feels valued and supported brings out the best in everyone, staff and students alike.

Teamwork

66 The most important thing is that you treat staff as equals. You are in charge, but it's really important to listen to and take on board the views and opinions of the staff you are working with. 99

Maria, special class teacher

- When designing your class timetable, try to play to the strengths of each staff member. You might have a member in your team who is very artistic or musical, has fantastic IT skills or has a knack for organizing. Not only will the task be done better than you could ever imagine but you are giving staff the opportunity to use their talents, leading to job satisfaction for everyone.
- Actively ask staff for their observations and opinions about what is going on in the classroom.
- Create a warm atmosphere in your classroom where both students and staff feel respected and accepted. Even though things can be quite busy in a classroom and the students' needs should take priority at all times, pick a moment in the day when you can check in with each other.
- The more the staff team is involved and is aware of what is going on, the more interested and motivated they are. Give them access to your planning and resources and discuss what you plan to do in the short and long term.
- Remind yourself that it is in everyone's best interest to work together as a team to support and teach the students. Put effort in creating a strong team bond and fostering morale.

Managing emotions

" I think when there is a conflict, it is important to try to take all the personalities out of it and focus on coming to a resolution. "

Teacher

- If conflict of any sort arises, nip it in the bud before it starts accumulating and takes on a life of its own.
- Be honest. Nobody is perfect. If you feel under pressure, or have said something in a way you fear might have come across differently than you intended, discuss this straight away.
- When you are presented with challenging situations in the classroom, emotions tend to run higher and opinions can grow stronger. Take time to listen to everyone's perspectives.
- If you are confronted with a disagreement between staff members, remind yourself that conflict often arises because everyone has the best interests of the students at heart.
- Aim to keep any disagreements within the classroom. Be vigilant of involving a number of colleagues; you only add a myriad of opinions and potentially spread the conflict.

Self-awareness

" When you go into a class as a new teacher, it's a bit like a principal starting in a new school. You can't just uproot everything. You need to rely on the staff that's already there. You have to tread carefully, but at the same time, staff have to respect that you are in charge. You just have to find the balance. "

Maria, special class teacher

- Regardless of your role in class, ask if you are unsure about something. Don't let your pride get in the way. Listen and learn. Whether you are a newly qualified teacher or a highly experienced teacher, we all can learn from one another.
- Be self-aware when bringing up an issue. Be conscious of your tone and try to remain calm. If you bring up a tricky issue, rehearse what you would like to say.

Team meetings

" I believe most problems are due to people not taking the time to listen to each other. "

Teacher

- Use your team meetings to check in with everyone and genuinely ask for everyone's contributions.
- Spend time discussing the rationale behind a particular approach you have decided to use with a student. If staff understand where you are coming from, they are more likely to be on board with what you are trying to do.

Part 5

The Special Class

❝ You forget that sometimes it's about changing the environment and the behaviours suddenly change then. ❞

Special class teacher

During the school year, you and your students spend a significant amount of time in the classroom. The classroom is the students' safe space. It is the place where they learn, interact, master new skills and grow. Putting thought and effort into setting up your classroom will pay off in so many ways. A good start for designing your special classroom is to familiarize yourself with the strategies of the TEACCH® Autism Program. Its key strategies are a clear physical organization of the classroom, individual visual work schedules, organized work systems and a clear visual structure of the task (Mesibov, Howley and Naftel 2016). By providing a visual and structured teaching approach, you are providing a predictable environment that promotes communication, understanding, learning and independence.

The guides in Part 5 provide further exploration of these strategies.

Guide 47

🧠 Physical Set-Up and Layout

A clear physical structure is one of the key components of a structured teaching approach. Creating a low-arousal environment and organizing the classroom into clear areas that each have a specific purpose will benefit the students in the following ways:

- More predictability: 'I know where I need to go for each activity and what I am supposed to do.'
- Increased independence: 'I move around the classroom confidently with minimal support.'
- Improved concentration: 'I have a space with no distractions where I can concentrate on my work.'
- Reduced chance of experiencing sensory overload: 'My classroom is calm and I am calm.'

Julian used to attend a mainstream preschool. The room was small and most materials were stored in open boxes on shelves within the children's reach. Julian spent his day going from one box of toys to another, leaving a trail of toys behind him. Sometimes he joined Story Time or Circle Time, but if he was too engaged in his play, he continued playing alone.

When Julian started in an early intervention class for autistic children, the class teacher ensured that unused equipment remained out of sight. Classroom materials were put on shelf cabinets on wheels turned towards the wall. Julian's teacher also made sure that each space in the room had a particular function that was clearly labelled. With the support of a schedule and a clearly organized classroom, Julian stopped browsing and engaged in class activities, as he now understood where he was supposed to be and what he was supposed to do.

💡 Areas in your classroom

Depending on the needs of the students, organize the following areas in your room:

- a play area where students engage in free play or can do an activity of choice
- a group area where students engage in group activities such as Art, Music, Circle Time or Story Time
- a lunch time area where students eat their lunch
- individual workstations where students complete their individual work

- a quiet area or quiet room where students can take a break from the busy classroom
- a teaching desk where you can teach students individually
- a transition area where students check their schedule
- a possible outdoor area adjacent to the classroom.

Organization of classroom areas

" I have taught children who couldn't cope with open space. I had to lay out the classroom in a way that there wasn't too much free space. Furniture needed to be placed with a lot of thought. "

Bláthnaid, special class teacher

Equipment
You can use visuals, furniture, dividers or coloured tape to distinguish between different areas in the classroom.

Function of classroom areas
Be consistent in the area you use for each subject, as this provides students with much needed predictability. For example, always use the same area for Story Time, Maths, individual work, etc.

However, this does not necessarily mean that you need to have a separate area for each subject. The group area, for example, can be used for a multitude of group activities such as Circle Time, lunch time, Music and Art, as long as they don't clash on your timetable.

If necessary, use a visual or an object to indicate the purpose of the area at that time. For example, a picture depicting 'lunch' or placemats positioned on the table can be used to show that the table is now used for lunch.

Distractions and clutter

- Keep desks away from windows or other potentially distracting features, such as the computer or interactive whiteboard.
- Keep displays and artwork to a minimum and within designated areas. Avoid banners or displays that span the length of the room.
- Keep windowsills free from clutter. Windowsills are usually situated low to the ground and the open space can tempt students to browse.

- Store resources, as much as possible, out of sight (see ⊕ Appendix 8 for a list of resources and equipment that might be useful).

Three-year-old Olive had lots of energy. She loved running across the classroom, jumping on and off tables and squeezing herself through some of the dividers. To encourage Olive to engage with what was happening in the classroom, her class teacher rearranged the location of some of the dividers so there was less opportunity to go in between them. She also moved the sand table and the sensory play table to a room adjacent to the classroom. Any tables that remained in the classroom were moved away from the windowsill to discourage Olive from jumping from one to the other.

Creative workarounds

It is rare that you start off with a perfect, purpose-built room. You may have to work creatively with whatever space you are given. For example, if you do not have access to a quiet room but require a quiet space, setting up a tent or playhouse inside the room can also work well.

Examples of classroom layouts

It is important to remember that no two classrooms look the same and that there is no one-size-fits-all approach to organizing your classroom. The amount of structure needed depends both on the needs of the students and on the supports available to you. Figure 5.1 and Figure 5.3 show examples of two different classroom layouts.

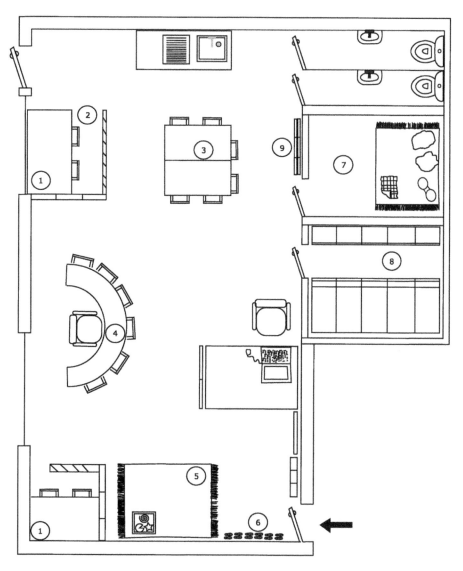

FIGURE 5.1 CLASSROOM LAYOUT 1

1. As all students in this class are able to learn in a group, there are only two individual workstations. These individual workstations are located as far as possible from each other to keep noise distraction to a minimum.
2. The individual workstations are mainly used for one-to-one reading, differentiated maths activities or oral language. They are separated by shelves and a divider.
3. The teacher opted for a square group table rather than a round group table to maximize space during group activities.
4. Both the horseshoe table and the square table are used for group activities. However, each table is associated with certain subjects. At the horseshoe table the students engage in circle time, concrete maths work, story time, Science and Geography. The square table is used for lunch time and Art.
5. As this is a class for young children, there is a large play area, which is demarcated by a carpet.
6. The laminated footprints by the door act as a visual support that shows the students where and how to line up.
7. The quiet room is a chill-out zone where students can browse through books on beanbags. Books are stored on high shelves.
8. The store cupboard stores all materials not in use such as toys, jigsaw puzzles and all other class resources.
9. Resources that are used frequently throughout the week are stored in baskets on shelves (see Figure 5.2).

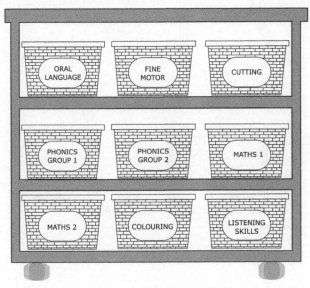

FIGURE 5.2 STORAGE SYSTEM FOR MATERIALS USED ON A DAILY BASIS

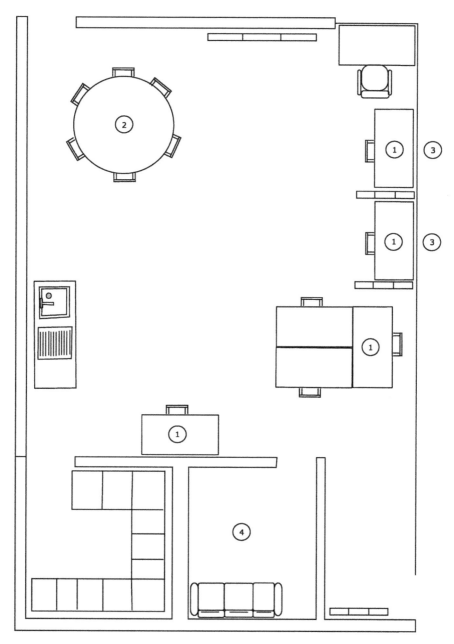

FIGURE 5.3 CLASSROOM LAYOUT 2

1. Each student has their own permanent workstation. Three students each have an individual workstation while three other students complete their work at workstations that are grouped together.
2. The needs of the students in this group vary significantly. Therefore, the students only meet as a whole group at the round table at lunch time.
3. Due to a lack of wall space, most of the individual workstations face windows. To limit potential distractions, the teacher has put a matte vinyl window sticker on the lower half of the windows, which still allows light to come in.
4. Some of the older students enjoy listening to music in the quiet room.

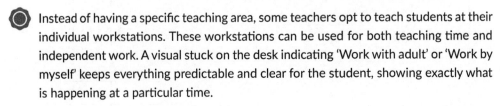 Instead of having a specific teaching area, some teachers opt to teach students at their individual workstations. These workstations can be used for both teaching time and independent work. A visual stuck on the desk indicating 'Work with adult' or 'Work by myself' keeps everything predictable and clear for the student, showing exactly what is happening at a particular time.

Choosing your own classroom

If you are lucky enough to be able to choose the location of your classroom in your school, it may be useful to consider the following questions:

- How much space do you need?
- What age are the students in your class? What age are the students in adjoining classrooms?
- Do you require access to toilets in your own classroom or is it sufficient to have toilets close to your room?
- Are some of the students inclined to abscond or be quite loud at times?
- Does the room have potentially distracting elements such as windows, other classes passing through or a view of the playground or road? Can you hear noise from adjoining classrooms or from outside that might be distracting for your students?
- Would you like to be close to the hall, school yard or other facilities?
- How often do your students join other classes? Consider the proximity to the classes they will be joining.
- Would you prefer to be in the centre of the school?

Guide 48

🧠 Workstations, Work Systems and Routines

FIGURE 5.4 A DISORGANIZED WORK SYSTEM

FIGURE 5.5 A WELL-ORGANIZED WORK SYSTEM

Compare both desks and try to imagine how you would feel being in either of these situations. Imagine what it would feel like to be the person in Figure 5.4: knowing that you have to get through what feels like a mountain of work every day in a busy and noisy environment. You feel dread and resentment towards the tasks and possibly towards the person who gave you the assignment. It is also unclear what will happen after you complete your tasks. The person in Figure 5.5 has a quiet workstation and a clear work system in place that helps him to get through his work fast and efficiently.

A well-organized workstation and consistent work system really helps students to complete tasks in a calm and relaxed manner.

Leonie, 9, loved a varied schedule and had a tendency to move quickly from activity to activity. As a result, she often became restless, which made it hard for her to concentrate on the task at hand. Her teacher set up an individual workstation, with dividers on both sides and to the back. This created a low-arousal environment with minimal distractions. She put three work baskets on the workstation shelves, with work inside each basket for Leonie to complete. This helped Leonie to easily understand that she was expected to complete these three baskets before she could check her schedule and move on to another activity. Using this system, Leonie was able to do two work sessions per day. Very soon, Leonie's workstation area became her safe space where she happily returned to throughout the day.

Individual workstations

Figure 5.6 shows an example of an individual workstation. A workstation usually consists of:

1. a table
2. dividers, which can be screen dividers or shelving units
3. work materials set up according to your preferred work system
4. a place to store finished materials.

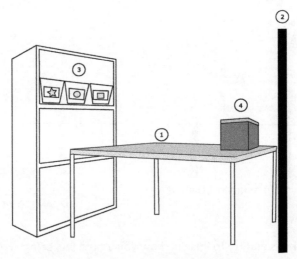

FIGURE 5.6 AN INDIVIDUAL WORKSTATION

An individual workstation is set up in a quiet part of the classroom, away from possible distractions such as windows, doors, screens, displays or noise. In time and if appropriate, the workstation can gradually be 'opened up' by taking away a divider or shelving unit.

Work systems

A work system is a structured way of organizing and setting up a student's work. A good work system gives the student four pieces of information (Mesibov and Howley 2003):

- What work do I need to do?
- How much work do I need to do?
- How can I tell that I am finished?
- What will I do next?

A work system is always organized from left to right or top to bottom (see Figure 5.7).

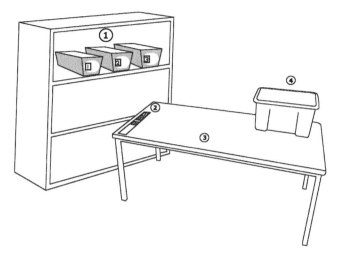

FIGURE 5.7 A WORK SYSTEM

1. **work to do**
   placed to the left of the table*. Work can be placed in:
   - plastic baskets on a shelf
   - a drawer unit with pull-out drawers
   - a document tray for worksheets or books.

   *If you don't have room on the left side you can also place the baskets in front of the student organized in a left-to-right manner.
2. **visual matching cards.**
3. **work being completed** placed on the table in front of the student.
4. **completed work placed**
   - on a visual indicating 'finished'
   - In an actual 'finished work box'
   - on a shelving unit.

Specifically teach a work system to your student to ensure that your student understands what is expected of him, especially when using a system that involves independent work. Your student should feel confident and motivated to navigate the system independently before you expect him to complete work independently.

Set up your work system so that your student progresses through his work in the following sequence:

1. The student matches the top matching card to the left basket on the shelf (Figure 5.8).

257

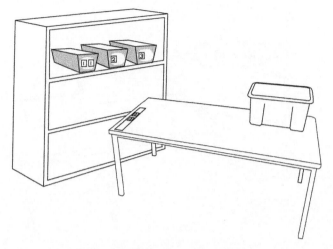

FIGURE 5.8 WORK SYSTEM STEP 1

2. The student places the basket on the table and takes out the work materials. The student then completes the work (Figure 5.9).

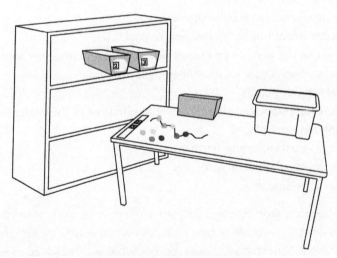

FIGURE 5.9 WORK SYSTEM STEP 2

3. When the task is completed, the student places the work materials back in the basket and places the whole basket in the finished area to the right (Figure 5.10).

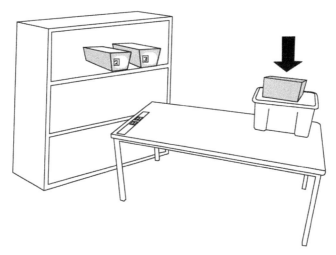

FIGURE 5.10 WORK SYSTEM STEP 3

4. The student matches the middle matching card to the middle basket, completes work and places it in the finished area (Figure 5.11).

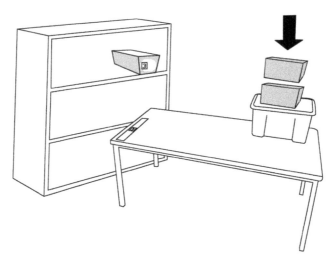

FIGURE 5.11 WORK SYSTEM STEP 4

5. Finally, the student matches the bottom matching card to the last remaining basket, which is the basket on the far right. The student completes the work and places completed work into the finished area (Figure 5.12)

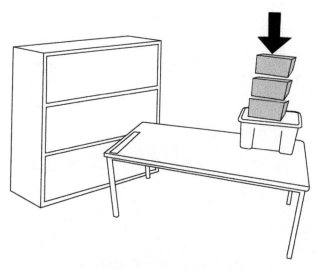

FIGURE 5.12 WORK SYSTEM STEP 5

6. Ensure that you have a system in place so the student knows what is next. For example, the student might check his schedule or get access to a favoured activity.

Foster independence

Always encourage your student to navigate the work system as independently as possible. This gives him control of his learning and builds confidence. Students can take ownership through completing the following tasks independently:

- matching the visual cards
- placing the basket on the table or opening the drawer
- taking out the work materials
- completing the task
- putting away the materials.

Tailor the work system

You can tailor the system to your own preference as long as you lay out everything in a visually clear and consistent manner.

- You can place the baskets at a distance from the workstation for students who need a movement break between tasks, provided it does not disrupt the student's work rhythm.
- You can use work systems in multiple ways: when teaching students new concepts or to complete independent work.

- Use a visual support to show a student whether he is expected to work independently or with an adult. You can also make this really clear by slightly altering the layout of the workstation by changing the colour of the baskets and corresponding matching cards or working with drawers rather than baskets.
- Select your learning materials carefully and make them as appealing as possible so the student wants to come to the workstation. Learning objectives can be accomplished through a wide variety of resources.
- Start with a highly motivating task if the student is reluctant to engage in tabletop work.

Four-year old Jack wasn't keen on any activity that required him to sit down. The minute he checked his schedule and saw the 'Work with adult' symbol, he dropped to the ground. To gain Jack's interest, his class teacher put one of his favourite activities, a shape inset jigsaw, in the first basket. Soon, Jack was much more interested in coming to his work desk.

Take the next step

Some teachers progress to working with one work basket that holds all the work the student needs to complete in a work session.

Other options include working with a checklist (see Figure 5.13) and corresponding work materials. The student ticks the completed work off the list as he progresses through the work.

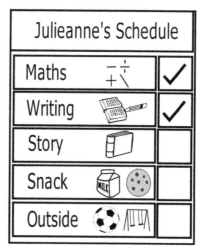

FIGURE 5.13 VISUAL CHECKLIST

 Use your student's interests to create visual matching cards: numbers, shapes, favourite TV characters or other special interest pictures.

Routines

66 Anything around having a routine was just a game changer. We could so clearly see a marked difference straight away. 99

Parent

 Class routines provide predictability and stability for your students. They help your students to understand what is happening in class, what they are supposed to do and how they are supposed to complete the task at hand. Once students are familiar with a particular routine, they will become more efficient at it and feel more confident.

Important class routines include:

- what to do when arriving in class, i.e. the morning routine
- what to do when finished work
- how to check the schedule
- what to do when returning back to class
- which classroom jobs need to be done
- how to know there will be a change in the timetable
- how to get ready to go home, i.e. afternoon routine.

See Guide 56: Teaching Daily Living Skills for guidance on how to teach routines to your students.

Guide 49

Timetables

 Everybody needs structure to their day, both adults and children. Everyone needs to know what is happening and when things are happening. It creates a calmness in the class. "

Bláthnaid, special class teacher

In a special class, your timetable is key. It provides a much-needed structure and acts as a reliable and comforting navigation system for both staff and students throughout the day. After all, everyone functions much better when there is a clear and established routine. Spending a few weeks figuring out your timetable at the start of the year will make the rest of the school year much easier.

A work in progress

You don't need to wait to devise your timetable until you have all school timetables. Start from the very first day by following these steps:

1. Write out a schedule for the first day. Observe what works and what doesn't work for each pupil and for the class as a whole. Adjust your schedule for the next day accordingly.
2. Observe which students work well together and how much support your students need during different lessons. More than likely, each student will need varying levels of support throughout the day.
3. Add lessons outside the classroom to your timetable as they become available, such as hall times, sensory room times or computer room times.
4. Continue altering this schedule until you have a schedule tailored to your students' needs.
5. Don't hesitate to alter your timetable at any stage during the year, in particular when you feel that your students' attention span and needs for support or breaks has changed.

 Some points to consider when devising a timetable:

- Is there a good balance between whole-class, small-group and individual activities?
- Are the time slots you allocated to each lesson realistic for your students?

For some students, lessons might have to be as short as ten minutes. Often you will be able to increase this as the year progresses.

- Is your timetable making the most out of support staff available to you?
- Is there enough staff support available during lessons you have planned? Take staff breaks into account. Plan group activities that require a minimum of staff input at these times. Also, if snack and lunch times are busy, schedule them outside staff break times.
- Don't be afraid to think outside the box. A special class is different from a mainstream class. Students don't necessarily have to do the same curriculum subject at the same time.
- While it is essential to have a clear structure every day, it can be a good idea to vary each day slightly to avoid an exact repetition of the previous day. This usually happens automatically when you are designing your timetable, as you might not have Music, P.E. or Art every day. While meeting your students' need for predictability and structure, you are also working on their ability to follow their schedule and cope with change.
- Ensure your afternoon timetable is less intense than the morning timetable as your students might find it much harder to concentrate in the afternoon.

“ One year, the needs of my students were so varied that I had to use all my creative thinking to construct a timetable that met all of their needs. This meant that I had to organize access to another room in the school, which we named the Rainbow Room. At different times throughout the day, the class was split up: while three students did Maths in class, three other students participated in Story Time in the Rainbow Room. Each activity was linked to either the classroom or the Rainbow Room so the students knew exactly what was happening. ”

Annelies

 Decide whether it is easier for you and class staff to navigate a daily, weekly, individual or group timetable. Each type of timetable has its own advantages. It all depends how much is going on in class and how you like to visualize your day.

See Appendix 9 for an example of a daily timetable in which it is clearly visible what each pupil does on that particular day. Appendix 10 provides a template for your use.

An example of a weekly class timetable can be found in Appendix 11, and you can find a template in Appendix 12.

- Ensure your timetable makes sense to whoever is setting up the students' schedules for the next day.
- Colour code slots when students leave the classroom to join their mainstream classes. This will be particularly useful when you have students attending different classes.

Planning

> " When planning is done right, it's worth doing. You get the most out of everyone. "
>
> *Special class teacher*

Your planning sets out what you want to achieve on a daily basis and where you want to go in the short term and long term. As a special class teacher, Individual Education Plans (IEPs) form an essential part of your planning (see 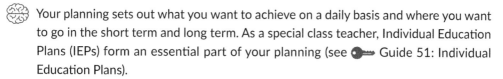 Guide 51: Individual Education Plans).

With regards to the planning format, most teachers are required to follow the guidelines stipulated by their own school or country. However, all teachers have some form of daily planning, short-term planning and long-term planning, as well as a review or evaluation of their planning. There are some particular aspects to keep in mind when planning for your students.

Long-term planning

Long-term planning can mean termly or yearly planning and indicates the general idea of what you would like your students to achieve.

Tips for long-term planning in a special class:

- Don't put yourself under pressure to have a long-term plan ready during the first month of the school year. Wait until you have a good picture of your students' long-term learning needs.
- As a long-term plan generally does not need to be very detailed, it can save a lot of time to use the goals that are set out in the curriculum in your long-term plan.

Make a list of all the non-curricular tasks you teach your students, such as daily living skills, social skills or organizational skills, and include them in your planning. It is easy to forget to include these non-curricular goals that are equally important for your students' development.

Short-term planning

Short-term planning can be weekly, fortnightly or monthly. It is usually much more specific than long-term planning.

" Every September, regardless of what class level I have, I always start with the theme 'myself and my family'. It's a nice, general theme, that usually works for everyone. It allows me to get to know the children in my class, it's easy to differentiate and it's a familiar topic for the children to relate to. "

Maria, special class teacher

Tips to support your short-term planning:

- Before the start of the school year, decide on a theme for the first few weeks and plan your lessons and activities around it. Realistically, this plan will change a lot as you get to know the students, but it gives you a good starting point.
- There are lots of sample planning templates available online. Rather than reinventing the wheel, select a template that you find useful and alter it, if allowed, to suit your needs.
- One useful way of altering a generic short-term plan to suit the needs of your special class is by inserting tables into your plan with the names of the students on top. This allows for differentiation without the plan becoming too long or wordy. (See ⬇ Appendices 13 and 14.)
- Your short-term planning can be either a whole-class plan, a plan for a group of students or an individual plan. (See ⬇ Appendix 15 for an example of an individual fortnightly plan and Appendix 16 for a template you can use.)

Reviewing your plan

Save time by using the same document for both your planning and your review. You can simply add a tick box to the document and allow space for additional comments. (See 🔑 Appendix 13.)

✓ When making a plan, keep the following in mind:

- If your plan is not informing your day-to-day practice, change it to make it work for you. Ensure your plan is actually guiding you rather than it only being additional paperwork.
- Always start from the academic level your students are currently at, without focusing too much on age-expected levels.
- Pay equal attention to achieving both curricular goals and non-curricular goals.

 It is likely that your students might be functioning at a variety of academic levels for different subjects (See 🔑 Guide 54: Tailoring the Curriculum). Making a table showing each students' level per subject will provide you with a clear overview, not to mention being a very useful tool to pass on to other professionals (see Table 5.1).

Table 5.1 Curricular levels of students in a special class

Subject	Student A	Student B	Student C	Student D	Student E
English					
Maths					
Science					
Geography					
History					
Art					
Music					
Physical Education					

Individual Education Plans

66 Plan your work and work your plan. 99

Napoleon Hill

 'I am going to be healthier this year' or 'This year, I am going to save more money' are examples of long-term goals that you might set for yourself on the first of January. In order to achieve your main goal, you will possibly create some short-term targets to keep yourself on track.

You might decide to:

- attend fitness classes three times per week
- bring your own lunch to work
- allow yourself a treat only on a Friday night.

Just like your New Year's resolution is personal to you, an Individual Education Plan is specifically designed for each student. It contains a set of yearly goals, which are then broken up into various short-term targets.

There are a number of steps involved in creating an IEP for your student (see Figure 5.14).

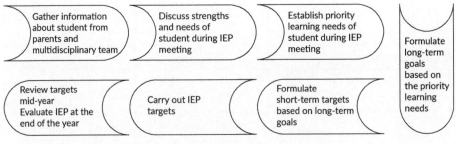

FIGURE 5.14 STEPS IN THE IEP PROCESS

Information gathering

66 IEPs are important because they are the link with home. Parents need to play a role in their child's education because they are the primary educators. 99

Special class teacher

Gather as much information as possible about the student before the IEP meeting. You can do this by:

- finding out your student's hopes and dreams for the year ahead and incorporating these into the plan
- asking your student what he would like to focus on this year
- meeting with the class team to get their perspective on the student's progress, strengths and needs
- sending out a questionnaire to parents through which they can share their opinions and ideas about their child (see ⊕ Appendix 17)
- acquiring information from members of the multidisciplinary team
- collating assessment tests, checklists, work samples and observations of the student.

Person-centred planning (PCP)

Person-centred planning is about listening to the voice of your student. It ensures that you always take the needs, wishes and desires of your students, their parents and their family into account whenever you make a plan about them. PCP plays to your students' strengths while also focusing on their needs.

PCP embodies the important ethos of 'Nothing about us without us' for your students.

The IEP meeting

At a minimum, the parents of the student and the teacher should be present at the meeting. The special needs coordinator, the principal, support staff and members of the multidisciplinary team might also be present.

As there is usually a lot to discuss during an IEP meeting, it is useful to have an agenda to keep the meeting as structured and productive as possible:

1. Welcome parents and explain the IEP process briefly.
2. Discuss the strengths and talents of the student and possibly record them on a flipchart.
3. Discuss the student's needs and record them next to the strengths on the flipchart.
4. Look at the identified needs and select priority learning needs for the upcoming school year.
5. Discuss parental involvement.
6. Establish a review date.

Sometimes a student can be present at some or all of the IEP meeting. For example, the student may be present for the 'celebrating strengths' part, showcase a portfolio of work or present a video clip made about her time in class. If possible and appropriate the student can also be involved in setting targets for herself.

Strengths and needs

Table 5.2 shows an example of Berfin's strengths and needs recorded during the IEP meeting.

Table 5.2 Record of Berfin's strengths and needs

Strengths	Needs
Has a great memory. Is a visual learner. Has a bubbly personality. Has a wide range of interests. Is motivated by rewards. Understands and copes with the use of a sand timer. Has excellent fine motor skills. Can read well. Has begun to seek interaction from peers. Is very musical, loves to dance. Is very creative, in particular when doing art. Has a great imagination when playing with toys. Is getting better at expressing what she needs. Is very gentle and friendly natured. Loves praise.	To walk independently around the school without running away. To do worksheets or activities that don't appeal as much. To concentrate for longer periods of time. To persevere when she finds a task difficult. To wait quietly. Neater handwriting. To participate in group activities. To work independently for more than five minutes.

Interests
Dress-up clothes, masks, pretend play, free drawing, Peppa Pig, puppets, stickers, colouring books, cycling, going for walks

Priority learning needs

During the IEP meeting, a collaborative decision is made which needs will be prioritized during the upcoming school year. When establishing the priority learning needs, take following factors into account (National Council for Special Education 2006):

- the student's current level of performance

- the student's strengths, interests and motivation
- the urgency and relevance of some of the student's needs
- the student's rate of learning.

 The student's strengths or interests are often used as a resource or strategy to meet her priority learning needs. For example, in order to increase Berfin's attention span when completing tabletop work (priority learning need), her teacher decided to use a sticker reward chart of Peppa Pig to motivate her.

 Priority learning needs might focus on the following areas:

- social interaction: playing games with peers, coping with winning or losing, coping in social situations, turn-taking, flexibility, sharing, waiting
- social communication: greeting, interrupting appropriately, asking for help, initiating, maintaining or ending a conversation, using the correct tone of voice or appropriate volume
- sensory processing: attention span and concentration, oversensitivity or under-sensitivity to touch, sound or light
- play skills: engaging in pretend play, following rules of a game, following others' play ideas
- language and communication: expressive language, such as grammatical errors, expansion of vocabulary; increasing length and depth of expression; or receptive language such as understanding of vocabulary, or following instructions
- academic skills: literacy, maths, general knowledge
- gross motor: jumping, ball skills, dancing, running, climbing
- fine motor: pre-handwriting skills, handwriting skills, hand-eye coordination, skills relating to manipulation of objects
- fitness: extending endurance and levels of fitness
- personal care: use of toilet, washing hands, brushing hair, dressing skills, eating skills
- personal independence: organizing school equipment, transitioning, checking a schedule
- diet: healthy food choices, eating foods of various food groups and textures
- joining mainstream classes

When selecting priority learning needs:

- It is considered good practice to select three to four priority learning needs during one academic year.
- A good rule of thumb is to select an area that you can practice in school at least three times per week during a set period of time.

Writing IEP goals and targets

Once you have established the priority learning needs of your student, you can formulate the goals and targets you would like your student to achieve.

Long-term goals or yearly goals

A long-term goal formulates the general progress you would like your student to make for each priority learning need for the duration of the school year (see Table 5.3). Long-term goals can be less specific than short-term goals.

Table 5.3 Priority learning need with associated yearly goal

Priority learning need	Yearly goal
Play skills	Enes will develop his outdoor play skills by inviting his peers to play with him. He will play a variety of outdoor games with minimal supervision.
Social interaction	Erica will gain an understanding of the preferences, strengths and personal characteristics of other people, including her peers in class and her brother.
Social communication	Carl will improve his ability to converse with his peers and adults such as asking appropriate questions, how to interrupt a conversation appropriately and taking turns in conversations.
Academic skills	Julieanne will improve her reading fluency and accuracy by developing and practising reading strategies when encountered with unknown texts and words.

Short-term goals or IEP targets

Short-term goals are much more specific than long-term goals. These short-term IEP targets need to be SMART:

- Specific
- Measurable
- Agreed and Achievable
- Realistic
- Timebound.

A SMART IEP target has the following characteristics:

- It includes a **specific** verb that stipulates visible behaviour such as sing, throw, sequence, read, write, run, summarize, retell, wait, name, recite, identify, classify, match, compare, describe, order, state, select, use, create, or imitate.

- The behaviour is **measured** by criteria for success: four out of five times, once a day or with 80 per cent accuracy.
- It is based on the priority learning needs **agreed** during the IEP meeting. With the use of suitable strategies and the right supports, the student should be able to **achieve** the target without any great difficulty.
- It is derived from a baseline assessment that indicates what the student can already do and is **realistic** in regards to what the student can achieve in a set amount of **time**.
- It might also include a condition, for example 'after having been presented with a two-step instruction'.

 Avoid vague, immeasurable verbs such as learn, become aware, improve, understand, know, increase, decrease, develop or remember.

Table 5.4 provides examples of SMART target writing.

Table 5.4 IEP target writing

Vague target	Problem description	SMART target
Helen will learn to wash her hands.	'Learn to' is an immeasurable, vague verb that doesn't tell us anything about what Helen is required to do. 'Wash her hands' on its own is not very specific as handwashing contains many steps. It makes more sense to break this skill down into manageable steps and emphasize which step or steps you want the pupil to achieve.	Helen will turn off the tap while she is scrubbing soap on her hands and in between her fingers.
Harry will exercise more.	This vague target is non-specific. A SMART goal details exactly what you want Harry to do, how often and with what amount of support.	Harry will run ten widths of the middle school playground three times weekly with minimal verbal prompting.
Maggie will develop her self-help skills and independence skills.	This target is too broad. It is more suitable as a long-term goal. It is also impossible to measure this goal.	Maggie will brush her hair independently, with a hair brush, using a minimum of five brush strokes.

An example of a completed IEP goal and target sheet can be found in ⬇Appendix 18.

Sections of an Individual Education Plan

While the sections of the entire Individual Education Plan depend on the requirements of the country you live in, there are some sections that occur in most IEPs (McCausland 2005):

- strengths and needs of the student
- special educational needs of the student
- the current level of educational performance of the student, which includes formal and informal assessments
- key teaching strategies
- support services provided to the student
- the names of all personnel who will be supporting the IEP
- yearly goals broken down into short-term goals
- the period of time and process for review of the IEP.

Carrying out IEP targets

Meet with your classroom staff after the IEP meeting to make them aware of the targets and how you plan to achieve them.

It is not always easy to remember each student's IEP targets. The following tips might help you to integrate IEPs into your daily practice:

- Keep a quick-glance A4 sheet with your students' current targets on your desk to serve as a reminder of what everyone is working on. For the purposes of confidentiality, you can code students' names or use initials instead of the students' real names.
- Put a star on your timetable or the students' schedules to remind you when you will focus on a particular IEP target.
- Inform parents and the mainstream class teacher of what target you are currently working on so everyone can work together to support the student with the IEP target.

 An IEP is a working document. It is possible that your student's needs will change throughout the school year or that you will need to change the priority of the original targets. You can discuss this at the review meeting or, if necessary, before the meeting.

Review and evaluation

Organize a review meeting midway through the school year where you can discuss the student's progress. Plan an evaluation meeting at the end of the school year, during which you evaluate the whole IEP. During this meeting, you can possibly discuss and indicate potential goals for the next school year. This can be particularly useful when the student will have a different class teacher in the upcoming school year.

Staff Organization

Listening to the voices of the support staff (Figures 5.15) we work with can give us a different but interesting perspective on how it is to work together.

I think respect, honesty and clarity are the most important things for me.
Aoife

No two teachers are the same. Some teachers want you to await their instruction, while others expect you to take initiative.
Mel

I thought it was a great idea to have an inbox during times when things were less busy: to do cutting, laminating or homework folder preparation.
Aoife

As a special needs assistant I work very closely with the children. It is important to me that teachers listen to what I observe.
Marcella

What really helped me was to have a specific timetable and routine.
Seán

It has its challenges being a 40+ SNA, working with a newly qualified 20+ teacher.
Liz

Obviously teachers have so much to do but when I don't know the plan, it's hard to know what to do and what not to do.
Karen

Please don't just tell me what to do, but also explain how you want me to do it too.
Mary

FIGURE 5.15 VOICES/PERSPECTIVES OF SUPPORT STAFF

Organization is key

In most special classes, the teacher and support staff work together to meet the needs of their students. While having support staff in the classroom opens up a wealth of opportunities, it also means extra considerations for you to manage your classroom successfully. As a teacher you often have to multi-task throughout the day, giving instructions to staff while trying to focus on teaching the students. Having a system in place that allows each team member to know exactly what they are doing and where they should be throughout the school day will ensure that the day runs as smoothly as possible, and that the individual needs of all students are met.

'Who works with who' rota

Table 5.5 shows an example of a 'Who works with who' rota. Students who have similar educational needs or who get on well are grouped together. Staff take turns working with each student or group of students. This simple system works because it:

- provides predictability for students as they know who they will work with in each session
- provides variety for both students and staff throughout the school day
- ensures that no team member works solely with the same student all the time.

You can easily tailor this rota based on the number of students and staff in your class.

Table 5.5 Example of a 'Who works with who' rota

Who works with who	
Student A and Student B	Staff 1*
Student C	Staff 2*
Students D, E and F	Staff 3*

* Staff names are written on laminated strips and are attached with Velcro. They are moved downwards on a daily or part-daily basis.

Colour-coded timetable

Another option is to colour code your timetable (see Table 5.6). Each member of staff has a specific colour so they can see at a glance who they are working with. As well as providing consistency for students and variety for staff, a colour-coded timetable has additional advantages:

- It allows you to be more specific compared to a 'Who works with who' rota in relation to which staff supports a student for a particular subject. You might decide that a certain member of staff will support a student for a particular subject for a period of time.

- It reduces the amount of explaining to staff about how you want the student to be supported, including what language to use and how much (or little) to prompt the student. This can save time and also provides much-needed consistency.

Table 5.6 Example of a colour-coded timetable

Monday	Student A	Student B	Student C	Student D	Student E
9:20–9:35	Fine Motor	Fine Motor	One-to-one work	Oral language	Oral language
9:35–9:50	Phonics	Phonics	Jigsaws	Jigsaws	One-to-one work
9:50–10:05	Reading	Reading	PECS training	PECS training	PECS training

Key:

Staff A	Staff B	Staff C

 Some points to consider when you are working with support staff in your classroom:

- Given the fact that many autistic students often have difficulties with receptive language, ensure that there is consistency in the language used in the classroom. Make sure that all staff use the same words for activities such as 'playground', 'lunch' or 'break time', and that commonly used phrases such as 'check your schedule' are used consistently by all staff.
- We are all social beings and have the need to chat and catch up with each other. However, encourage the class team to keep personal chat to a minimum during lesson times. This will really help students who are noise-sensitive or whose attempts at communication are very subtle.
- Ensure that staff members know what to do during less busy times, such as when the teacher is taking the whole group for an activity. Setting up schedules for the next day, organizing resources or making new visuals are tasks that all aid the smooth running of the class.
- Be very clear and specific when giving instructions to staff. It is easy to assume that all team members know exactly what to do. You can avoid a lot of frustration by providing clarity and checking that everyone is on the same page.
- Try to avoid repeating instructions given to a child by another staff member. Your students could easily become dependent on hearing instructions multiple times before acting on them.

“ When I was working in a special class, I always wondered how teachers were missing some of the things I observed. Now that I am a teacher, I understand how easy it is to miss things as your head is constantly full with so many competing priorities. ”

Annelies

- Often, you are so busy that there is not enough time to discuss situations that crop up throughout the day. Set up a notebook in which staff can write down observations that you can then discuss at a later stage. It can be useful to code students' names in order to comply with data protection guidelines.
- If regular formal staff meetings are not an option, plan brief informal meetings on a weekly or fortnightly basis to check in with the team.

Guide 53

The First Day

66 When you get off to a good start, it sets the tone for the rest of the year. 99

Special class teacher

 First days are exciting and difficult at the same time. There is so much to observe, organize, and do. You need to get to know your students and find out their likes, dislikes, sensory sensitivities, attention spans, academic levels, learning styles, and pace of learning.

Communication Passport

A Communication Passport (see ⬇ Appendix 20) containing information from the student's previous setting can be very useful to get to know the student. Parents, the previous school, preschool or home tutor will all have valuable information about your new student.

If a student moves class within the school, organize a good handover between the previous class teacher and the current teacher, both at the end of the school year and at the beginning of the new school year. Information given at the end of the year can help you with the preparations for the first few weeks. A handover at the start of the school year can give you more detailed information about the student's learning needs.

Preparing the student

You can support the transition to a new school and make it a much more predictable experience in a variety of ways:

- Create a visual story with photos of staff, the classroom and what will happen on the first day.
- Organize a visit to the school and class to introduce the new student to the setting, staff and possibly other children. During this visit, plan an activity based on the student's interests. If necessary, plan the visit just before the start of the school year as young children in particular might not remember an earlier visit before the summer holidays.
- A video walk-through of the empty school or classroom emailed to parents can also be useful, as the child can re-watch this on a device during the summer holidays.

Plan for the first week

❝ I often set up 'treat type' of activities to gauge what the students like and what I could use as a reward later on. ❞

Jessica, special class teacher

During the first week, your main aim is to have the right combination between:

- settling the students and getting to know them
- finding out their particular interests and devising work tasks around these
- providing a clear structure.

Table 5.7 shows a good structure for young students on their first day.

Table 5.7 Schedule for first day for young students

One-hour day	Half day
• free play based on the interests of the students • snack • yard • structured activity such as manipulative play, jigsaws, Play-Doh or inset shapes.	Add on a combination of: • group work: Circle Time, Story Time, Art, P.E. or Music • small group work: a tabletop game with a member of staff and another student or a fine motor activity in a small group • individual activities: reading a book with a staff member, engaging in sensory play.

✓ On the first day, it is useful to have the following things ready before you begin:

- an organized classroom with clearly defined areas (see Guide 47: Physical Set-up and Layout)
- a plan of what you will do on the day
- the children's schedules, organized according to your plan
- a rota indicating which staff will be allocated to each student (see Guide 52: Staff Organization)
- a system that indicates how students are expected to check their schedule and how to transition to the playground
- some basic routines such as where the students put their notebooks, lunches and coats, routines around going to the playground and what to do when someone finishes lunch early
- key points from each student's Communication Passport placed on your desk, ready to be consulted at a glance when needed
- labels or visuals for bags, coats, schedules and chairs.

Measure your progress

For the first few weeks, settling your students and getting to know them is your most important task. Don't worry about achieving many academic goals at this time. Set a few goals for each of your students during the first few weeks that focus on settling the student and make them part of your plan. For example, in a class of six students, your initial goals might be:

- Student A: To be settled and happy when saying goodbye to parents.
- Student B: To learn the meaning of the schedule visuals and follow the system of checking the schedule.
- Student C: To call staff and students by name.
- Student D: To form a bond with other students by playing with them during play time.
- Student E: To sit down on the carpet during play time.
- Student F: To sit alongside other peers during Circle Time.

Consider a reduced school day

If the guidelines of your country allow it, you could consider a reduced day in specific circumstances. The idea of a reduced day is to make the transition to a new school as smooth and positive as possible. A reduced day can have the following advantages:

- It reduces the likelihood of challenging behaviours due to tiredness and sensory overload.
- It gives students the chance to settle in and become familiar with their peers, staff and classroom routines before more educational demands are placed on them.
- It gives staff more time to observe behaviour carefully and implement appropriate strategies.

Seven-year-old Josie had moved school. A visit to her new school and the information in her Communication Passport showed that she needed a tight schedule at all times. Otherwise, she started making her own plan for the day, which then caused her a lot of distress. In order to set up a solid new routine, the class teacher reduced each day in Josie's first school week to three hours. Even though this caused some logistical problems in relation to transport, these problems were solved with some creative thinking. As a result, Josie's gradual introduction into the routine of her new school took place as seamlessly as possible.

A reduced day can also be a good idea for students who have already attended school the previous year, but who might struggle with the demands of a full day after the summer holidays. Naturally this needs to be decided in liaison with the parents and school management before the start of the school holidays.

 If you have a whole class of new students starting, consider staggering their time slots for the first few days. A higher staff ratio ensures that each student will get more attention and facilitates teaching class routines to the students. For example, if you have six new students starting, you can have a morning slot for a group of three students and an afternoon slot for the other three students. As their time in class gradually increases, they will all be in class at the same time in a matter of days or weeks.

Guide 54

Tailoring the Curriculum

66 When I changed from working in a special school to working in a mainstream school with special classes I felt so overwhelmed. The new school seemed like such a picture-perfect school. I felt isolated and under pressure to achieve the curriculum like my colleagues in mainstream classes did. It was only after a while that I realized that I was putting this pressure on myself. I needed to adapt my teaching to my students' needs, rather than focusing on what I thought was expected of me. 99

Special class teacher

Teaching in a special class is different from teaching in a mainstream class. Not only is your class organized differently, but there are also differences in the pace of teaching, the length of your lessons and the strategies, methodologies and resources that you use.

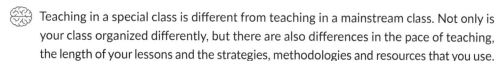 **Pace and length of lessons**

The old adage is true: 'Repetition is the key to all learning'. Don't hesitate to revise as much as you need to. There is no point in rushing ahead if your students cannot keep up. Therefore it is completely possible that you might need more than one school year to teach a curricular year.

66 Teaching one new maths concept a day was just too much for some of my students. I had to change my plan to teach one maths concept a week. Each new concept was revised and practised daily. By the end of the week, the students had a much better grasp of the new concept and they were ready to move on to the next step. 99

Annelies

Even though your students might remain at the same class level for subjects such as History, Science, or Geography, this doesn't mean that you have to repeat teaching the same themes year in and year out.

66 Even though my students' level of understanding was limited, I kept teaching new themes but tailored the language, and the amount of information and detail. 99

Special class teacher

Lessons in a special class might have to be shorter than in a mainstream class. Additionally, it is not always possible to follow the typical steps of a mainstream lesson.

" My Maths lessons used to consist of short stints of multiple, but completely different, concepts. My students each had a Maths work basket that consisted of a number concept, a time concept and one other concept, which they practised daily. In this way, they didn't only revise and practice continuously, but it also kept them interested and attentive. "

Annelies

Strategies and methodologies

Think about the methodologies you use to teach your lessons. Group projects, pair activities, treasure hunts, table quizzes or role-play might not always suit the needs of the students in your class. Trying to make your lessons as interesting as possible is commendable, but it is important to ensure that your students understand the core concept of what you are teaching. You might have to teach your students the social aspects of some methodologies before actually using them to teach.

" One year, I had to teach a sequence of lessons relating to personal safety. As I looked through the programme I realized that all lessons were illustrated with case studies. I knew that my students would not understand the language used in these stories and they would not understand the link between the story and the key message, no matter how much I simplified it. Instead, I focused on teaching the objective of each lesson and created a simple lesson plan around it. Most of the time, this entailed teaching my students a rule of what to do in a social situation and role-playing this rule multiple times. "

Annelies

Learning in group

Learning as part of a group is an important skill, but you might have to teach this skill gradually to your students. Group learning requires a number of social skills, including turn-taking, dealing with distractions, joint attention and adhering to rules such as waiting to answer until the teacher addresses you. In the meantime, teaching students in small groups can be more efficient.

Selecting strategies

Use the visual strengths of your students to your advantage and incorporate as many visual strategies as possible into your teaching.

" My students found retaining facts during History lessons really difficult. I used a variety of methodologies: PowerPoints, specially designed worksheets, used video footage, etc., but what worked best was the use of Mind Maps. It was like a light-bulb moment for some of my students on how to recall information. "

Maria, special class teacher

When teaching mental maths strategies, teach your students one strategy that corresponds with their individual learning style. For example, when teaching the 'bridge through ten' strategy, it can be very confusing for your student to learn a multitude of strategies (splitting, doubles, near doubles) and have to decide which strategy to choose each time.

Be prepared to try out different strategies if traditional methods of teaching do not suit your students' learning styles.

Sally, 6, had learned all the letter sounds but she didn't manage to blend them into words even though her class teacher Phil had patiently tried for many months. Phil decided to change his approach completely and started teaching her word lists. For one whole month Sally practised CVC (consonant–vowel–consonant) words ending in -at. Once she was able to read these words, she started work on another word list, with each list taking less and less time. After about three months, Sally was able to blend unknown CVC words.

Note: Some students can find it difficult to learn to read using phonics and may prefer to learn to read by using sight words instead.

Matching, selecting and naming

When teaching a new concept, it can be very useful to follow a matching, selecting and naming strategy (Bird, Beadman and Buckley 2001). This can be done during tabletop work with actual objects or pictures, but also while doing activities on the interactive whiteboard or iPad.

For example: when teaching about zoo animals:

- **Match** identical or non-identical pictures of zoo animals.
- **Select** a particular zoo animal by pointing, touching or giving a picture of a zoo animal.
- **Name** the zoo animals.

The same procedure can be used to teach numerals; money; sight words; concepts such as long/short, big/small, open/closed; or when teaching vocabulary such as prepositions.

Generalizing concepts

During a turn-taking game, Juanita, 5, matched coloured drawings of vehicles to a coloured baseboard. The next day she successfully placed coloured blocks onto small, coloured circles. However, when her teacher instructed her to match a variety of coloured plastic animals to coloured placemats, she was not able to complete this task. Her class teacher knew she had to create more colour matching activities so Juanita could truly acquire this concept.

Generalizing a skill is the ability to apply a skill in different settings and situations, with different people, at a different time of the day or in a different way.

Difficulties with generalization come in all shapes and sizes:

- counting blocks during tabletop work but finding it hard to count how many pupils are present in class during Circle Time
- being able to unbutton a coat, but finding it impossible to open the button of a shirt or pants
- not recognizing that a flashcard of a bike, a photo of a bike and the object bike all refer to the concept 'bike'
- accepting to wear a seatbelt in the car with Mum, but not with Dad
- taking turns while playing 'pop up pirate' but not taking turns when playing a lotto game, or happily taking turns while playing a board game in school but refusing to take turns when playing a board game at home
- waiting in line in the grocery store but finding it really hard to wait when ordering in a fast-food restaurant
- being able to read words on flashcards but being unsuccessful at reading the same words on flashcards that use a different font.

The main strategy to ensure generalization of skills and concepts is to practise, practise, practise with different materials, with a variety of people and in different settings:

- Practice daily living skills such as tying shoelaces, undoing buttons and putting on a coat both at home and at school.
- When teaching academic skills, use a variety of resources to ensure the student has actually learned the concept rather than merely having memorized it.
- Apply a rule to all settings from the moment you are teaching this rule, for example wearing a seat belt in the car or putting on a coat when going outside.

- When role-playing social skills, practise lots of different scenarios. For example, when teaching greeting people, role-play scenarios relating to greeting people in class, in the corridor of the school, in a shop, at a party, etc.
- Use visuals, stories or video footage to explain in which settings a learned behaviour applies.

 Plan for generalization before teaching a new skill so the new skill gets acquired across a variety of settings, people and situations.

Resources

Use resources tailored to the level of understanding of your student. Similar to the order of visuals explained in ⚿ Guide 6: Using a Schedule, there is also a hierarchy in the abstraction of learning materials. Resources can be ordered from concrete to abstract:

1. concrete material
2. coloured photos
3. coloured line drawings
4. black and white line drawings
5. symbols or written text.

A resource might look amazing and colourful, but it might not suit the learning style of your students.

Finding the right resource might make all the difference. If your student appears disinterested in the task, consider trying out a different resource.

> Five-year-old Sarah loved making jigsaws, but she wasn't very keen on completing other tabletop tasks. In order to encourage her to identify and name 2-D shapes, her teacher put jigsaws that focused on this concept in her work baskets. Sarah absolutely loved it and she became much more interested in looking at, manipulating and naming 2-D shapes. Once the teacher had Sarah's interest, she was able to replace some of the jigsaws with 2-D matching activities.

If suitable, use ready-made resources, but consider tailoring them to suit your needs.

" An IEP target for one of my students required me to teach him about feelings, in particular the feeling of 'jealousy'. I found a really good resource that involved matching a variety of feelings to different situations. It was exactly what I was looking for, however, the feeling of 'jealousy' wasn't included. I still wanted to use the resource so I created a few additional situations relating to jealousy and added them to the game. It worked a treat! "

Maria, special class teacher

The curriculum

66 I always explain it like this to my friends and colleagues: teaching a special class is like multi-class teaching. 99

Maria, special class teacher

Despite their age and no matter how long it takes, teach your students at their current curricular level. If necessary, you might even have to teach multiple curricular levels within a subject.

66 I once taught a 12-year-old student who found the concept of adding and subtracting extremely difficult. For years he had been stuck at the same class level for Maths. However, he didn't have the same problem with other parts of the Maths curriculum. I moved him on to the next class level for measures, time and fractions but kept him at the same level for addition and subtraction. 99

Annelies

Non-curricular tasks

Non-curricular activities and tasks such as organization skills, dressing skills and personal independence skills are as important as the official curriculum.

66 Don't be afraid to exercise your autonomy. When teaching in a special class, your focus shouldn't primarily be on following the curriculum, it should be on catering for what the children need. During my first year teaching in a special class, I was surprised how much time I spent teaching social skills, organizational skills, conversation skills and life skills. You have to know when to use your teacher autonomy. Thankfully, this has become second nature to me now. 99

Maria, special class teacher

Step by step

Teach one concept at a time. If a student finds a particular concept quite difficult, teach him one element of the concept first before moving on to an associated concept. For example, when teaching rhyming, teach words that rhyme first, then tackle words that don't rhyme. Similarly, when teaching concepts such as long and short, focus on one of the concepts first rather than teaching both concepts simultaneously.

Homework

You might have to show some flexibility around giving homework because your students might think of schoolwork as something that is only supposed to happen in school and not at home. This might mean reducing the amount of homework to the bare essentials or supporting parents with implementing a homework routine.

> ❝ Have a decent understanding of the person's challenges. Don't discriminate, be gentle and be fair. ❞
>
> *Michael, teenager on the spectrum*

- Be empathetic and patient. Keep in mind that your students might have to work ten times as hard to learn compared to their mainstream peers.
- Always ensure you make time for your students to experience the joy of practising a newly acquired concept rather than quickly moving on to the next topic.

 You will teach a wide variety of class levels throughout your teaching career. It is more than likely that you will also use numerous resources to support your students' learning. It is so handy to print hard copies for yourself as you go along and file them in a folder according to class level. Also, save a copy online in a cloud application.

Guide 55

Assessment

 In most special classrooms, the number of students is comparatively lower than in a mainstream classroom. It is often not necessary to do as many academic tests compared to a mainstream class, as you are usually able to assess learning on a continuous basis. However, it can be very useful to complete more comprehensive testing to get a better picture of your students' functioning and to support you in identifying their learning needs.

End-of-term tests

Consider whether it would be beneficial for your student to do an end-of-term formal assessment. Make note if you decide to give your student additional time or other allowances to complete the test. Ideally you agree on a whole-school approach to testing, as it might be confusing for parents if students' scores vary greatly each year depending on whether allowances are being made or not.

Test kits

 There are a lot of tests available, and it can be hard to decide which one to choose. Here are some tips to put you on track:

- Consider what information you are looking for and ensure your chosen test provides you with this information. Some tests only provide you with a level of functioning; other tests also include follow-up targets and tasks, or even possible IEP targets.
- Check the age range the test is aimed at and the time needed to complete the test. Some tests allow you to score based on observation, other tests require you to complete each step of the assessment. Some tests are strictly timed. Other tests allow you to break up the tasks in as many chunks as you desire.
- Consider cost versus need. Test kits are not cheap. Perhaps you can share a kit between a few schools.
- Before administering a test, prepare yourself thoroughly by familiarizing yourself with the test guidelines. Take note of the amount of language used, the level of prompting involved and the recommended set-up. If you need concrete material, ensure you have it ready, stored in a box out of sight of the student.

- If you are planning to test more than one student and are completely unfamiliar with the test itself, start off with a student who likes doing tabletop work.

" I decided to complete the PEP-3 kit with all my students to obtain a better picture of their functioning. When going through the results of the test, I found that I had learned a lot more about the students who I had only been teaching recently but less so of the students who had been with me for more than one year. "

Annelies

Table 5.8 gives an overview of four different assessments that are aimed at primary school–aged autistic students.

Table 5.8 Overview of assessments for autistic students

	Basic Skills Checklist (Breitenbach 2000)	Psychoeducational Profile, Third Edition (PEP-3)	Assessment of Basic Language and Learning Skills Revised (ABLLS-R®)	Verbal Behaviour Milestones Assessment and Placement Program (VB-MAPP)
Focus	Gives an overview of home and school functioning in the following areas: basic concepts, Maths, English, fine motor, personal independence and personal care.	Tests verbal and pre-verbal cognition, receptive and expressive language, fine and gross motor skills, visual-motor imitation, affective expression, social reciprocity, characteristic motor behaviours and characteristic verbal behaviours.	There is a big focus on language acquisition. Tests 544 skills in 25 areas such as language, social interaction, self-help, motor, writing, spelling, grooming, play and leisure skills, motor imitation, group instruction and dressing skills.	Contains 5 components: Milestones Assessment, Barriers Assessment, Transition Assessment, Task Analysis and Supporting Skills and Placement and IEP goals.
Age range	Officially preschool and primary school–aged children, but can also be done with older students as the scores are not age based.	From 2 years old to 7 and a half years old.	From 0 to 12 years old.	While it is focused in theory on autistic younger children or children, it can also be used for teenagers or adults.

Outcome	Administrator scores items as 'correct/ independent', 'emerging/ prompting', or 'incorrect/no response'.	Provides a developmental age for each area. Also gives an indication of delay compared to other autistic children and compared to mainstream peers of similar age.	Identifies language and other skills that are in need of intervention.	Milestone assessment gives a detailed overview of child's language functioning. Barriers Assessment determines what barriers might impede the child from learning. Transition Assessment identifies if the child has the necessary skills for a transition to another educational setting. The Task Analysis and Supporting Skills breaks above skills down further. The Placement and IEP goals section provides suggestions for IEP goals.
Advantages	It shows an itemized list of various steps for each skill. For example, non-identical matching: object-to-object, picture-to-picture (of object), picture-to-picture (of action), picture-to-object, object-to-picture, object-to-picture symbol, picture symbol to object.	It is quite a comprehensive test covering a wide range of skills and behaviours. The test kit includes a wide variety of attractive testing materials. The test kit also includes a caregiver report.	Can be purchased with accompanying testing materials but this comes at a price. It gives guidelines to devise associated IEP targets. It gives a very clear sequence of the developmental order or complexity of tasks.	This is a very comprehensive test. It provides follow up IEP goals for each milestone. There is space for follow-up assessment so results can be compared easily. Barriers Assessment and Transition Assessment are quite unique.
Disadvantages	It doesn't tell you how to work on each skill. As the name indicates it is a basic skills checklist and will not be suitable for those with lower support needs currently.	It only provides a current level of functioning; there is no indication of follow-up tasks or goals.	This is a very long assessment (90 pages) and requires an enormous number of materials.	Materials are not provided but a clear list of what is needed is included. This a very long test.

🧠 Teaching Daily Living Skills

" You have no idea what a simple thing like learning to tie shoelaces can do. When he is in P.E. with all the other boys and his shoelaces become untied, he no longer stands out. It's been a fabulous thing. "

Jacinta, mother of Michael

As a special class teacher, your job often goes further than just teaching academic skills. Explicit teaching of daily living skills is crucial. In fact, having well-developed daily living skills has been shown to be an important predictor of certain life outcomes, such as access to third-level education, employment and independent living for autistic people, more than cognitive ability (Bagatell 2019). Spending time teaching daily living skills not only helps your students to be more independent, but also generates a sense of achievement and success.

While it is generally best practice to teach life skills in their natural setting, distractions or the pressure of time might inhibit successful learning of a skill in real time, as it occurs. Sometimes it may be more suitable to teach these skills in a quieter, more controlled environment.

Daily living skills can be divided into three categories:

- personal skills: dressing, grooming, toileting, handwashing
- domestic skills: sweeping, cleaning, cooking, making a cup of tea, washing dishes
- community skills: taking the bus, ordering in a restaurant, buying groceries, safely crossing the road.

" Children are totally different in school than at home. It makes life a lot easier for parents if the teacher introduces a new skill and the parents follow on with it at home. Parents might not always see how able their children can be. They might do a lot more for their children. Independence is key. "

Bláthnaid, special class teacher

Gustav, 7, found it really hard to put on his jumper, including holding the jumper the right way up, putting his head in and finding the sleeves. His parents reported that mornings were really busy in the house as the whole family was rushing to get to work or school on time. Because of the hectic morning situation, attempts at teaching Gustav how to put on his jumper had failed. It got to the point where

Gustav was refusing even to try. After discussing this issue during a parent–teacher meeting, Gustav's teacher started teaching him how to tackle this task step by step in class.

Task analysis

Task analysis is the process of breaking a task down into manageable steps. As a general rule, each step should consist of one behaviour. Breaking skills down into steps is an interesting process as it makes you aware of how many steps a simple task actually consists of. Table 5.9 shows an example of an incomplete versus a correct task analysis when teaching handwashing skills.

Table 5.9 An example of incomplete task analysis versus correct task analysis

Incomplete task analysis	Correct task analysis
Turn on tap. Wash hands. Turn off tap. Dry hands.	Turn on tap. Wet hands. Turn off tap. Press soap dispenser to release soap. Rub hands together to form bubbles. Turn on tap. Rinse hands. Turn off tap. Dry hands.

Note: This is an example of incomplete task analysis when you are teaching a student to wash his hands. This can be a good task analysis if a student can already wash his hands but forgets one step, such as turning off the tap or drying his hands.

Chaining

Once you have broken down a task into manageable steps, it is a matter of linking these steps in a particular sequence. This is called chaining, because each step links to the next step like the links in a chain. The student only moves on to the next step of the chain when the previous step has been accomplished. The key is to support the student while mastering new steps but to retain independence of steps already achieved. Chaining can be used for teaching life skills as well as teaching academic and behaviour skills.

There are three types of chaining (DuCharme 2003).

Forward chaining

Forward chaining involves the student successfully completing the first step of a sequence before the next step is taught. The advantage of forward chaining is that the student starts off with a sense of achievement as he is successful in achieving the first step. While the student is learning to complete each step, you simply carry out the next steps yourself.

Forward chaining is really useful for teaching skills such as tying shoelaces or brushing teeth.

Examples of forward chaining can be seen below.

PHONE NUMBER

Rather than teaching your student to memorize a whole phone number in one go, you can start by teaching the first three digits. Once the student has mastered these digits, you can teach the next set of digits until he has memorized the full phone number.

SHOELACES

Start by teaching your student to hold both laces. Model this step and practise it until your student can do this completely independently without any verbal instruction.

Sequence 1

1. Hold both laces. ✓
2. Cross them over. ✗
3. Thread green lace underneath the blue lace. ✗
4. Pull tight. ✗
5. Make loop with green lace and pinch together. ✗
6. Wind blue lace around green lace. ✗
7. Pull blue lace through hole. ✗
8. Pull both laces. ✗

Once the student has achieved holding both laces, you can move on to teaching the student to cross the laces.

Sequence 2

1. Hold both laces. ✓
2. Cross them over. ✓
3. Thread green lace underneath the blue lace. ✗

4. Pull tight. ✗
5. Make loop with green lace and pinch together. ✗
6. Wind blue lace around green lace. ✗
7. Pull blue lace through hole. ✗
8. Pull both laces. ✗

The student continues following the sequence, accomplishing one step and moving onto the next step.

Backward chaining

As the name indicates, backward chaining involves working backward. You start by teaching your student the last step of a sequence. The student starts off by completing the last step of a task, leading to a sense of fulfillment. Backward chaining is particularly useful for dressing skills such as putting on clothes or zipping up a coat. The reason for this is that the first steps of a dressing skill are often trickier than the last steps.

FIGURE 5.16 CHAINING: PUTTING ON A JUMPER

Sequence 1	Sequence 2
1. Pull jumper down. ✓	1. Pull jumper down. ✓
2. Put in one arm. ✗	2. Put in one arm. ✓
3. Put in other arm. ✗	3. Put in other arm. ✗
4. Pull jumper over head. ✗	4. Pull jumper over head. ✗
5. Hold jumper out in front of self. ✗	5. Hold jumper out in front of self. ✗

Sequence 3

1. Pull jumper down. ✓
2. Put in one arm. ✓
3. Put in other arm. ✓
4. Pull jumper over head. ✗
5. Hold jumper out in front of self. ✗

Sequence 4

1. Pull jumper over head. ✓
2. Put in one arm. ✓
3. Put in other arm. ✓
4. Pull jumper over head. ✓
5. Hold jumper out in front of self. ✗

Sequence 5

1. Pull jumper over head. ✓
2. Put in one arm. ✓
3. Put in other arm. ✓
4. Pull jumper over head. ✓
5. Hold jumper out in front of self. ✓

Total chaining

When you use total chaining, you teach your student all the steps of a sequence simultaneously. Total chaining can be suitable for teaching certain skills and routines such as completing morning, evening or lunch-time routines. However, be aware that total chaining expects your student to complete all of the steps and that you might be more successful when teaching the student one step at a time.

Steps of a morning routine in school might include:

1. Take off coat.
2. Hang up coat.
3. Hang up bag.
4. Take pencil case out of bag.
5. Place pencil case on desk.
6. Take out homework.
7. Place homework in an allocated homework basket.
8. Sit down on chair.
9. Wait for teacher.

Most skills such as washing hands or wiping a table can be taught with either forward or backward chaining. It simply depends on how your student learns best.

Prompting

When teaching daily living skills, there is usually a certain level of prompting needed in order for your student to master the new skill. The type of prompting you use depends on the skill you are teaching and on the learning style of the student:

- Physical prompting: You physically guide the student to do the task while ensuring that you have the student's attention so that he is actively participating rather than passively experiencing the physical prompt.
- Modelling: You actually model a particular step. This can be a good option when teaching skills such as blowing your nose or pulling a lace through a loop when tying shoelaces.
- Video modelling: The student watches a video of someone completing a task in its entirety and then carries out this particular task. Video modelling can be useful for skills such as loading a dishwasher, setting the table or washing hands. Video modelling makes great demands on the student's memory skills as the student is watching an entire video before attempting the task himself.
- Video prompting: The student practises a single step after having watched a video clip of this step.
- Verbal prompting: Verbal prompting can range from prompting the student with one word only to prompting with sentences. Ensure all staff use the same vocabulary and talk in clear, short sentences to avoid confusing the student.
- Gestural prompt: Using any type of gesture such as pointing or touching an object can direct the student to do the right action. For example, touching the tap to encourage the student to turn on the tap.
- Visual prompting: Visuals are a widely used support to portray the steps of task analysis. When using visuals, ensure that they are clear and to the point, free of any unnecessary elements.

 Be vigilant that you purposely fade your prompts away once your student has learned the steps, as students can easily become prompt-dependent.

> “ I was trying to teach my son how to dress himself. But then I realized he had become too dependent on the visuals. I had to take them away, because if they weren't there, he wouldn't do it. He had become too dependent on them. ”
>
> *Jacinta, mother of Michael*

Daily living skills and technology

Technology offers not only a multitude of options when teaching daily living skills but can also be more motivating for autistic students. Video prompting can be more successful compared to video modelling or visuals when teaching daily living skills

(Domire and Wolfe 2014). Ideally, the person who is modelling the behaviour is of similar age and gender as the student.

There are a wide variety of apps available that can support autistic people with daily living skills, such as iDo Hygiene, Living Safely, Everyday Skills, iDo Getting Dressed and MagnusCards.

Apps are also great for setting reminders, finding the way or making lists. Here are some additional tips when teaching new skills:

- Ensure you only have the items that you need present, for example toothbrush, cup, toothpaste and mirror when brushing teeth.
- You might need to be discreet when teaching an older student life skills, as they may feel self-conscious about their lack of skill in a particular area.
- Always check with your student's parents if your task analysis is correct. It is important that the sequence of steps that you have developed is exactly the same that the parents are using at home.
- Ask another adult to practise the sequence of steps you devised to check if they are clear and logical and to ascertain if you have left out anything important.
- Ensure the student generalizes the learned skill to all settings. One way is to ensure the student practises each learned step at home too.
- A new skill should be practised at least once a day. Leaving a long interval delays the acquisition of a skill.
- Teaching new steps can be tedious, and it requires patience and time. Ensure you don't rush the student, and remain positive at all times.
- Ensure that you make rules for new-found independence. For example, when you have taught a student how to use a cooker, a rule such as 'You can only put the cooker on when I am in the room' might have to be implemented.

 Keep a folder with visuals depicting steps of life skills such as the hand washing sequence. You will be surprised how often you will use them throughout your teaching career.

Guide 57

Circle Time

Circle Time is probably one of the most common activities in a special class. It offers fantastic opportunities for social interaction, oral language and listening skills. However, it can be a difficult activity for some students due to increased social demands and a need for joint attention.

> " A few years ago, my Circle Time sessions used to consist of singing songs and identifying the weather, the date, day, month and season. I felt that the session was very stilted and that the students were not getting a lot out of it. Students who understood these concepts were getting bored of re-hashing them daily. Students for whom these concepts were difficult still didn't grasp them after months of doing them. I decided to revamp my Circle Time sessions and introduced playing a game, reciting a rhyme and doing a dance. The sessions became so much more fun and interactive. "

Annelies

Circle Time can consist of a wide variety of activities. It can last any time from 10 minutes to 30 minutes. You might have to take into account that some students may only be able to attend part of it. If this is the case, organize your activities in such a way that they can attend the activities that are of most interest to them before they check their schedule and move on to another activity. You can then continue your Circle Time session with different activities for the remaining group. Depending on the attention span of your students you could have two to three layers in a 'layered Circle Time'.

News

If you choose to do news as part of your Circle Time, ensure that it is suitable for your group and that it does not go on for too long, as this places huge demands on students' receptive language, attention and listening skills.

Ask parents to provide you with some information, as not all students may remember or be accurate when retelling what happened at home. Parents can fill out a simple template (see Table 5.10) that allows you to ask some targeted questions about what the students did at home.

Table 5.10 Home–school news template

	I played with...	I watched...	I ate...	I went to...
Monday				
Tuesday				
Wednesday				
Thursday				
Friday				

For students who need more visual support, you can use a home–school communication sheet similar to the one mentioned in ☞ Guide 44: Communicating with Parents. In this case, it displays visuals of activities the student might do at home. Based on the activities that the parents have circled, a short discussion about the student's home activities can take place.

Songs and rhymes

Circle Time songs can range from a 'Good Morning' or 'Hello' song, action songs or songs relating to the current class theme. Find a balance between repeating some songs so the students anticipate them and learn them and adding in new songs to keep everything interesting.

Rhymes can be nursery rhymes, counting rhymes or other fun rhymes to short poems. Rhymes encourage the students to talk in unison and practise their memory skills.

Social interaction games

Making social interaction games fun not only teaches your students that playing and interacting can be enjoyable but it also prepares them for playing with their peers during yard time or playing with family members at home. Find out what games children are currently playing or practise old favourites such as chase, the traffic lights game, duck, duck, goose or musical statues.

🔑 Help me to navigate the social world of school

Social skills games

Circle Time is the ideal opportunity to practice skills such as:

- Imitating actions or rhythm: Students imitate a gesture and then pass on a smile, a clap, a wave, etc. to the next student, or they imitate the actions of the teacher or another student who is 'the conductor of an orchestra'.
- Requesting and handing items: Make up simple games whereby pupils each get an object and need to request objects from each other.
- Taking turns: Play 'person swap', where one student calls out another student's name and they swap places. That student then calls out another student's name and they swap places again. Students can also take turns when playing a simple version of 'wink murder'.
- Practising conversation skills: Conversation skills such as listening skills or asking each other questions can be practised by playing a variety of listening games such as variations of Simon says or asking a student questions about a mystery object hidden under a blanket.

Dance

Dancing provides students with a necessary movement break. It also increases body awareness and makes students more confident to move around the space. Ensure you include a mixture of guided and free dances. You can use visual supports such as plastic dots, laminated feet or an area marked by tape to ensure students remain in place during a stationary dance.

Sensory activities

Circle Time can also be a nice opportunity for your students to experience a variety of sensory activities. Activities such as touching different textures or hot and cold materials or blowing feathers are not only fun but can also act as calming activities that regulate your students. Gently encourage but never force a student to do something they are not comfortable with.

Oral language opportunities

Circle Time is the ideal occasion for short games that develop students' language skills such as guessing games, show and tell, feely bag games, talking about favourite things or following instructions by engaging in treasure hunts.

For older students you can also add the following activities:

- calendar activities
- topic presentations
- short drama or improvisation activities.

Additional tips

- Draw your students in by incorporating as many fun elements as possible.
- Use visuals: Some students might need a mini Circle Time schedule to understand what is coming up. You can also use visuals to support desired behaviours such as 'good sitting' or to explain how to play a game.
- Make it active: Get everyone moving.
- Build up a routine: Establish a Circle-Time routine with a set number of activities. Once the students understand what is expected of them, you can alter the routine to keep it interesting and flexible.
- Order your activities to suit the emotional and cognitive needs of the group: Follow up an energizing game with a more calming activity. Also, follow a task that some of the students might find hard with a task that they are comfortable doing.

Guide 58

Participating in Whole-School Events

School fundraisers, performances, musicals, open days or religious ceremonies are part and parcel of most schools' yearly calendar. These events can be quite overwhelming for some autistic students, as they often contain a number of unexpected situations and make demands on the student's sensory system.

It's all down to: 'Can they do this?' If they can, great! But if they are stressed and it's a negative experience, then why are we doing this? It shouldn't be about the parents' expectations either.

Special class teacher

School performances

There are many strategies that can support a student to partake in school performances. Putting thought and effort into planning the event and preparing the student can make a big difference to the student and enable him to participate successfully.

- Make an assessment of what is expected of the students and determine if these expectations are realistic for your student.
- If any of the available roles don't suit your student, consider if the student can be given a role that is more suitable.
- If being on stage is not one of your student's strengths, look into other roles such as handing out flyers before the play or helping out with the sound.
- On stage, position the student close to another student who serves as a good model.
- Use a visual story or a First/Then schedule to explain what will happen.
- Explain to parents the whole process of what is involved in participating: unplanned and possibly lengthy practices, raised noise levels, the expectation of remaining quiet and standing still for a prolonged time. Ensure that everyone has the same expectations.
- Consider the possibility of using visual markers such as plastic dots to show the student where he needs to be.
- If possible, organize that students who find standing difficult can sit down.
- Consider whether it matters to you or the parents if a student is present on stage but is not fully participating.

- During the final rehearsals, assess how the student copes with wearing a costume, being in front of an audience and using a microphone.
- Have a plan in place if something doesn't work out during the performance.

School trips

Providing support during a school trip can turn a daunting prospect into a positive experience and enjoyable trip:

- Plan the trip from the moment you step onto the bus to what will happen when you arrive back in school. Think of seemingly small things such as the seating plan for the bus, the availability and location of a toilet and the range of activities that are planned.
- Use visual supports such as pictures, schedules or stories appropriate to your student's needs. Visit the website of your destination and show the student real pictures of how everything looks. Some websites even have a 360° view feature.
- Explain to the students what you expect of them *before* you leave. Be clear and explicit about your expectations in relation to desired behaviour, and go through rules. Discuss what you expect from the students while waiting or during free time.
- If needed, allocate a member of staff to support the student.
- If a student is anxious about a particular destination, ask parents to visit the venue prior to the trip so that the student becomes familiar with the location and is less overwhelmed by the new surroundings.

Nadia's teacher always prepared his students ahead of time when they were going on a class trip. He created a photo slideshow of each trip that illustrated all the things the students would do while on the trip. Nadia always enjoyed going on a trip but when she was on the bus back to school, she often started crying and asked to be dropped home rather than going back to school.

Upon reflection, Nadia's teacher realized that the preparations only included what happened during the trip and that he had omitted what the students were expected to do when they arrived back to school. From then on, he added another section to his slideshow that included specific information about what the students would do upon return.

66 In a mainstream school there are a lot of expectations to attend all events in the same way mainstream students do. 99

Special class teacher

305

Whole-school assemblies

Depending on the size of the school, whole-school assemblies can be busy events. If your student finds this difficult you can:

- prepare your student to help them understand what to expect through a visual story or video footage of a typical assembly
- practise desired behaviour ahead of time in the hall with a smaller group
- provide the student with a safe place. Maybe the student can stand slightly to the side of the group rather than in the middle of a crowd.

Part 6

Keep It Positive

“ I was taught by a behaviour expert to treat anyone displaying behaviours that are considered challenging with both compassion and respect. ”

Claire

A refusal to participate in a P.E. lesson, pushing someone in the playground, sitting at a desk quietly avoiding work or running away – just like any other child, autistic students can act in ways that are difficult for teaching staff to comprehend. In this chapter, we will focus on looking at behaviour through the lens of autism. We will try to figure out why certain behaviours happen, and what we can do to help everyone involved.

This may involve strategies such as changing:

- the environment
- our understanding of autism
- the students' understanding of what is happening and how it affects other people.

The key to understanding behaviour is to understand autism.

A note on language

You will have noticed that instead of using the term 'challenging behaviour', we have chosen to use 'behaviours that may challenge' and 'behaviours of interest'. This is because 'challenging behaviour' implies intention, as if a child is deliberately misbehaving in order to challenge you, when often they are simply trying to cope with the school environment and everything that entails.

In fact, many students can act in ways that appear illogical to others but are actually very functional for the child himself. For example:

> Shane, 7, used to hide under his desk whenever the school bell rang out like a siren four times a day. He was simply trying to block out the noise of the bell in the most effective way he could think of at that time.

Think about:

- What does 'behaviour that may challenge' mean to you?
- What is the most pressing behaviour of concern in your class that you would like to help someone with right now?
- Why do you think the person is engaging in this behaviour?

Guide 59

Looking at Behaviour in a Different Way

" Start with what you know about autism – and use that to try to figure out why someone is acting in a certain way. "

Claire

 All behaviour is communication, and all children display behaviours that may present challenges for staff.

A child's behaviour can be compared to an iceberg. There are two levels:

- what we see (above the waterline)
- what we do not see (below the waterline).

As most of the iceberg sits below the waterline, what you see on the outside is just a small proportion of everything that is going on underneath (see Figure 6.1). You often have to dig deeper to find out exactly what is causing the actions that bubble to the surface.

For example, think about a 12-year-old girl who suddenly loses concentration in class and who forgets her homework every day for a week. Instead of labelling her as 'lazy', you might look below the surface to find out that she has been looking after her three younger siblings on her own every night for the last week because her mum is in hospital.

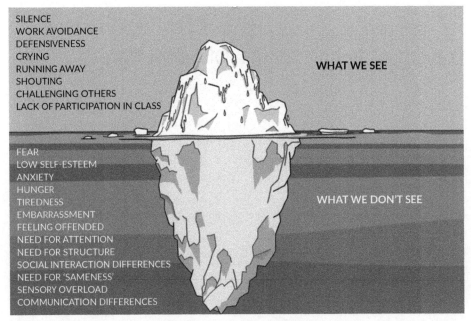

SILENCE
WORK AVOIDANCE
DEFENSIVENESS
CRYING
RUNNING AWAY
SHOUTING
CHALLENGING OTHERS
LACK OF PARTICIPATION IN CLASS

WHAT WE SEE

FEAR
LOW SELF-ESTEEM
ANXIETY
HUNGER
TIREDNESS
EMBARRASSMENT
FEELING OFFENDED
NEED FOR ATTENTION
NEED FOR STRUCTURE
SOCIAL INTERACTION DIFFERENCES
NEED FOR 'SAMENESS'
SENSORY OVERLOAD
COMMUNICATION DIFFERENCES

WHAT WE DON'T SEE

FIGURE 6.1 BEHAVIOUR ICEBERG

For an autistic child, there is often even more going on below the waterline. As a result, it is important to look at and analyze behaviours in a different way than you might do for non-autistic children.

It is highly likely that the behaviour that is seen as challenging may actually be linked to one of the key areas of difference in autism and may be a very functional and logical solution for the child himself.

Behaviour bubbles

Based on the key areas of difference in autism, as outlined in the DSM-5 dyad of impairments (APA 2013), the following could be seen as possible reasons for behaviours that may be seen as challenging at school:

- social communication differences
- social interaction differences
- sensory needs
- a need for structure
- a need for sameness.

These are a good place to start when trying to better understand behaviours of interest.

Whenever you analyze a student's behaviour:

- look at each behaviour bubble (see Figure 6.2) and consider whether or not it could be a potential reason behind the behaviour

- select the behaviour bubble(s) that are relevant to a particular situation
- figure out ways to help your student cope better in this situation.

By understanding that behaviours are usually not deliberate and by using behaviour bubbles to analyze behaviour, staff often feel more positive about what is happening in the classroom and are better able to view the student and their actions with compassion.

FIGURE 6.2 BEHAVIOUR BUBBLES

Case studies

Which of the behaviour bubbles best fit as a possible explanation for why these students are acting in a particular way?

Melanie, 11, upset her classmate by saying that her artwork was 'disgusting'.

Possible reasons

Social interaction: Melanie does not currently understand the effect of her words on her classmate.

What to do

- Teach Melanie about the difference between being honest and telling 'white lies' in order to protect someone else's feelings.
- Practise this using a variety of different scenarios that could arise at school. For example, 'What would you say if your friend arrived into school with a new haircut that didn't look very nice?'

John, 8, always gets into some kind of trouble either with classmates or adults during play times. By the end of play time, he can usually be found either crying on his own or being reprimanded by a member of staff for being too physically rough with the other students.

Possible reasons

Social communication and interaction, sensory needs, structure: Playground time feels unstructured and too open-ended for John. He is never really sure what to do out there. While keen to make friends, he often tries to get other students' attention in unexpected ways and then gets into trouble.

311

What to do
Structure playground time for John by doing the following:

- Set up simple organized games.
- Give him a clear role, e.g. litter warden or helping a younger student.
- Create a zoned reading area for all students, which happens to contain a selection of John and his friends' favourite Minecraft annuals, amongst other books.

Fergus, 5, refused to leave the classroom when it was time to go to the hall to practise for the Christmas carol concert.

Possible reasons
Structure, sameness: Going to the hall is unexpected, as the daily routine has now changed.

Sensory needs: It is cold and very noisy in the hall.

What to do

- Put 'Hall' on the schedule, and use a photograph to show Fergus where he is going.
- Allow Fergus to take a favourite toy with him to ease the transition.
- Consider allowing Fergus to attend the hall practice for a certain amount of time before going on a sensory break with an adult and another student.

Juan, 10, checks his watch continuously during playground time. As soon as his watch beeps at 11 a.m., and even before the school bell rings, Juan has started to walk off alone back to the classroom, where he waits, unsupervised, for his teacher and class.

Possible reasons
Structure, sameness: As soon as his clock strikes 11 a.m., Juan considers that it is time to go inside. In his mind, there is no room for manoeuvre on this.

What to do

- Teach Juan the concept of 'around' in relation to time, so that he understands that 11 a.m. can also mean a few minutes before or after 11.
- Give Juan a visual rule explaining that he must line up in the playground with his class and wait for his teacher. Explain that this is so everyone stays safe by going back to the classroom together.

Guide 60

🧠 Preventative Strategies

❝ If a behaviour is recurring, you have to look at how you can prevent the behaviour rather than only dealing with the behaviour afterwards. ❞

Jessica, special class teacher

Preventative strategies are general, autism-friendly strategies that help your students to stay calm, relaxed and ready to learn. They are key in the prevention of behaviours that might be seen as undesirable or challenging.

They are the hard-working, behind-the-scenes strategies that can be embedded into everyday practice and can support not only autistic students but also their non-autistic peers. These are another example of Universal Design for Learning (UDL). See 🗝 'Make Everything Visual for Me' in Part 2 for more discussion on UDL.

Examples of preventative strategies are detailed throughout Part 2. They include:

- schedules
- visual supports
- reward systems
- increased motivation
- structure, routines, and predictability throughout the school day.

Preventative strategies provide a solid foundation for behaviour management in the classroom. However, because they often do not yield dramatic and immediate results, these strategies can fall by the wayside.

In fact, it is not always obvious that they are actually working. Instead, just as teeth flossing quietly helps you to maintain a healthy set of teeth and avoid frequent visits to the dentist, these strategies are there to maintain a calm classroom and create happy students.

> Class staff felt that Jack, 8, no longer needed a visual schedule. He never asked for one, and he knew the schedule off by heart, often reminding his teacher what was happening next throughout the day. However, over the following six weeks, Jack began to put his head on his desk during work time, and often seemed anxious, constantly questioning staff and looking for reassurance about whether they would be doing his favourite subject, Irish, that day.

313

Possible reasons

Structure: Jack feels anxious all the time now because he is no longer sure that his daily schedule will happen in the same way as before. He is afraid he will miss out on doing his Irish lesson.

What to do

During an after-school meeting, class staff brainstormed a range of strategies for Jack's new behaviours, including stories about social situations and a reward system for focus and motivation. It wasn't until a member of staff wondered aloud whether it was the lack of structure that was affecting Jack that they decided to reinstate the daily visual schedule. Within a few weeks Jack was back to himself, and no longer anxious about what was happening during the day.

In fact, having structure in place every day will pay dividends on a day when a student is finding it particularly difficult to manage.

Shonice, 7, loved going to the swings for five minutes daily as a reward after completing her work. When the timer beeped, she stopped the swing and went back to her classroom. One day, Shonice arrived into school upset because her bus had been late. She started to run around the school, followed by staff. When staff asked her whether she'd like to go on the swings and showed her the timer, she began to calm down and went to the swings quite happily. Shonice recognized this predictable activity, and it gave her some boundaries and comfort in the midst of all of the chaos. Once the timer beeped after 15 minutes, she went back to class.

 Part 2 of this book provides detailed guidance and strategies on a number of preventative strategies.

Guide 61

🧠 Reactive Strategies

❝ It's important to stop and think before you say something or act. When you are heightened and stressed over a behaviour, you might be inclined to act too quickly. ❞

Jessica, special class teacher

❝ To understand someone, you need to know them first. To help them with strategies, you need to know them first. You need to know what gives them anxiety, and what they like, what they don't like, what textures they like, what textures they don't like, and just like the subtle things that nobody else would notice, to just help bring out and to be aware of, so that you know when, maybe they're struggling, and maybe when they're about to break. ❞

Erin Davidson, autistic advocate and narrator of 'Walk in My Shoes' (Donaldson Trust 2020b)

Reactive strategies are used in response to any behaviours that may challenge and aim to calm a situation down. They manage and prevent any escalation of the current situation and help a student to become calm-alert again.

Unlike preventative strategies, which are used to prevent a behaviour from occurring, reactive strategies are used once the behaviour has started.

Reactive strategies include:

- distracting the student
- diverting the student's attention to something else
- giving reassurance
- giving the student time and space by offering him a break
- planned ignoring
- diffusing the situation with humour
- triggering a 'plan B' day where you reduce immediate work expectations
- having a written behaviour plan in place. This details what staff should do as soon as a student begins to show signs of anxiety or enters the agitation phase.

Preventative strategies are put into place in order to reduce the need to use *reactive strategies*.

Brian, 7, was having a hard day at school. He told his special education teacher, Melanie, when she collected him from his classroom that he was feeling tired. She offered him some water and sympathized with him, and then wrote out a reduced schedule with him on a mini whiteboard (see Figure 6.3) as soon as he sat down in her resource room, mentally knocking off two other tasks she had planned to do with him that day.

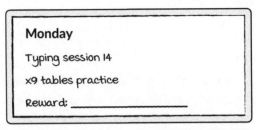

Monday

Typing session 14

x9 tables practice

Reward: _____

FIGURE 6.3 ALTERED MINI WHITEBOARD SCHEDULE

Brian usually picked a reward from a list they had devised together at the start of the year. However, this time, Brian wasn't motivated by anything on the list. He complained that he didn't want to do his multiplication tables or typing, put his head on the desk and began to slide slowly off his chair. Melanie knew that she had to act fast, as this was usually a precursor to more pressing behaviours that may challenge.

Possible reasons

Social communication and interaction: Brian clearly felt overwhelmed by something (as yet unknown) and simply did not have the communication skills at that time to tell Melanie that he needed a break.

What to do

Melanie remembered that Brian had recently mentioned that he was reading Harry Potter at home. She suggested that they think of a better reward together. Ignoring the chair-sliding behaviour, she did the following:

- She offered him five minutes of learning to draw some Harry Potter characters on YouTube.
- She googled the website there and then to give him a taste of what he could expect to earn.
- She rubbed the multiplication tables task off his schedule and told him that she would do every second typing task for him.

In this way, Melanie's quick-thinking reactive strategies prevented Brian from becoming upset and potentially disrupting his own learning for the rest of the day. She did this by:

- giving Brian the predictability and structure that he needed by more or less sticking to the schedule
- reducing Brian's workload on a day when he just was not able to do it.

❝ Consistency is key. All staff have to be on board for any strategy to work. ❞

Mags, special class teacher

 Planned ignoring

Sometimes, consciously turning a blind eye to low-level behaviour of concern can stop it in its tracks. Planned ignoring is a planned active response to low-level, attention-seeking behaviours that may challenge.

Even though it may feel like you are doing nothing to react to a behaviour of concern, planned ignoring is in fact considered to be a reactive strategy. The 'ignoring' is the reaction.

> **CASE STUDY: PLANNED IGNORING**
>
> In the previous case study, the special education teacher Melanie used planned ignoring well. In the past, whenever Brian began to slide off his chair, Melanie used to react by telling him to sit up, showing him photos of what 'good sitting' looked like or offering him a reward for 'good sitting'. However, this usually only served to draw attention to this behaviour, and Brian frequently ended up being under the table for prolonged periods of time.
>
> Melanie decided that chair sliding was pretty low-level behaviour for her and something that she would tactically ignore from now on.
>
> She also used the following reactive and preventative strategies to help Brian during the session.
>
> - Reactive strategies: To distract Brian so that he might forget to slide off his chair, rather than drawing attention to it.
> - Preventative strategies: She wrote a story for Brian about 'Why Melanie is so proud of me for staying in my chair', which they read frequently, and she encouraged Brian to tell her when he felt upset so that staff would be able to help him. They also did daily focused work on identifying emotions and figuring out ways to deal with these emotions.

 Planned ignoring is not suitable for behaviours that can potentially be dangerous for the student or for other students. Be really sure that you can actually safely ignore the behaviour and that it will not intensify further if ignored.

Ensure that everyone in school knows about the agreed planned ignoring strategy. Otherwise, other staff members may assume that you have a lackadaisical approach to behaviour management and may try to intervene on your behalf.

Triggering a 'plan B' day

Some children can experience recurring periods of anxiety or upset. In this case, it is really useful to trigger a 'plan B' day, for days when everything just feels too much for your student.

On days like this, simply reduce work expectations, add in more frequent sensory breaks and chances to earn rewards and make the reward time longer, if needed. In other words, adopt a 'softly, softly' approach for absolutely everything.

At the same time, do try to continue using the visual schedule, albeit with different activities on it to suit the needs of your student at that time.

 Behaviour plan

It is really helpful to outline preventative and reactive strategies on a written behaviour plan. A behaviour plan includes information about what to do when the student is in each phase (see ⟿ Guide 62: The Behaviour Curve). Familiarizing yourself regularly with this plan allows you to react quickly and have the necessary resources to hand when needed.

> Whenever Anthony became overwhelmed, he began to bang his hands repeatedly on the desk. Class staff knew that this marked the beginning of Anthony becoming increasingly distressed.
>
> **What to do**
> Following the steps in the behaviour plan, staff wordlessly took Anthony's sensory bag, showed Anthony the 'Sensory Room' card without using any language and brought him there, where he stayed until he was calm again.
>
> Because staff were fluent in this plan, there was no need to discuss what needed to be done, which would create further noise around Anthony. They also felt more confident in knowing that they had a plan in place.
>
> Crucially, staff also practised this 'take a break' routine daily with Anthony, when he was relaxed, so that he knew the routine when the time came to put it into action.

- Make sure that you share the behaviour strategy you are currently implementing with all school staff, either informally or during a staff meeting. In this way, staff will know whether or not to intervene when passing a student and staff member who are working through something.
- A good general rule in a school is for other staff to wait for a nod or pre-planned phrase from classroom staff before jumping in to help.

Analyzing Behaviour

Analyzing and responding to other peoples' actions is a constant part of everyday life and human interaction. You observe how the other person is behaving, try to figure out the reasons why, and together come up with a mutually acceptable solution that allows everyone to feel valued, understood and listened to.

After a behaviour of interest has happened, and everyone is calm again, it is useful to sit down with the class team and figure out what happened, why it happened, and what strategies can be put into place to prevent it from happening again.

This section contains a number of ideas to analyze behaviour in order to help your students feel calm at school. These include:

- the behaviour curve
- ABC charts
- logging behaviours.

🧠 The Behaviour Curve

A behaviour curve is a really useful way to map out what happens at each phase of a behavioural event.

Completing a behaviour curve often helps staff to:

- recognize that there are different phases during a behavioural event
- identify what is happening during each phase
- figure out strategies to support the student during each phase.

💡 Being able to recognize when a student is becoming anxious and implementing reactive strategies can often halt the behaviour in its tracks, and help your student to return to the 'calm' phase, or at least feel more at ease. Taking control of the event also builds staff's confidence in their ability to support a student who is having a hard time.

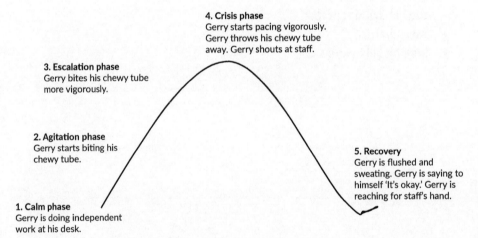

4. Crisis phase
Gerry starts pacing vigorously.
Gerry throws his chewy tube
away. Gerry shouts at staff.

3. Escalation phase
Gerry bites his chewy tube
more vigorously.

2. Agitation phase
Gerry starts biting his
chewy tube.

5. Recovery
Gerry is flushed and
sweating. Gerry is saying to
himself 'It's okay.' Gerry is
reaching for staff's hand.

1. Calm phase
Gerry is doing independent
work at his desk.

FIGURE 6.4 BEHAVIOUR CURVE FOR GERRY

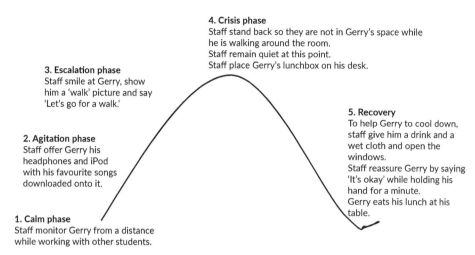

4. Crisis phase
Staff stand back so they are not in Gerry's space while he is walking around the room.
Staff remain quiet at this point.
Staff place Gerry's lunchbox on his desk.

3. Escalation phase
Staff smile at Gerry, show him a 'walk' picture and say 'Let's go for a walk.'

2. Agitation phase
Staff offer Gerry his headphones and iPod with his favourite songs downloaded onto it.

1. Calm phase
Staff monitor Gerry from a distance while working with other students.

5. Recovery
To help Gerry to cool down, staff give him a drink and a wet cloth and open the windows.
Staff reassure Gerry by saying 'It's okay' while holding his hand for a minute.
Gerry eats his lunch at his table.

FIGURE 6.5 STAFF SUPPORTING GERRY

As you can see from Figures 6.4 and 6.5, staff can step in *at any stage* to help a student try to regain some equilibrium.

Behaviour curves are different for every student. For example:

- Kevin bangs a pencil on the table = crisis phase
- Sheila bangs a pencil on the table = agitation phase.

Table 6.1 shows some general behaviour strategies that can be used at each phase. Staff can use this for ideas when analyzing an individualized behaviour curve for a student.

Table 6.1 Behaviour strategies

	Characteristics	Strategies
Calm phase	The student is calm, responds to instructions and can be directed to complete tasks.	Maintain the situation by: • observing the student • teaching the student new skills • helping the student to regulate his own sensory needs • using strategies such as visuals, a schedule and rewarding positive behaviour.

	Characteristics	Strategies
Agitation phase	The student shows signs of stress: There are changes in facial expression, vocalization, tone of voice, pacing, fidgeting, engaging in self-stimulatory behaviours or refusal to engage in an activity.	• Use calm short phrases. • Listen to the student. • Offer choice. • Distract. • Take away the trigger if appropriate. • Display a positive, relaxed disposition. • Be supportive and empathic. • Activate your behaviour plan (☞ See Guide 61: Reactive Strategies).
Escalation phase	The student is clearly distressed. The intensity of any of the behaviours in the previous phase increases significantly. The student might start displaying more behaviours that may challenge, both verbal and non-verbal.	• Give him space. • Ensure that your own body language is relaxed. • Avoid doing anything that might upset the student more. • Redirect in clear, short terms. • Use a quieter voice. • Activate your behaviour plan.
Crisis phase	The student is at a peak crisis level.	• Give the student space. Don't enter the student's personal space unless absolutely necessary. • Keep everyone safe. • Avoid giving directions or instructions. • Prioritize everyone's safety and don't worry about material items in the room. They can always be replaced. • Activate your behaviour plan.
Recovery	The situation is calming down: The student and staff are, more than likely, physically and emotionally drained.	• Look after yourself and the student. • At the end of the recovery phase, debrief with the student. See ☞ Guide 65: Three Things Staff Can Do After an Event. *This is possibly the most important phase. If the recovery is not completed properly, you can easily go back into the escalation or crisis phase.*

❝ Each child is individual. What works for one may not work for another. ❞

Mags, special class teacher

It is important to personalize the plan for each student, with his likes, dislikes and interests in mind. What works to calm one student down might exacerbate the situation for another.

- Remember, the best teaching and learning occurs when your student is calm. Trying to teach your student about *what they should be doing* while still in the agitation, escalation or crisis phase may just make the situation worse. It is best to wait until your student is calm again.

For example, if Charlie, 6, throws his pencils on the ground, asking him to pick them up may not help. Instead, wait until Charlie has completely calmed down, or simply pick up the pencils yourself later on. The next day, you could begin to teach him why pencil throwing is not appropriate, followed up by learning about and rehearsing the expected ways to act in class over the next few weeks.

- If you feel your presence is possibly preventing the student from becoming calm again, ask an experienced second person to take over temporarily. This can also be written into the behaviour plan.

" The most important thing is to keep going. Sometimes it feels like you are getting nowhere and then suddenly you're there because of everything you have done before. "

Mags, special class teacher

 Even in the middle of a difficult situation, try to remind yourself that all behaviour is communication and that your student is simply trying to tell you something. It is usually not personal, even though, some days, it may feel like it.

Guide 63

🧠 ABC Charts

What is an ABC chart?

An ABC chart is a tool used to analyze behaviours of interest.

- A= antecedent
- B = behaviour
- C = consequence.

Using an ABC chart can give staff an insight into factors that play a role in the behaviour. For example, they can work out:

- what caused the behaviour
- what the student is trying to communicate via this behaviour.

The theory that underpins ABC charts is rooted in Applied Behaviour Analysis (ABA). One of the main principles of ABA is that behaviour is controlled (either repeated or stopped) by its consequences.

For example, if you put your finger on a hot plate and get hurt, you will more than likely avoid touching a hot plate in the future.

If, on the other hand, what you do is followed by a positive experience such as praise, or receiving a reward, you are more likely to repeat this behaviour. For example, when a teacher praises a student for sharing a toy with a friend, it is likely that he will share the toy again another day.

Please note: The term 'Applied Behaviour Analysis' as used above refers to the scientific method of behaviour analysis, and not to the specific named approach or therapy called 'ABA' that is often used with autistic children.

Main components of an ABC chart
Antecedent

The antecedent is what happened directly before the behaviour of interest occurred. When defining the antecedent of a situation, consider the following:

- What were you or other people present doing or saying?
- What was the student doing?
- Was there any environmental change in the room, such as people entering or exiting, an increase in noise or a change in activity?

Behaviour

This describes what the student did.

Consequence

The consequence is what happened immediately after the behaviour. When establishing the consequence, consider the following:

- How did staff respond to the behaviour?
- Did the student obtain or avoid something after displaying the behaviour of interest?

An ABC chart also includes information about the day, time of the day, the activity and the location of the behaviour you are recording.

Note: Consequence in this context refers to *what happened as a result of the behaviour*, and not to the punitive meaning of consequence as 'punishment'.

Analyzing an ABC chart

Further analysis of the antecedent and the consequence are key to understanding the behaviour of interest and making steps towards changing it. Essentially, you are trying to identify if a pattern exists between:

- the antecedent and the behaviour

or

- the consequence and the behaviour.

By sitting down with the class team and analyzing the event, you may be able to come up with a possible reason why the behaviour of interest happened.

The antecedent

When looking at the antecedent, you are trying to identify potential triggers for the behaviour of interest. Sometimes a behaviour can be triggered by an accumulation of factors. Other times a single trigger can cause a behavioural response.

CASE STUDY: IRINA, 4

Table 6.2 ABC chart for Irina

Antecedent	Behaviour	Consequence
Staff turned on the 'Storm' song they were using as part of their weather theme. It was turned up loud and contained lots of fast-moving images.	Irina got out of her seat and ran out of the classroom.	Irina avoided having to listen to the song.

Possible reasons

Staff analyzed Irina's behaviour using an ABC chart (see Table 6.2) over a few days, and quickly figured out that the song was just too loud and busy for Irina.

What to do

As the other children really loved the song, and there was only another week left of the weather theme, staff decided to take Irina for a scheduled movement break before the song came on every day.

CASE STUDY: SUZIE, 8

Table 6.3 ABC chart for Suzie

Antecedent	Behaviour	Consequence
The children were put into groups to design a banner as part of a project on the environment.	Suzie started to walk from table to table, disrupting others' work.	Suzie avoided participating in the group work.

Possible reasons

After filling out the ABC chart (see Table 6.3), Suzie's teacher realized that Suzie was probably trying to avoid group work. She did not know how to participate in such an unstructured activity and found it hard to cope with the various demands placed on her.

What to do

The teacher came up with a variety of strategies aimed at teaching Suzie what to do during group work. These included:

- using a visual chart outlining group work rules, which illustrated the desired behaviour during group work. These were: use a soft voice, listen to others, take turns answering and stay with your group

- assigning everyone in the group a clear role. For example, Suzie was the 'recorder' with a pen and paper and now had a very concrete task to focus on
- teaching Suzie how to ask for help by modelling the phrase 'I need help' and role-playing how to ask for help appropriately
- introducing a 'Break' card that Suzie could use if the situation was too overwhelming.

In the above examples, staff helped the students to cope better by either:

- modifying the environment and changing the trigger (Case study: Irina, 4)
- teaching the student strategies to cope with a particular trigger, as well as modifying the environment (Case study: Suzy, 8).

The consequence

When analyzing the consequence, consider the following:

- Does the student gain anything from displaying the behaviour? This can be something tangible (a desired object), a reaction (increased attention) or a sensory stimulus (quiet time).
- Does the student avoid something as a result of the behaviour? For example, avoiding a task or an overloud situation.
- What is the student trying to communicate?

Once you figure out that a student is behaving in a particular way in order to achieve a particular consequence, then you can change the behaviour of interest by changing the consequence.

As well as looking at the antecedent and the consequence, it can be useful to take note of the following environmental factors such as:

- What day is it?
- What time of the day is it?
- Where did the behaviour occur?

When staff have inadvertently triggered a behavioural response

Sometimes an ABC chart analysis identifies that something that a staff member did actually fuelled a situation, rather than defused it. This is so common and not something to be ashamed of or embarrassed about. All you can do, as a teacher or support staff, is to learn from your mistakes and remember that you did your best at the time.

The best way to move forward is to take note of what happened, share the information with all staff working with the student and try a different strategy.

Tips for recording

- Write down your observations as soon as possible after the behaviour occurred.
- Record exactly what the student or staff member said, using quotation marks.
- Describe the situation as objectively as possible by giving an exact description of the behaviour in neutral terms. Someone who was not there should be able to visualize exactly what happened. Using the phrase 'he had a tantrum' does not describe what actually occurred and does not provide you with the level of detail you require for analysis.
- Involve all professionals that were present as their contributions might assist you in building a better picture.

Often, you will need to complete a few ABC charts over a period of time to gain more insight into behaviours.

 Logging Behaviours

Behaviour logging is a way to record recurring behaviours in order to:

- get a baseline measurement of how often a behaviour of interest is occurring
- establish whether there is a pattern to the behaviours. For example, if the behaviour of interest occurs more at particular times, during specific subjects or on certain days
- identify times when a behaviour does not occur and possibly identify reasons for this
- evaluate the efficacy of your behaviour plan by noting any increases or decreases in a behaviour.

There are several different ways to log behaviours.

Frequency chart

A frequency chart gives you an overview of how often a behaviour occurs in a given period of time (see Table 6.4). This type of chart is suitable for recording frequently occurring behaviours such as speaking out of turn, stereotyped behaviours (for example pacing or repetitive questioning) or more physical behaviours of interest.

Staff can:

- choose a behaviour to focus on
- record the behaviour of concern over an hour, a day, a week or a month
- tally in the appropriate slot, whenever the behaviour occurs.

Table 6.4 Example of a weekly frequency chart

Name student: Charlie, 5

Behaviour: Running around the classroom and trying to engage with others while they are working by shouting at them

	Monday	Tuesday	Wednesday	Thursday	Friday
9:00–9:30					
9:30–10:00	I I I I	I I I I	I I I	I I I I	I I I I I
10:00–10:30					
10:30–11:00	Break				
11:00–11:30	I I		I I I		I
11:30–12:00					
12:00–12:30					
12:30–1:00		I I	I I I	I I	I I I I I I I I I
Total	6	6	9	6	14

Reading the chart

This weekly chart provides you with a clear overview of when the behaviour of interest occurs most frequently.

The shaded areas in Table 6.5 show the times of day that Charlie found it difficult to focus or manage. Staff can then:

- cross-check the chart with the daily class timetable to see if there is a pattern to Charlie's behaviour
- check what times of day the behaviour of interest is not occurring, note what Charlie was engaged in then and add more of that into Charlie's daily schedule
- try to establish what factors could be responsible for the increase and decrease at specific times during the day once you have made these observations.

Table 6.5 Analyzing a weekly frequency chart

Name student: Charlie, 5

Behaviour: Running around the classroom and trying to engage with others while they are working by shouting at them

	Monday	Tuesday	Wednesday	Thursday	Friday
9:00–9:30	Jigsaws	Threading	Play-Doh	Stickle Bricks	LEGO®
9:30–10:00	Literacy station teaching 4	Literacy station teaching 4	Literacy station teaching 3	Literacy station teaching 4	Literacy station teaching 5
10:00–10:30	Whole-class phonics	Whole-class phonics	Whole-class phonics	Whole-class phonics	Whole-class phonics
10:30–11:00	Break				
11:00–11:30	Maths 2	Maths on the computer	Maths 3	Maths on the computer	Maths 1
11:30–12:00	P.E.	P.E.	P.E.	P.E.	P.E.
12:00–12:30	Swimming	English	English	English	Art
12:30–1:00	Swimming	History 2	Geography 3	Science 2	Golden time 8

In the above example, it is clear that:

- the behaviour of interest happened most frequently during station teaching, golden time, in the afternoons and, to a lesser extent, during Maths
- the behaviour happened far less frequently during Phonics, and when there were physical activities such as P.E. or swimming, and more project-based subjects such as History, Geography and Science.

Some possible ways to support Charlie include the following:

- Give him more structure during station teaching, perhaps by allowing him to stay at his own desk while all of the other groups move around to the different stations.
- Ensure he has closed-ended tasks to do during station teaching. For example, give him his own set of phonics card or letter fans, or incorporate his special interest of Sonic the Hedgehog by making a Sonic Play-Doh mat to encourage him to participate.
- Offer a sensory break during station teaching, as this is often a noisy session.

- Add in another Maths on the computer session for him, as he seems to enjoy this.
- Structure golden time so that he has a set game to play, and ensure that he manages to take a sensory break during this very busy session too.

It is really useful to continue to use a frequency chart while implementing a strategy over a few weeks, as it will tell you clearly whether or not your strategies are working.

Calm spots and hot spots

Frequency charts help you to find a clear pattern of behaviour and enable you to pinpoint 'calm spots' and 'hot spots' throughout the school day.

- **Calm spots** are times when your student is participating calmly and is engaged in the task.
- **Hot spots** are times that your student finds tricky, and they may display behaviours that may be seen to be challenging as a result.

The aim is to look at your student's school day and find ways to:

- increase calm spots
- reduce hot spots, or further structure or incentivize these to make them easier.

Duration chart

A duration chart (see Table 6.6) allows you to record how long a behaviour of interest lasts. If you complete a duration chart before and after you implement strategies, it is then easy to gauge whether or not your strategies are making a difference for your student. For example, you can clearly see whether the student is displaying the target behaviour for a shorter or longer period of time.

> Mary, 8, had a tendency to leave her seat during whole-class sessions and individual work time and wander around the classroom.

To get an accurate picture of how long she was able to sit down for, staff completed a duration chart measuring time spent in her seat.

After looking at just one week's worth of data, they figured out that Mary was able to sit at her desk for about ten minutes on average, either doing her work or listening to the teacher during a whole-class session.

Table 6.6: Example of a duration chart

Name: Mary			
Behaviour of interest: Time spent in seat			
Day/location	Start	End	Duration
Monday	9:30	9:40	10 minutes
Tuesday	10:40	10:53	13 minutes
Wednesday	12:15	12:24	9 minutes

Staff sat down together and looked at some ways to encourage Mary to stay sitting at her desk for longer in order to complete her work and not miss out on any key learning. Strategies included:

- asking Mary what she found hard about sitting down at her desk and if she had any ideas about what might help her
- giving Mary increased sensory breaks throughout the day
- trialling a Move 'n' Sit cushion with her in her seat, which she loved
- giving her permission to take a break by leaving her seat (and outlining exactly where she could go in the classroom)
- giving her some fiddle toys to use while sitting and passively listening
- ensuring that work was closed-ended and it was clear what Mary had to do
- offering Mary an incentive for completing work
- praising Mary whenever she managed to complete her work
- making the whole-class work more visual by using more images on the interactive whiteboard or a visualizer when doing an art lesson.

When staff completed the duration chart a month later, they were delighted to see that she was now able to sit for up to 20 minutes and was no longer missing out on key learning.

General tips for behaviour logging

When logging behaviours, it is useful to keep the following in mind:

- Clearly define the behaviour you are recording. For example, 'shouting out during class time'.
- It is usually simpler to focus on and record a single behaviour of interest at a time. Choose the most pressing behaviour first. Once you have implemented strategies for this, you can move on to the next behaviour of concern.
- If you choose to record a group of behaviours that are related, you can write the code for each behaviour on the behaviour chart (see Table 6.7).

Table 6.7 Recording recurring behaviours

R= raised voice

Q = repeated questioning

If the repeated questioning occurs twice in the time slot, simply code it as
QQ. The same applies for multiple instances of raised voice.

	Monday	Tuesday
9:00–9:30	QQ	Q
9:30–10:00	RRR	RR

- If this is too confusing for staff to record, simply write the behaviours at the top of the behaviour log and code them as 'E' for event (see Table 6.8 for example).

Table 6.8 Recording multiple behaviours

E = raised voice; repeated questioning

	Monday	Tuesday
9:00–9:30	EE	E
9:30–10:00	EEE	EE

- If you forget to log the behaviours on a particular day or at a certain time, draw a line through this day, and write 'not done'. This prevents your data from being skewed and ensures that you get a really accurate picture of the behaviour.

The Recovery

 When a behavioural event has occurred, both staff and students can feel vulnerable and exhausted. Handling the recovery in a careful and thoughtful manner will help prevent the situation from recurring, as well as enabling the student to emerge from the situation with dignity and self-esteem.

A well thought-out behaviour plan could also include a brief outline of what to do when everything has settled down again.

💡 Three Things Staff Can Do After an Event

1. Show kindness to your student

Keep in mind that your student has just been on an emotional rollercoaster and is more than likely exhausted. The most important part of the recovery now is to show empathy, to support the student to become calm again and to remain so.

Examples of this include:

- giving her something to eat or drink
- breathing exercises
- allowing her to relax by listening to music or taking some quiet time in the cosy corner.

Staff gave Stuart, 6, a drink and a cold cloth to help him calm down after he had had a difficult morning. They sat down with him, and helped him to take off his shoes. There was no teaching done at this point or any discussion about right and wrong. Staff were simply helping a very confused and exhausted little boy to regain his equilibrium in as dignified a way as possible.

2. Show kindness when reporting back to parents or guardians

An important part of dealing with a behavioural event is how you communicate to parents about what happened. Many parents need and want to know if anything unusual has happened during the school day so that they can monitor their child's mood when they arrive home. They might also want to discuss the school day and support their child when she gets home, confident that they know all the details about the situation.

However, it can often be difficult for parents to hear about what their child has done at school on a particularly hard day.

Staff can:

- consult with parents at the start of the year about their preferred way of communication with you about their child
- take a deep breath and jot down key facts about the event before ringing a parent, and let them know about the event in a calm and neutral manner
- consider ringing or emailing parents whenever something good happens at school too to balance out communication about difficult days

- remember that it can be really upsetting to receive a phone call from school, and that some parents can become defensive at times. Be aware this is usually never directed personally at staff, but arises rather from embarrassment or fear that their child will be excluded from school. See ⚷ Guide 44: Communicating with Parents.

3. Show kindness to yourself and the class team

An extended period of behaviours that may challenge can be emotionally and physically exhausting for staff. If events happen frequently in your setting, ensure that you have agreed procedures in place to help staff feel supported and heard. For example:

- Give members of the staff team a break after the event, if appropriate.
- Have a staff debrief as soon as possible afterwards.
- Chat to trusted colleagues about the situation.
- Don't be afraid to seek advice from outside professionals. It can be hard to have a clear perspective on something you are living and breathing daily.
- Ensure that there is a culture of positivity in the classroom – celebrate every success no matter how small.
- When your behaviour strategies are working nine days out of ten, and then you have one particularly difficult day, just put it down as a blip and move on.
- Find something outside of school that relaxes you and do it regularly.

I discovered Kundalini yoga during a particularly stressful time at work, and it became the best two hours of my week. *Claire*

After work, I go straight to my garden or polytunnel. *Annelies*

I make my favourite salad and watch my favourite programme on TV. *Marcella*

It helps me to talk to my partner because he says 'Why would you worry about this?' *Jessica*

Guide 66

Helping Your Student to Learn from the Event

As discussed earlier, very little learning happens until your student feels calm again. If handled carefully, choosing the right moment to discuss the event with him will not cause it to reoccur. In other words, 'Strike while the iron is cold.'

Talking through the event (see Table 6.9) provides an opportunity to gain insight and also avoids future recurrence. 'Debriefing is about repair and recovery. It is the aftercare of de-escalation' (Brown 2015, p.71).

It is useful to wait until both staff and the student have fully recovered their equilibrium. Otherwise, staff risk choosing the wrong words or tone of voice, and the student risks becoming upset all over again.

This chat may happen later on during the same day, the next day or even the next week.

66 We often feel that we have to address a behaviour immediately. If you know that the child can talk about it later, I would always opt for that. It gives you time to think about it too. 99

Jessica, special class teacher

Table 6.9 Debriefing dos and don'ts

Dos	Don'ts
• Provide your student with relevant coping strategies. • Set out clear expectations. • Teach your student the more expected way to act in the situation. • Use a 'Playback' form (see 🔑 Guide 37) to draw or write down what happened. This will help him to understand what actually happened as well to learn about the effect his actions had on other people.	Don't ask a student why he displayed a certain behaviour. Even as adults, it might only be after a lengthy reflection that we begin to understand why we behaved in a certain way.

Guide 67

Five Positive Behaviour Management Strategies

Please note: Whenever analysing 'possible reasons' behind any behaviour of interest, it is useful to refer back to Figure 6.2 'Behaviour Bubbles' in Guide 59.

1. Remember that patience is a virtue – just wait!

Chen, 5, didn't always check his schedule when prompted. Sometimes he picked a random activity from his schedule and refused to engage in the current activity. He usually started shouting 'No' and lay on the ground. When staff tried to reason with Chen or when they showed him a visual of what he was expected to do, he just shouted louder and louder.

Possible reasons
Social communication: Shouting is the only way that Chen knew how to communicate that he did not want to do something.

What to do

- Class staff decided to give Chen more time. They simply waited until he was ready to move on. After a few minutes, he usually began to participate happily in the class activity.
- Staff also started modelling the phrase 'I don't want to do this' so Chen would learn how to communicate how he felt.

Think about
Consider the number of instructions that you give to your students in one day. Some students are not able to communicate that they just need a moment. It is a natural response to start reasoning with your students, which can often result in them feeling overwhelmed. It is often much more beneficial to wait until your student is ready to collaborate with you. It is usually just a matter of waiting for a few moments before he is ready to move on.

2. Tackle one thing at a time, but use as many strategies as you can

Since the Christmas holidays, Anja seemed slightly unsettled in school. She did not want to engage in some activities and answered back to staff when she was asked to do something. Her mother also reported that she had difficulties getting Anja ready for school in the morning.

Possible reasons

Structure, sameness: Coming back to school after a long break had unsettled Anja. She needed time to settle back into school life after the lack of routine over the Christmas holidays.

What to do

- Anja's teacher made a visual calendar clearly displaying school days and weekend days so Anja knew exactly what days she had to go to school and when she could stay at home.
- The teacher also tweaked Anja's daily schedule slightly, providing her with more breaks.
- Every afternoon, support staff spent ten minutes with Anja discussing what had gone well during the day and what could have gone better.

After a few weeks, Anja was right back on track, following her usual routine.

Think about

Sometimes it can be hard to identify the exact root of the problem. Implementing numerous strategies simultaneously can help to tackle many aspects of a situation.

3. Avoid viewing a potentially difficult situation as a competition between yourself and the pupil – diffusing a situation is not the same as 'giving in'

Ali, 6, did not want to leave his mainstream classroom to go to a phonics group with the special education teacher, Donna. Whenever Donna arrived into the classroom, holding a 'Learning Room' photo card, Ali usually chose to sit under a table. It often took up to 15 minutes of coaxing before Ali went to the phonics classroom. This proved difficult logistically, as Donna also had four other students in the group.

During the phonics session, Donna used a visual schedule and a rewards system. When Ali had completed four phonics activities, he was allowed to look at pictures of Sonic the Hedgehog on the iPad for five minutes at the end of the session.

Possible reasons

Structure, sameness: Ali found it hard to cope with change during the school day.

Social communication: Ali did not know how to communicate that he felt scared about moving classrooms, even though he did it every single day.

What to do

Using a written social narrative and a First/Then Board saying 'First: walk to learning room, Then: Sonic for three minutes', Donna explained to Ali that he would now be able to have the iPad as soon as he arrived in the learning room. In this way, the iPad would become a 'transitional object' to help Ali to move into the other classroom.

After a few weeks, Ali became more used to going with Donna and being in the learning room.

Think about

At times, it might feel counterintuitive to give a reward first, but in this instance, Ali needed something to help him to transition successfully to another classroom, rather than needing a reward for the work session itself.

Focus on what you want to accomplish and how this can be achieved. It is not a failure to adjust your expectations or meet the student halfway. Recognize that the road to success is paved with small milestones.

4. Plan ahead: If you know the student will find an upcoming situation difficult, be as proactive as possible to come up with solutions

Last year, Emmet, 10, really enjoyed preparing for his school's annual Christmas concert. He participated in the dance sessions with his classmates and practised endlessly at home. However, when the time came, Emmet refused to attend school for a few days before the show and ended up missing the show altogether.

When Emmet's parents and teacher met, they concluded that, in hindsight, this had all been due to performance anxiety. This school year, the school was planning a similar event and Emmet started to miss school in the weeks leading up to the event.

Possible reasons

Social communication: Emmet had become so anxious about the show that he could not communicate what he wanted.

Structure, sameness: Emmet was frightened of the unknown and needed to know exactly what was expected of him and how he could escape, if he needed to.

What to do

- His teacher emailed a written story explaining to Emmet that he didn't have to participate if he didn't want to and what he could do instead while the show was on.

- When Emmet came back to school, the teacher went through the options with him, discussing what he felt most comfortable to do.
- She also asked an adult to be on stand-by in case Emmet decided he wanted to leave the stage.

With these measures in place, Emmet felt confident enough to participate in the show and told everyone he felt proud of himself afterwards.

Think about
If you know your student is going to find a particular situation difficult, put as many strategies as possible in place to support him.

5. For a student to change their behaviour, you might have to change your approach completely

Mary, 9, had a tendency to interrupt lessons with an endless flow of questions that were unrelated to the topic. This included why certain school rules were in place, when they would start to learn about her special interest, the *Titanic*, and when they would practise her new favourite song again. Initially, her teacher answered these questions patiently as they were always phrased so reasonably. However, the questions were endless and disrupted a smooth running of many lessons.

Possible reasons
Social communication and interaction: Mary did not realize the impact of her actions on other people. She was very keen to chat to others about her special interests and things she found interesting in class. She needed a structured approach around asking questions, in particular around her special interest, the *Titanic*.

What to do

- Mary's teacher decided that once she had given a definite answer to the whole class, she would only repeat her answer one more time, clearly stating that this was the last time this issue was being discussed.
- She inserted a 'talk with teacher' time onto Mary's schedule, during which Mary could ask her any questions she might have.
- She wrote a social narrative explaining to Mary how difficult it was for the teacher and the class when Mary constantly interrupted lessons.

After a few weeks, Mary's questioning during class time reduced significantly. She was now happy to hold on to her questions until 'talk with teacher' time, as she was reassured that they would get answered then. She also had a better understanding of how her actions were affecting other people.

Think about

Your students will not change their behaviour solely because you want them to change it. Staff's response to a behaviour is an essential part of positive preventative and reactive strategies. If what you do is not working, a simple change of approach might be all you need.

Also remember

- **Be calm, consistent and confident at all times: If you have said it, help your students to achieve it.** Being consistent makes school life much more predictable for your students. It also forms the basis of trust developing between you and your students. If your students don't follow your first instruction, repeat it a second time while guiding them to carry out the task.
- **Never take away everyday scheduled activities. These are non-negotiable.**
  Anything already on a child's schedule, like swimming, P.E. or playground time, are non-negotiable and should never be removed. If your student consistently fails to follow a routine or request, rather than making an immediate change, you might have to analyze the situation further by completing an ABC chart or logging the behaviour and seeing what strategies might work better.
- **Show your student what you want him to do, rather than telling him what not to do.** By stating the desired behaviour, you are focusing on what you want your students to do. Saying 'No running' to a student may encourage him to run, as this is the last word he has heard. If, instead, you simply say 'Walking', he knows exactly what he is supposed to do.
- **Develop a positive relationship with your student. Praise your students as much as you can for their achievements.** Take some time out to have fun with your students. Most students will put their best foot forward if they have a great relationship with you. Building a positive relationship takes time and effort, but really does pay dividends.
- **Sometimes you have to go backward to go forward.** Revisiting issues that you thought were resolved can feel like a step backward. However, letting a situation slip can make it much harder in the long run. Strategies need to be based on the student's current needs, rather than where you think he should be.

Five essentials for staff when implementing positive behaviour supports

Flexibility

Sometimes you have to gauge what is working and what is going to be an uphill battle. Sometimes it is the adults who need to learn how to be flexible. While it is commendable to challenge your students, it is sometimes wiser to back down. For example, if a student arrives into school after being stuck in traffic for an hour and has not eaten breakfast, then you might consider allowing him to relax for ten minutes or reducing their workload slightly.

A small ego

Sometimes you have to let your students think that they are in charge when really you are in charge. For example, if you know the student does not want to write ten sentences, you can instead offer him a choice of three or five sentences. In this way, at least he is getting some work done while sticking to the schedule, albeit in a reduced way.

Courage

Don't be afraid to ask for help. Ask your principal or a colleague for advice, sign up for some training or put in a request for a visit from your local outreach team or autism team advisor. Often getting an outside perspective can really help.

Confidence

It takes confidence in your ability to ignore certain behaviours of interest, particularly in front of other staff who may be fully paid-up members of the 'He has to learn' brigade. It also takes chutzpah to hunker down beside a child who is lying on the floor of a main corridor and calmly sit there using visual supports to encourage the child to stand up and come back to class.

A sense of humour

It goes without saying that this is key for anyone who regularly works with all children. Most school staff have this in bucket loads already.

Frequently asked questions

Q: I tried all the strategies and they didn't work.

A: It sounds like you have put so much thought and effort into helping everyone to have a better time at school. First of all, give yourself and the class team a pat on the back. Next, think about whether it would be useful now to take a step back and ask for help. Sometimes, just chatting over situations with someone new (be it an outreach worker, a behaviour consultant or a colleague in another class) can illuminate the way forward for you.

Time and time again, I have seen staff leave these meetings feeling recognized and appreciated for all of their hard work and with fresh ideas that *they have come up with themselves* – they just needed some time out to think, discuss and reflect.

Q: Does this mean my student can get away with doing whatever he wants in order to avoid conflict in the classroom?

A: Always try to bring it back to what you think your student can manage on a particular day – it's not 'giving in' to allow someone to take a break or to have a reduced workload, it's levelling the playing field for every student, depending on their needs at that time.

If you change the schedule on a whim, dependent on his needs, make sure to display the new schedule and let the student know that this has changed. Most students still want clear boundaries in place throughout the school day, as it makes them feel safer.

Try to keep using those preventative strategies – and keep going back to these questions:

- What does my student love to do?
- What can we do to help him to feel calmer (possibly using all the resources and activities he loves in a creative way, as an incentive)?

Q: My student was already stressed when he arrived at school this morning. We didn't even see the different phases.

A: When this happens, it is probably because your student is already in the agitation phase by the time he arrives into school. This might be as a result of a sleepless night, having missed breakfast or having taken a different route to school. If this happens frequently, ask parents for any useful information about what happened before the student came to school. As changes in some students' behaviour can be very subtle, good observation skills are essential. Implement a 'plan B' day for such days.

References

Altomare, A.A., McCrimmon, A.W., Cappadocia, M.C., Weiss, J.A., Beran, T.N. and Smith-Demers, A. (2017) When push comes to shove: How are students with autism spectrum disorder coping with bullying? *Canadian Journal of School Psychology 32*(3–4), 209–227.

American Psychiatric Association (APA) (2013) *Diagnostic and Statistical Manual of Mental Disorders* (5th ed.). Arlington, VA: American Psychiatric Association.

AsIAm (2019) *Invisible Children: Survey on School Absence and Withdrawal in Ireland's Autism Community.* AsIAm Policy Office. Accessed on 21.02.2021 at https://asiam.ie/wp-content/uploads/2019/04/Invisible-Children-Survey-on-School-Absence-Withdrawl-in-Irelands-Autism-Community-April-2019.pdf

Attwood, T. (2015) *The Complete Guide to Asperger's Syndrome.* London: Jessica Kingsley Publishers.

Ayres, A.J. (1972) *Sensory Integration and Learning Disabilities.* Los Angeles, CA: Western Psychological Services.

Bagatell, N. (2019) Individuals with autism spectrum disorder and skills for daily living. In R. Jordan, J.M. Roberts and K. Hume (Eds.) *The Sage Handbook of Autism and Education.* London: Sage.

Baker, M.J., Koegel, R.L. and Koegel, L.K. (1998) Increasing the social behavior of young children with autism using their obsessive behaviors. *Journal of the Association for Persons with Severe Handicaps 23*, 300–308.

Baranek, G.T. (2002) Efficacy of sensory and motor interventions for children with autism. *Journal of Autism and Developmental Disorders 32*, 397–422.

Baranek, G.T., David, F.J., Poe, M.D., Stone, W.L. and Watson, L.R. (2006) Sensory experiences questionnaire: Discriminating sensory features in young children with autism, developmental delays, and typical development. *Journal of Child Psychology and Psychiatry 47*(6), 591–601.

Baron-Cohen, S., Leslie, A.M. and Frith, U. (1985) Does the autistic child have a 'theory of mind'? *Cognition 21*(1), 37–46.

BBC Two – Horizon (2006) *The Woman Who Thinks Like A Cow* [Documentary]. London: BBC Two.

BBC Two – Horizon (2013–2014) *Living with Autism* [Documentary]. London: BBC Two.

Bellini, S., Peters, J.K., Benner, L. and Hopf, A. (2007) A meta-analysis of school-based social skills interventions for children with autism spectrum disorders. *Remedial and Special Education 28*(3), 153–162.

Bird, G., Beadman, J. and Buckley, S. (2001) *Reading and Writing for Children with Down Syndrome.* Hampshire, UK: Down Syndrome Educational Trust.

Blackburn, R. (2019) *Autism* [Lecture]. The Bridge London Trust Islington, London. September.

Breitenbach, M. (2000) *Basic Skills Checklist.* Arlington, TX: Future Horizons.

Brown, S. (2015) *Autism Spectrum Disorder and De-Escalation Strategies.* London: Jessica Kingsley Publishers.

Burgess, R. (2016) *Understanding the Spectrum.* Theorah. Accessed on 21.02.2021 at https://theoraah.tumblr.com/post/142300214156/understanding-the-spectrum

REFERENCES

Cachia, R.L., Anderson, A. and Moore, D.W. (2016) Mindfulness in individuals with autism spectrum disorder: A systematic review and narrative analysis. *Journal of Autism and Developmental Disorders 3*(2), 165–178. doi:10.1007/s40489-016-0074-0

Caldwell, P. (2011) *Intensive Interaction: Using Body Language to Communicate.* Intellectual Disability and Health, University of Hertfordshire. Accessed on 21.02.2021 at www.intellectualdisability.info/how-to-guides/articles/intensive-interaction-using-body-language-to-communicate

Carnegie, D. (2009) *How to Win Friends and Influence People.* New York: Simon & Schuster. (Original work published 1936.)

Centers for Disease Control and Prevention (CDC) (2020) *Data and Statistics on Autism Spectrum Disorder.* Accessed on 24.03.2021 at www.cdc.gov/ncbddd/autism/data.html

Chang, Y.C. and Locke, J. (2016) A systematic review of peer-mediated interventions for children with autism spectrum disorder. *Research in Autism Spectrum Disorders 27*, 1–10.

Cirillo, F. (2019) *Do More and Have Fun with Time Management.* Cirillo Consulting GMBH. Accessed on 21.02.2021 at https://francescocirillo.com/pages/pomodoro-technique

Cook O'Toole, J. (2013) *The Asperkids Secret Book of Social Rules.* London: Jessica Kingsley Publishers.

Cridland, E.K., Jones, S.C., Caputi, P. and Magee, C.A. (2014) Being a girl in a boys' world: Investigating the experiences of girls with autism spectrum disorders during adolescence. *Journal of Autism and Developmental Disorders 44*(6), 1261–1274.

Csikszentmihalyi, M. (1990) *Flow: The Psychology of Happiness.* London: Rider Books.

Cummins, C., Pellicano, E. and Crane, L. (2020) Autistic adults' views of their communication skills and needs. *International Journal of Language and Communication Disorders 55*(5), 678–689.

Dachez, J. (2017) *La Difference Invisible.* Paris: Delacourt/Mirages.

Davies, G. (2014, July 28) *Attention autism – therapy ideas live* [Video]. YouTube. www.youtube.com/watch?v=nFYnc4xcZ6k

Dawson, G., Toth, K., Abbott, R., Osterling, J., Munson, J., Estes, A. and Liaw, J. (2004) Early social attention impairments in autism: Social orienting, joint attention, and attention to distress. *Developmental Psychology 40*(2), 271–283.

Delaney, S. (2017) *Become the Primary Teacher Everyone Wants to Have.* Oxon and New York: Routledge.

Department for Education (2014) *Children and Families Act 2014.* Her Majesty's Stationery Office. Accessed on 21.02.2021 at www.legislation.gov.uk/ukpga/2014/6/contents/enacted

Department of Health (2018) *Estimating Prevalence of Autism Spectrum Disorders (ASD) in the Irish Population: A Review of Data Sources and Epidemiological Studies.* Accessed on 21.02.2021 at https://assets.gov.ie/10707/ce1ca48714424c0ba4bb4c0ae2e510b2.pdf

Domire, S. and Wolfe, P. (2014) Effects of video prompting techniques on teaching daily living skills to children with autism spectrum disorder: A Review. *Research and Practice for Persons with Severe Disabilities 39*(3), 211–226.

Donaldson Trust (2020a) *Walk in my shoes* [Interview]. Donaldson Trust. Accessed on 26.03.2021 at https://www.donaldsons.org.uk/walk-in-my-shoes

Donaldson Trust (2020b) *Walk in my shoes* [Video]. YouTube. Accessed on 21.02.2021 at www.youtube.com/watch?v=KSKvazfTLv8&feature=emb_logo

Droney, C. (2017) Promoting autism peer awareness in mainstream schools. *Impact: Interim Issue, Journal of the Chartered College of Teaching 1.*

DuCharme, R. (2003) Evidence based instruction for children with Asperger syndrome. In R. DuCharme and T. Gulotta (Eds.) *Asperger Syndrome: A Guide for Professionals and Families.* New York: Springer Science+Business Media.

Frith, U. (1989) *Autism: Explaining the Enigma.* London: Blackwell.

Frith, U. and Frith, C.D. (2003) Development and neurophysiology of mentalizing. *Philosophical Transactions of the Royal Society of London, Series B, Biological Sciences 358*(1431), 459–473.

Fuller, E.A. and Kaiser, A.P. (2019) The effects of early intervention on social communication outcomes for children with autism spectrum disorder: A meta-analysis. *Journal of Autism and Developmental Disorders 50*, 1683–1700.

Gagnon, E. and Smith-Myles, B. (2016) *The Power Card Strategy 2.0: An Evidence-Based Strategy.* Shawnee, KS: AAPC Publishing.

Galanopoulos, A., Robertson, D., Spain, D. and Murphy, C. (2014) Mental health and autism. *National Autistic Society: Your Autism Magazine 8*(4).

Gorman, J.C. (2004) *Working with Challenging Parents of Students with Special Needs.* Thousand Oaks, CA: Corwin Press.

Grandin, T. (2002) *Teaching Tips for Children and Adults with Autism.* Indiana Resource Centre for Autism. Accessed on 21.02.2021 at www.iidc.indiana.edu/irca/articles/teaching-tips-for-children-and-adults-with-autism

Grandin, T. (2009) *My experiences with autism, from early childhood to a successful career* [Lecture]. The Irish Society for Autism. 28 March.

Grandin, T. (2014) Different kinds of minds contribute to society [Video]. *The Biomedical & Life Sciences Collection, Henry Stewart Talks.* https://hstalks-com.ucc.idm.oclc.org/bs/2834

Gray, C. (1993) *The Original Social Stories Book.* Arlington, TX: Future Horizons.

Griffin, C., Lombardo, M.V. and Auyeung, B. (2015) Alexithymia in children with and without autism spectrum disorders. *Autism Research 9*(7), 773–780.

Grindal, T., Hehir, T., Freeman, B., Lamoreau, R., Borquaye Y. and Burke, S. (2016) *A Summary of the Evidence on Inclusive Education*, Abt Associates. Accessed on 21.02.2021 at www.edu-links.org/resources/summary-research-evidence-inclusive-education

Grove, R., Roth, I. and Hoekstra, R.A. (2016) The motivation for special interests in individuals with autism and controls: Development and validation of the special interest motivation scale. *Autism Research: Official Journal of the International Society for Autism Research 9*(6), 677–688.

Happé, F. and Baron-Cohen, S. (2014) *Remembering Lorna Wing (1928–2014).* Spectrum News. Accessed on 21.02.2021 at www.spectrumnews.org/opinion/remembering-lorna-wing-1928-2014

Harris, A. (2019) *Creating inclusive schools for autistic students.* [Lecture]. Scoil Triest, August.

Healy, S., Nacario, A., Braithwaite, R.E. and Hopper, C. (2018) The effect of physical activity interventions on youth with autism spectrum disorder: A meta-analysis. *Autism Research 11*, 818–833. doi:10.1002/aur.1955

Hebron, J. and Humphrey, N. (2014) Exposure to bullying among students with autism spectrum conditions: A multi-informant analysis of risk and protective factors. *Autism 18*(6), 618–630.

Humphrey, N. and Symes, W. (2010) Perceptions of social support and experience of bullying among pupils with autistic spectrum disorders in mainstream secondary schools.' *European Journal of Special Needs Education 25*(1), 77–91.

James, L. (2018) *Odd Girl Out.* London: Bluebird.

Jung, S. and Sainato, D.M. (2013) Teaching play skills to young children with autism. *Journal of Intellectual & Developmental Disability 38*(1), 74–90.

Kapp, S.K., Gillespie-Lynch, K., Sherman, L.E. and Hutman, T. (2013) Deficit, difference, or both? Autism and neurodiversity. *Developmental Psychology 49*(1), 59–71.

Kasari, C., Freeman, S. and Paparella, T. (2006) Joint attention and symbolic play in young children with autism: A randomized controlled intervention study. *Journal of Child Psychology and Psychiatry 47*, 611–620.

Kasari, C., Gulsrud, A.C., Wong, C., Kwon, S. and Locke, J. (2010) Randomized controlled caregiver mediated joint attention intervention for toddlers with autism. *Journal of Autism and Developmental Disorders 40*(9), 1045–1056.

Kasari, C., Rotheram-Fuller, E., Locke, J. and Gulsrud, A. (2012) Making the connection: Randomized controlled trial of social skills at school for children with autism spectrum disorders. *Journal of Child Psychology and Psychiatry and Allied Disciplines 53*(4), 431–439.

Kenny, L., Hattersley, C., Molins, B., Buckley, C., Povey, C. and Pellicano, E. (2016) Which terms should be used to describe autism? Perspectives from the UK autism community. *Autism 20*(4), 442–462.

Klin, A., Danovitch, J.H., Merz, A.B. and Volkmar, F.R. (2007) Circumscribed interests in higher functioning individuals with autism spectrum disorders: An exploratory study. *Research and Practice for Persons with Severe Disabilities 32*, 89–100.

Kloosterman, P.H., Kelley, E.A., Craig, W.A., Parker, J.D.A. and Javier, C. (2013) Types and experiences of bullying in adolescents with an autism spectrum disorder.' *Research in Autism Spectrum Disorders 7*(7), 824–832.

Kohls, G., Antezana, L., Mosner, M.G., Schultz, R.T. and Yerys, B.E. (2018) Altered reward system reactivity for personalized circumscribed interests in autism. *Molecular Autism 9*(9), 1–12

Kossyvaki, L. and Papoudi, D. (2016) A review of play interventions for children with autism at school. *International Journal of Disability, Development and Education 63*(1), 45–63.

Kouklari, E.C., Tsermentseli, S. and Monks, C.P. (2018) Hot and cool executive function in children and adolescents with autism spectrum disorder: Cross-sectional developmental trajectories. *Child Neuropsychology 24*(8), 1088–1114.

Kretzmann, M., Shih, W. and Kasari, C. (2014) Improving peer engagement of children with autism on the school playground: Randomized controlled trial. *Behavior Therapy 46*, 20–28.

Lang, R., Regester, A., Lauderdale, S., Ashbaugh, K. and Haring, A. (2010) Treatment of anxiety in autism spectrum disorders using cognitive behaviour therapy: A systematic review. *Developmental Neurorehabilitation 13*(1), 53–63.

Lindl, J.C. (1989) What do parents want from principals and teachers? *Educational Leadership 47*(2), 12–14.

Lindsay, S. and Edwards A. (2013) A systematic review of disability awareness interventions for children and youth. *Disability and Rehabilitation 35*(8), 623–646.

Little, L. (2002) Middle-class mothers' perceptions of peer and sibling victimization among children with Asperger's syndrome and monverbal learning disorders. *Issues in Comprehensive Pediatric Nursing 25*(1), 43–57.

Loraine, S. (2008) *What are basic concepts?* Super Duper Publications Inc. Accessed on 21.02.2020 at www.superduperinc.com/handouts/pdf/161%20Basic%20Concepts.pdf

Luxford, S., Hadwin, J.A. and Kovshoff, H. (2017) Evaluating the effectiveness of a school-based cognitive Behavioural therapy intervention for anxiety in adolescents diagnosed with autism spectrum disorder. *Journal of Autism and Developmental Disorders 47*(12), 3896–3908.

Mazurek, M. (2013) Social media use among adults with autism spectrum disorders. *Computers in Human Behavior 29*(4) 1709–1714. https://doi.org/10.1016/j.chb.2013.02.004

Mazurek, M.O. and Wenstrup, C. (2013) Television, video game and social media use among children with ASD and typically developing siblings. *Journal of Autism and Developmental Disorders 43*(6), 1258–1271.

McCausland, D. (2005) *International Experience in the Provision of Individual Education Plans for Children with Disabilities.* Dublin: National Disability Authority.

Mesibov, G. and Howley, M. (2003) *Accessing the Curriculum for Pupils with Autistic Spectrum Disorders.* Oxon: David Fulton Publishers.

Mesibov, G., Howley, M. and Naftel, S. (2016) *Accessing the Curriculum for Learners with Autism Spectrum Disorders.* Oxon and New York: Routledge.

Middletown Centre for Autism (2017) *Social and Leisure Skills: Research Bulletin No 24.* Accessed on 13.02.2021 at www.middletownautism.com/files/uploads/682a0ef3230f92198342bbc99fb06e62.pdf

Milton, D. (2012) *So What Exactly Is Autism?* Autism Education Trust.

Morewood, G.D., Humphrey, N. and Symes, W. (2011) Mainstreaming autism: Making it work. *Good Autism Practice 12*(2), 62–68.

Murza, K.A., Schwartz, J.B., Hahs-Vaughn, D.L. and Nye, C. (2016) Joint attention interventions for children with autism spectrum disorder: A systematic review and meta-analysis. *International Journal of Language & Communication Disorders 51*(3), 236–251.

NASEN (2016) *Girls and Autism: Flying Under the Radar.* Accessed on 21.02.2021 at https://nasen. org.uk/resources/girls-and-autism-flying-under-radar

National Autistic Society (NAS) (2020a) *What Is Autism?* Accessed on 21.02.2021 at www.autism. org.uk/advice-and-guidance/what-is-autism

National Autistic Society (NAS) (2020b) *Autistic Women and Girls.* Accessed on 21.02.2021 at www. autism.org.uk/advice-and-guidance/what-is-autism/autistic-women-and-girls

National Autistic Society (2020c) *Strategies and Interventions.* Accessed on 21.02.2021 at www. autism.org.uk/advice-and-guidance/topics/strategies-and-interventions/strategies-and-interventions

National Council for Special Education (2006) *Guidelines on the Individual Education Plan Process.* Dublin: The Stationery Office.

National Council for Special Education (NCSE) (2019a) *Initial teacher education for inclusion: Final report to the National Council for Special Education, November 2019.* NCSE Research Report No. 27. Accessed on 21.02.2021 at https://ncse.ie/wp-content/uploads/2019/12/04611-NCSE-Teacher-Training-RR-Proof05.pdf

National Council for Special Education (NCSE) (2019b) *Policy Advice on Special Schools and Classes: An Inclusive Education for an Inclusive Society?* Trim, Ireland: NCSE.

National Institute for Health and Care Excellence (NICE) (2013) *Autism Spectrum Disorder in Under 19s: Support and Management.* Clinical Guideline [CG170]. Accessed on 21.02.2021 at www.nice.org.uk/guidance/cg170

Neilson, S. (2018) *Looking at sensory loads: Autism in the home* [Lecture]. University College Cork. 4 December.

Neilson, S. (2019a) *Creating autism: Exhibition opening and panel discussion* [Lecture]. St Peter's Cork, Ireland. 7 February.

Neilson, S. (2019b) *Sensory Issues and Social Inclusion.* Accessed on 21.02.2021 at http://wordpress. stuartneilson.com/sensory-issues-and-social-inclusion

O'Brien, E.Z. (2016) *Psychology for Social Work: A Comprehensive Guide to Human Growth and Development.* London: Palgrave Macmillan.

O'Byrne, A. (2018) Including parents right from the start. In E. Ring, P. Daly and E. Wall (Eds.) *Autism from the Inside Out.* Oxford: Peter Lang.

Ofcom (2019) *Children and Parents: Media Use and Attitudes Report 2019.* Accessed on 13.02.2021 at www.ofcom.org.uk/__data/assets/pdf_file/0023/190616/children-media-use-attitudes-2019-report.pdf

Parten, M.B. (1932) Social participation among preschool children. *Journal of Abnormal and Social Psychology 27*(3), 243–269.

Pellicano, E. (2012) The development of executive function in autism. *Autism Research and Treatment* 2012, 146132.

Peterson, C.C., Wellman, H.M. and Slaughter, V. (2012) The mind behind the message: Advancing theory-of-mind scales for typically developing children, and those with deafness, autism, or Asperger syndrome. *Child Development 83*, 469–485.

Płatos, M. and Wojaczek, K. (2017) Broadening the scope of peer-mediated intervention for individuals with autism spectrum disorders. *Journal of Autism and Developmental disorders 48*(3), 747–750. https://doi.org/10.1007/s10803-017-3429-1

Ratto, A.B., Kenworthy, L., Yerys, B.E., Bascom, J. et al. (2018) What about the girls? Sex-based differences in autistic traits and adaptive skills. *Journal of Autism and Developmental Disorders 48*(5), 1698–1711.

Rodgers, J., Goodwin, J., Parr, J.R. et al. (2019) Coping with Uncertainty in Everyday Situations (CUES©) to address intolerance of uncertainty in autistic children: Study protocol for an intervention feasibility trial. *Trials 20*, 385.

Rodgers, J., Hodgson, A., Shields, K., Wright, C., Honey, E. and Freeston, M. (2016) Towards a treatment for intolerance of uncertainty in young people with autism spectrum disorder: Development of the coping with uncertainty in everyday situations (CUES©) programme. *Journal of Autism and Developmental Disorders 47*(12), 3959–3966.

Rowe, A. (2013) *The Girl with the Curly Hair: Aspergers and Me.* London: Lonely Mind Books.

Rubin, E. (2017) *The SCERTS model: An introduction* [Lecture]. The Bridge London Trust Islington, London. 30 October.

Sam, A., Cox, A., Savage, M.N., Waters, V. and Odom, S. (2020) Disseminating information on evidence-based practices for children and youth with autism spectrum disorder: AFIRM. *Journal of Autism and Developmental Disorders 50*(6), 1931–1940.

Semple, R.J. (2018) Review: Yoga and mindfulness for youth with autism spectrum disorder: Review of the current evidence. *Child and Adolescent Mental Health 24*(1), 12–18.

Siegel, D.J. (2010) *Mindsight: The New Science of Personal Transformation.* New York: Bantam Books.

Siegel, D.J. and Bryson, T.P. (2011) *The Whole-Brain Child: 12 Revolutionary Strategies to Nurture Your Child's Developing Mind.* New York: Bantam Books.

Simpson, J. (2019, February 4) *Special interests* [Video]. YouTube. www.youtube.com/watch?v=a5DbDPBB8Mo&feature=emb_logo

Singh, N.N., Lancioni, G.E., Manikam, R., Winton A.S.W., Singh, A.N.A., Singh, J. and Singh, A.D.A. (2011) A mindfulness-based strategy for self-management of aggressive behavior in adolescents with autism. *Research in Autism Spectrum Disorders 5*(3), 1153–1158.

South, M. and Rodgers, J. (2017) Sensory, emotional and cognitive contributions to anxiety in autism spectrum disorders. *Frontiers in Human Neuroscience 11*(20). doi:10.3389/fnhum.2017.00020

Sowa, M. and Meulenbroek, R. (2012) Effects of physical exercise on autism spectrum disorders: A meta-analysis. *Research in Autism Spectrum Disorders 6*(1), 46–57. doi:10.1016/j.rasd.2011.09.001

Steinbrenner, J.R., Hume, K., Odom, S.L., Morin, K.L. et al. (2020). Evidence-based practices for children, youth, and young adults with autism. The University of North Carolina at Chapel Hill, Frank Porter Graham Child Development Institute, National Clearinghouse on Autism Evidence and Practice Review Team.

Sterzing, P.R., Shattuck, P.T., Narendorf, S.C., Wagner, M. and Cooper, B.P. (2012) Bullying involvement and autism spectrum disorders: Prevalence and correlates of bullying involvement among adolescents with an autism spectrum disorder. *Archives of Pediatric & Adolescent Medicine 166*(11), 1058–1064.

Steward, R. and Knight, J. (Hosts) (2018, November 17) Turn down the studio lights [Audio podcast episode]. In *1800 Seconds on Autism.* BBC Sounds. www.bbc.co.uk/programmes/p06sdq0x

Ury, W. (1991) *Getting Past No: Negotiating in Difficult Situations.* New York: Bantam Books.

van Schalkwyk, G., Marin, C., Ortiz, M., Rolison, M. et al. (2017) Social media use, friendship quality, and the moderating role of anxiety in adolescents with autism spectrum disorder. *Journal of Autism and Developmental Disorders 47*(9), 2805–2813.

van Steensel, F.J.A. and Heeman, E.J. (2017) Anxiety levels in children with autism spectrum disorder: A meta-analysis. *Journal of Child and Family Studies 26*, 1753–1767.

Vermeulen, P. (2012) *Autism as Context Blindness.* Shawnee, KS: AAPC Publishing.

Vermeulen, P. (2019) *Autism and context blindness [interview with Paul Micallef]* [Lecture]. Autism Explained Online Summit, 16 October.

Wainscot, J.J., Naylor, P., Sutcliffe, P., Tantam, D. and Williams, J. (2008) Relationships with peers and use of the school environment of mainstream secondary school pupils with Asperger syndrome (high-functioning autism): A case control study. *International Journal of Psychology and Psychological Theory 8*(1), 25–38.

Ward, D.M., Dill-Shackleford, K.E. and Mazurek, M.O. (2018) Social media use and happiness in adults with autism spectrum disorder. *Cyberpsychology Behaviour and Social Networking 21*(3), 205–209. https://doi.org/10.1089/cyber.2017.0331

Watkins, L., O'Reilly, M., Kuhn, M., Gevarter, C., Lancioni, G.E., Sigafoos, J. and Lang, R. (2015) A review of peer-mediated social interaction interventions for students with autism in inclusive settings. *Journal of Autism and Developmental Disorders 45*(4), 1070–1083. https://doi.org/10.1007/s10803-014-2264-x

Webster, A. (2016) *Autism, Sport and Physical Activity.* NAS. Accessed on 21.02.2021 at https://england-athletics-prod-assets-bucket.s3.amazonaws.com/2018/11/National-Autism-Society-Autism-sport-physical-activity-PDF-2.1MB-.pdf

Wharmby, P (2018) It is a commonly held view that #autistic people can't empathise, sympathise or show emotion (!). Twitter. Accessed on 28.06.21 at https://twitter.com/commaficionado/status/976179620285382656

Williams, R.R. (2016) Life, Animated. New York: The Orchard.

Wing, L. (1996) Autistic spectrum disorders. *BMJ 312*(7027), 321–327.

Wolfberg, P., Bottema-Beutel, K. and DeWitt, M. (2012) Including children with autism in social and imaginary play with typical peers – integrated play groups model. *American Journal of Play 5*(1), 55–80.

Wood, C., Littleton, K. and Sheehy, K. (2006) *Developmental Psychology in Action.* Milton Keynes: The Open University.

World Health Organization (2004) *The ICD-10 International Classification of Diseases and Related Health Problems* (Tenth revision, 2nd ed.). Geneva: World Health Organization.

Young, K., Mannix McNamara, P. and Coughlan, B. (2017) Authentic inclusion: Utopian thinking? Irish post-primary teachers' perspectives of inclusive education. *Teaching and Teacher Education 68*, 1–11.

Appendices

Appendix 17: Parental Input Individual Education Plan

Appendix 18: Sample Individual Education Plan Goals and Targets

Appendix 19: Template: Individual Education Plan Goals and Targets

Appendix 20: Sample Communication Passport

Appendix 21: Template: Communication Passport

Index